State of the Art of Preparation and Practice in Student Affairs: Another Look

STATE OF THE ART OF PREPARATION AND PRACTICE IN STUDENT AFFAIRS: ANOTHER LOOK

EDITED BY
NANCY J. EVANS
AND
CHRISTINE E. PHELPS TOBIN

American College Personnel Association

University Press of America,® Inc.
4720 Boston Way
Lanham, Maryland 20706

12 Hid's Copse Rd.
Cummor Hill, Oxford OX2 9JJ

Printed in the United States of America
British Library Cataloging in Publication Information Available

Library of Congress Cataloging-in-Publication Data

ISBN 1-883485-09-6 (cloth: alk. ppr.)
ISBN 1-883485-10-X (pbk: alk. ppr.)

™ The paper used in this publication meet the minimum requirements of American National Standard for information Sciences—Permanence of Paper for Printed Library Materials, ANSI Z39.48—1984

Contents

Preface

This monograph is a revised and updated version of *The State of the Art of Professional Education and Practice* (1988) which was edited by Robert B. Young and Leila V. Moore as a joint project of the American College Personnel Association, National Association of Student Personnel Administrators, and Association for Counselor Education and Supervision. The papers included in the original *State of the Art* monograph were intended to serve as discussion pieces for a national forum on the interface between academic preparation and practice in student affairs, called in response to the establishment of the CAS standards for preparation and practice and the fiftieth anniversary of the publication of the *Student Personnel Point of View*. The intent was to assess the current status and future needs of preparation and practice in student affairs work. Although the forum did not take place, the prepared papers were collected and published in monograph form by the American College Personnel Association. Unfortunately, this monograph was distributed only on a limited basis by Commission XII (Professional Preparation).

The goal of this revised monograph is to present a visionary reexamination of the status of student affairs preparation and practice by some of the field's leading thinkers. Preparation and practice in student affairs are constantly evolving. Our work is informed by new scholarship in the field of student affairs and related areas as well as by changing societal forces affecting higher education. It is important to examine the "state of the art" on a regular basis to track the progression of the profession and to chart the course for its future development.

In the years since the original *State of the Art* monograph was prepared, important changes have taken place within student affairs and in higher education generally. Increasingly, the profession is being influenced by outside forces ranging from state and federal government and governing boards to the changing demographics of the nation. Institutions are downsizing and outsourcing services in response to enrollment decreases and budget crises. Student affairs is in the midst of a paradigm shift moving from an objective, mechanistic, and reductionistic interpretation of its role to one that is perspectival, holonomic, and complex (Kuh, Whitt, & Shedd, 1987).

Obviously, student affairs preparation programs must adjust their curricula to address these changes. They are also faced with the challenge of incorporating recent research and theoretical advances, particularly related to multiculturalism and student development, into an already full curriculum. In addition, in light of the rapid changes occurring in higher education, the need for continuing education for student affairs practitioners is greater than ever before. Unfortunately, student affairs preparation programs, like other components of the university, are facing budget cuts, staffing problems, issues related to student recruitment, and outside regulation which make adequate response to the changing needs of the field particularly difficult.

Given the limited distribution of the first *State of the Art* monograph and the changes that have occurred during the last several years, a revised and updated examination of student affairs practice and preparation is warranted. To effectively prepare for the challenges of the future we must assess and analyze the current "state of the art." In this monograph, leading student affairs practitioners and scholars examine the current status of student affairs practice and preparation as well as the linkages between practice and education. Both practitioners and educators will benefit from the collective wisdom of some of the field's best thinkers.

In contrast to the first monograph, the revised monograph more clearly delineates four sections: student affairs practice, preparation of student affairs professionals, linkages between preparation and practice, and concluding commentary. Specifically, Part One, Student Affairs Practice, has been greatly expanded to include examination of societal forces influencing the field, institutional pressures, issues facing student affairs professionals, and issues facing professional associations. In Chapter 1, Doug Woodard introduces the concept of societal "changedrivers" and discusses their impact on higher education and student affairs. In Chapter 2, Carolyn Bair, Bill Klepper and Christine Phelps Tobin look at the influence of institutional mission, values, and pressures on student affairs practice. In Chapter 3, Joan Hirt and Don Creamer review the changing personal and professional demands on student affairs professionals. To conclude this section, in Chapter 4 Leila Moore and Carmen Neuberger examine the role of student affairs professional associations in addressing the issues facing the student affairs field.

In Part Two, the focus shifts to preparation of student affairs practitioners to meet the challenges outlined in the first section. The chapters in this section have been updated and expanded to reflect the need for multiculturally sensitive individuals in the student affairs profession as well as to address other issues facing preparation programs. In Chapter 5, Christine Phelps Tobin discusses issues, trends, and directions concerning the recruitment, screening, selection and retention of well qualified, committed graduate students who will become quality student affairs professionals. Using data from a survey of student affairs faculty, in Chapter 6 Nancy Evans and Terry Williams provide a profile of current student affairs faculty and identify the characteristics and qualifications essential to prepare faculty members for a rapidly changing and challenging academic climate. In Chapter 7, Marylu McEwen and Donna Talbot discuss curriculum issues in student affairs preparation. This chapter has been expanded and revised to include a review of the CAS preparation standards and to address current issues that must be addressed to maintain a current and comprehensive curriculum at both the masters and doctoral levels.

In Part Three, linkages between student affairs practice and preparation programs are examined. In Chapter 8, Stan Carpenter stresses the increasing need for ongoing education in student affairs in light of a rapidly changing society and discusses strategies for involving preparation faculty in such efforts. In Chapter 9, Susan Komives examines ways in which practice can inform preparation in student affairs and quality preparation can enhance the performance of student affairs practitioners.

In Part Four, three student affairs professionals reflect on the material presented in the earlier chapters of this monograph, highlighting ideas they think are particularly important, critiquing points with which they disagree, and adding material they find missing. Russ Jablonsky provides a new professional point of view. Jane Fried adds her perspective as a mid-career professional who has had extensive experience both as a practitioner and a faculty member, and Lee Upcraft comments from his position as a recently retired student affairs professional who has had a distinguished career as a practitioner-scholar.

In an epilogue entitled "A Heretical Bit of Whimsy," Bob Young concludes with an "Alice in Wonderland, through the looking glass" examination of the student affairs field.

Higher education is being bombarded with issues resulting from the rapid changes in society. If student affairs is to continue to play a positive and meaningful role in the educational enterprise, its practitioners must be thoroughly familiar with these issues and take the lead in developing strategies to address them. Student affairs educators must see that the new professionals they teach are prepared to assume leadership roles. The intent of this monograph is to assist practitioners and educators with these challenges.

REFERENCES

Kuh, G. D., Whitt, E. J., & Shedd, J. D. (1987). *Student affairs work, 2001: A pradigmatic odyssey.* Alexandria, VA: American College Personnel Association.

Young, R. B., & Moore, L. V. (Eds.). (1988). *The state of the art of professional education and practice.* Alexandria, VA: American College Personnel Association.

Part One

Student Affairs Practice

Student affairs practice has been greatly influenced by societal forces, institutional pressures, issues facing student affairs professionals, and issues facing professional associations. In Chapter 1, Doug Woodard examines societal influences on higher education and student affairs. Setting the context for the entire monograph, this chapter provides a framework regarding the likely forces that will shape postmodern higher education institutions, and then provides an understanding of these forces in the context of the profession of student affairs. The first part of the chapter introduces the concept of "changedrivers." Change-drivers are the forces that will transform higher education by causing destabilization within the academy. They include economic restructuring, technology, demographic changes, globalization, regulatory grid-lock, redefinition of family and home, and recycled activism. The second part of the chapter examines these forces from the perspective of student affairs and outlines some of the issues which will be discussed throughout the monograph.

In Chapter 2, Carolyn Bair, Bill Klepper, and Christine Phelps Tobin consider the institutional issues facing student affairs programs, specifically the influence of institutional mission, values, and pressures on student affairs practice. These issues are examined by contrasting Woodard's challenges from Chapter 1 with Brown's (1972) recommendations from *Student Development in Tomorrow's Higher Education—A Return to the Academy.* Beginning with a retrospective view, the authors revisit the original academy and then consider today's higher education in an effort to provide a clearer vision of the future.

The changing personal and professional demands on student affairs professionals are the focus of Chapter 3. In this chapter Joan Hirt and Don Creamer examine the impact that the critical changes and issues discussed in Chapters 1 and 2 have on the daily lives of individual practitioners. The components of contemporary professional life, the demands and subsequent tensions created by these demands, and the influence of these tensions on the nature of the work administrators perform on a daily basis are the focus of this chapter. Hirt and Creamer approach this chapter from the four realms in which practitioners regularly operate: the personal, the institutional, the extra-institutional, and the professional. Each context uniquely effects the experience of the practitioner. Hirt and Creamer provide an overview of each realm, suggesting that increased understanding and appreciation of each will enable professionals to better understand the demands of student affairs practice.

To conclude Part One, Chapter 4 focuses on the role of professional associations in student affairs practice. Leila Moore and Carmen Neuberger begin by providing an overview of student affairs professional associations, followed by a discussion of the current role of professional associations. Specifically, the response of professional associations to societal issues is outlined, with particular focus placed on four recent issues in higher education raised in Chapters 1 and 2. These issues include identification and assessment of student outcomes, increased attention to the learning process, economic constraints, and technological advances for managing information. Moore and Neuberger suggest that a new role be assumed by professional associations with respect to these issues. Moore and Neuberger conclude Chapter Four with a discussion of the future role of professional associations in higher education.

This section provides a framework for the remainder of the monograph. Student affairs practice is examined from four influencing forces: society, the institution, the individual, and student affairs professional associations.

REFERENCE

Brown, R. D. (1972). *Student development in tomorrow's higher education–A return to the academy.* Washington, DC: American College Personnel Association.

Chapter One

Societal Influences on Higher Education and Student Affairs

Dudley B. Woodard, Jr.

Imagine sitting around the hearth in the year 995 A.D. and discussing the coming millennium. What issues were discussed? What forces were identified as likely shaping the future? And, what was the sense of our ancestors regarding the future? Despair? Hope? Trepidation? Thinking about the future is like trying to imagine what your preschoolers will be like as adults and trying to identify the forces and events that will influence their development. It is exciting and interesting to make predictions and discuss future trends; however, it is much more difficult to think about the ways to address the challenges posed by these changes.

Today, modern universities are scrambling to respond to changing financial conditions, shifting enrollment patterns, an unfavorable public opinion of higher education, and attacks by postmodernists which call into question higher education's legitimacy and purpose (Bloland, 1995). Commenting on these perilous conditions in higher education,

---

The author wishes to acknowledge with appreciation the assistance of Sherry Mallory in the writing of this chapter.

Guskin (1994) observed that higher education has the capability to survive creatively, but will be able to do so only with significant and radical changes in the ways that administrative structures and faculty roles are organized. A survey conducted by the American Council on Education in 1994 found that over half of all public institutions were involved in academic and administrative restructuring activities (El-Khawas, 1994a). It is quite clear that modern American higher education institutions are undergoing some kind of transformation as we head into the 21st century.

The purpose of this chapter is twofold: (1) to provide a backdrop for the reader regarding the likely forces that will shape postmodern higher education institutions and (2) to provide an understanding of these forces in the context of the profession of student affairs. There is no returning back to the "good old days" (whatever those were); rather, there is a new reality and, as professionals, we need to understand this new reality and the emerging constructs and organizational structures that will shape and transform our work. The chapter is divided into two parts. The first part describes "changedrivers" into the third millennium (United Way of America's Strategic Institute, 1990, p. 1). Changedrivers are the forces that will transform higher education by causing destabilization within the academy and which will require us to examine roles, functions, and structures in order to achieve a level of homeostasis (Leslie, 1995) and to meet the expectations and challenges posed by a global society. The second part examines these changedrivers from the perspective of student affairs and introduces some of the issues which will be further discussed in subsequent chapters.

CHANGEDRIVERS INTO THE THIRD MILLENNIUM

The United Way of America's Strategic Institute (1990) identified over 100 trends that likely will influence society into the 21st century and grouped them into nine changedrivers. Each of these changedrivers should be understood for its social, economic, political, and technological power to transform higher education. I have modified these changedrivers and will use them as a framework for examining the forces which will influence the evolving postmodern colleges and universities.

Economic Restructuring

There seems to be a growing consensus about the economic future of higher education. Breneman (1993) describes this new reality as a "rethinking of the structure and mission of colleges and universities in a more austere world" (p. 5). Robert Atwell, President of the American Council on Education, doesn't see any financial improvement until after 2010 and Harold Shapiro, an economist, sees the current trend continuing for several years since the growth in revenues will not be sufficient to "maintain the quality, scope, and method of production of the current system" (Richard A. Harvill Conference, 1992, p. 6). Future government support for higher education may be restricted by policies that limit spending in order to control budget deficits. In addition, higher education faces increased competition from other national and state priorities such as health care, law enforcement, and correctional facilities (Horton & Andersen, 1994). Adjusted for inflation, federal appropriations per full-time equivalent (FTE) higher education student (including students enrolled at both public and private institutions) were slightly higher in 1980 than in 1993 ($3,300 vs. $3,000). And, in the 1992 fiscal year, approximately 9.2% of state tax revenues were allocated to higher education, compared with 10% of state budgets a decade before (Horton & Andersen, 1994). Moreover, state funds now account for just half (50.5%) of the operating budgets of public institutions down from 56.6% just five years ago (El-Khawas, 1994b).

The results of a national survey found that the financial conditions of the early 1990s are having wide repercussions on institutional life. "Substantial redirection and change is underway, with uncertain long-term consequences for the nature of higher education in the United States. . . . and many acknowledge that the changed financial environment has caused them to plan academic programs with an eye to their ability to generate revenue for the institution" (El-Khawas, 1994b, p. 25). With support from both federal and state sources decreasing, institutions need to look at other alternatives for generating revenue—both internally and externally.

The recent trend toward restructuring activities directed at organizational changes to produce savings and efficiencies has been stymied because of the persistent difficulty in achieving savings in a growth industry where human resources comprise most of the capital. Levin (1989), in a very thoughtful analysis, described why higher education cannot achieve the same level of efficiency and cost savings through restructuring as does the corporate world. For most institutions, tuition has risen faster than inflation and overall costs have outstripped revenue. The actions institutions have taken to achieve savings and to support new programs and demands for services still have not been adequate to reduce debt and fund new programs and initiatives. Levin (1989) noted that for institutions to stay even they need to increase revenues at a rate which is greater than increases in price levels. Drawing on William Baumol's work, Levin pointed out that higher education is unlike industry in that, as unit prices increase, industry can take advantage of labor saving techniques such as technology. However, because higher education is labor intensive, the services offered by the labor force do not benefit from technical progress. It is very difficult to "adopt innovations or substitute instructional technologies that would raise productivity" (Levin, 1989, p. 2).

The question, then, becomes how institutions of higher learning can raise productivity given the constraints of a labor intensive setting which requires a highly skilled workforce. Levin (1989) states that this objective can be achieved by "substituting more valuable activities for less valuable ones as well as by improving the quality and quantity of existing activities relative to budgetary and other resources" (pp. 3-4). The approach must be systematic and take into account the overall structure of the institution in order to succeed. How can incentives be used to stimulate ways to raise productivity without increasing unit costs? How can escalating administrative costs be reduced? Should we reallocate time spent on existing tasks/activities? Can we take advantage of technology to reduce personnel costs? Are there other sources of revenue that can be used without passing the cost on to students?

Technology

Technology has significantly changed what we do, how we do it, why we do it, and where we do it. Rossman (1992) contrasts today's infotech world with the dawn of the university in the 12th century; he suggests that the way students now travel the information highway is not unlike the way 12th century students wandered from country to country, in search of the course they wanted. John Sculley, former president of Apple Computers, predicted that "universities as networks of interdependence are going to be at the center of a new renaissance" (Rossman, 1992, p. xi). Global universities are emerging using technology to connect students, teachers, and researchers. Programs such as VideoPhone make it possible to use the Internet for interactive dialogue between students and faculty from almost anyplace in the world. New teaching tools like interactive programs using holograms or virtual-reality experiences will build on students' preferred ways of learning and increase the trend toward consumer based learning opportunities. There will be a boom in packaged educational products, such as automated tutors, and students will have access to electronic libraries and databases which will exponentially increase knowledge and cause conflicts over what to learn (Cornish, 1996, pp. 5-6). Wilson (1994) warns us to be cautious and not "embrace technology with the abandon we see all around us" (pp. 14-15). Her argument is that we need to make certain that technology serves our needs in higher education and not the marketplace needs generated by the manufacturers of technology. Equally important, we need to place ourselves in a position to raise questions about the impact of technology on teaching and learning. We need to raise questions about the impact of distance learning on cognitive and personal development as well as on community. How will the explosion in information change what will be accepted as knowledge? How will our way of viewing reality change? How will moral reasoning and reflective judgement develop when the interactive vessel is an impersonal computer station? How will community standards be defined and enforced if students and faculty spend more time connected through a modem than through personal relationships? How beneficial is it to spend hours surfing the highway? Will cocooning (spending a high percentage of time during the day interacting with a terminal) desocialize people and lead to antisocial behavior? (Cornish, 1996, p. 4). As we think about the effects of this changedriver on student affairs and how practitioners will be transformed by this emerging technology, we need to keep in mind Wilson's (1994) admonishment:

> Every technology has a philosophy which is given expression in how the technology makes people use their minds, in what it makes us do with our bodies, in how it codifies the world, in which of our senses it amplifies, in which of our emotional and intellectual tendencies it disregards. . . . (E)verything looks like . . . data, instead of thought; calculation, instead of judgment; ubiquitous access, instead of introspection; individual omniscience, instead of social interdependence. . . . We need to think about that. (p. 15)

Demographic Changes

Most of our campuses do not look anything like they did during the 1960s and early 1970s. A colorful human mosaic pattern will usher in the third millennium. College enrollments will continue to grow at a modest rate and women will continue to enroll and graduate from college at higher rates than men. The 35 and older population will increase from 19% to 23% of the total enrollment and the under 35 age cohort will drop (Evangelauf, 1992, p. A1). Likewise, it is expected that the enrollment of racial and ethnic minority students will increase. According to Justiz (1994), "between now and the year 2000, college classes will increasingly be made up of diverse groups, including Hispanics, African Americans, Native Americans, immigrants, and foreigners" (p. 7). The ethnic diversification and the graying of America will be two powerful forces in shaping the enrollment patterns and needs of tomorrow's learner. The characteristics, competencies, and interests of today's and tomorrow's students are so diverse and reflective of societal needs that institutions will need to continually redesign the learning environment in order to effectively meet the educational and career interests, preparation, and needs of these students.

While a demographic profiling of the 21st century student allows us to capture a mental picture of what our campuses might look like, it really doesn't tell us too much about who these students are—what their interests, values, beliefs, abilities, and purposes will be. Much has been written about past, present and current generations (Coupland, 1992; Loeb, 1994; Strauss & Howe, 1991; Wexler & Hulme, 1994). Students have been described as (1) belonging to the Silent, Boomer, Xer, 13er, or Millennial generation; (2) committed to social justice or committed to self; (3) filled with a sense of hope for tomorrow or with oozing despair; and (4) adaptive or reactive. What we have learned about the characterization of students is that no one label is appropriate for any generation and that there may be just as much diversity within a generation as there is among generations. Generations are both influenced, shaped by, and reflective of the social, political and economic conditions of their time. But generations are not static; they continue to change throughout their life cycle. So, what do we know about the current generation of students and what are some of the future conditions likely to influence and change these students?

Toffler (1990) described today's society as a throw away society; a society challenged by a crumbling family structure, escalating violence toward others, and a genetic revolution. The so called generation gap of the 1960s was between college-age students and their parents; the so-called generation gap of the 1990s is between working age adults and retirees. This issue is often posed in terms of intergenerational conflict and divisiveness based on resource scarcity and resource distribution.

Strauss and Howe (1991) view American history through a lens of social movements—"an era, typically lasting about a decade, when people perceive that historic events are radically altering their social environment" (p. 71). There are two types of social movements—secular crises and spiritual awakenings. A secular crisis is a time when individuals band together to protect the community (such as during a war) and a spiritual awakening is a period when the focus is inward and change is driven by values (such as the civil rights movement). These social movements are timed and roughly occur in an alternating cycle of every 80 years; subsequently, Strauss and Howe believe that we are headed for our next secular crisis as we enter the 21st century, sometime around the year 2020. If we are headed for another secular crisis, what will it be? A global conflict fueled by hunger, poverty, ideology? A generational conflict between the moralizing Boomers and the alienated 13ers? A cultural clash driven by the increasing disparity in wealth and the dismantling of affirmative action programs? An intergenerational conflict based on scarcity of resources and resource distribution? The conditions for any one of these conflicts currently exist and these conditions will be powerful influences in shaping future students' attitudes, beliefs, behavior, and subsequent campus communities. What role will student affairs play on our campuses in helping students, faculty, and staff to understand the reasons for and destructive power of these forces? What role will student affairs practitioners play in helping to change these conditions in order to avert a secular (global) crisis?

Globalization

Globalization as a concept refers both to "the compression of the world and intensification of consciousness of the world as a whole" (Robertson, 1992, p. 8). Fueled by technological, scientific, and telecommunications changes, globalization has caused us to reexamine how we think about and interact with other people—their values, beliefs, and assumptions about knowledge. Trade agreements such as NAFTA and economic unions such as the European Economic Community are examples which illustrate the changing patterns of social and economic behavior found in education, government, and communities. The complexity introduced by globalization will require us to move from a centrist position in order to understand and visualize what it will mean to live and work in a global society. Some view globalization as the eventual homogenization of the world; in doing so, these individuals fail to grasp the complexity of globalization and what it means to forge worldwide social relations among people of distinct and differing cultures.

Slaughter and Leslie (in press), in examining the role that globalization has played in higher education, claim that as state and federal resources declined during the past twenty years, faculty have increasingly had to compete for external dollars that were tied to the market place. They describe this activity as *academic capitalism*—that is, institutional and professorial market or market-like efforts to secure external monies. According to Slaughter and Leslie, higher education in the United States, Australia, and the United Kingdom has increasingly moved ". . . toward academic capitalism, emphasizing the utility of higher education to national economic activity on the part of the faculty and institutions" (p. 33). This shift has resulted in less money for social welfare and higher education funding, with the exception of educational programs and research that are market specific. As a consequence, universities have had to move toward emphasizing research that is entrepreneurial rather than basic, developing curricula that supports programs directly related to the market, and providing the training required to support multinational corporations.

If globalization leads to increasing multinational conglomerates and increased competitiveness, what are the implications for higher education? Do we understand what a global community means? Are we preparing our students for the complexities and issues of a global community? Will there be less money for higher education activities? Will the money allocated to higher education be targeted mostly for programs and research that are close to the market? Will multinational corporations assume an increasing responsibility for the education of the global workforce? Will traditional programs such as the social sciences and humanities struggle for survival? Will poverty increase thereby moving us closer to a global crisis?

Regulatory Gridlock

For many years, higher education has enjoyed "an implied immunity from the norms that govern society as a whole" (Cloud, 1992, p. 10). However, during the 1960s, a dramatically changed social context led to the switching of an institution's authority, in student matters, from the doctrine of in loco parentis to contractual and constitutional doctrines. The passage of the Twenty-Sixth Amendment in 1971, which lowered the voting age from twenty-one to eighteen, paved the way for most states to lower the age of majority from twenty-one to eighteen giving students the right to enter into binding contracts, sign consent forms for medical treatment, declare financial independence, or establish legal residence apart from their parents (Kaplin & Lee, 1995). This change in student status ushered in for the first time external regulations directed at protecting student rights—the Family Rights and Privacy Act of 1974 (FERPA), Title XI (1972), Section 504 of the Rehabilitation Act of 1973, the Right to Know and Campus Security Act of 1990, and the Americans With Disabilities Act of 1990.

The redefined contractual and institutional relationship with students and the enactment of several regulatory statutes has changed the work environment in higher education. Some examples will illustrate this changed state of affairs. The doctrine of official immunity is no longer a defense for public university and college officials since they act under the color of law and, therefore, are subject to Section 1983 of the Civil Rights Act of 1871. This means that they can be sued for official misconduct and held personally liable for monetary damages. Section 1983 does not extend to private institutions since officers in these institutions are not acting under the color of law (Cloud, 1992, p. 11). This has been a positive change in that officials could no longer over reach their authority to violate student and employee rights but, on the other hand, it has invited some unnecessary and frivolous lawsuits which have used scarce resources and detracted from the educational purposes of the institution.

Affirmative action offices did not exist until the 1970s. A major responsibility of these offices has been to act on the behalf of all employees and students in protecting their civil rights as granted under the Civil Rights Act of 1964 and subsequent titles to the 1964 Act. Both public and private institutions are held accountable for meeting the requirements of the Civil Rights Act and subsequent titles. There have been many positive outcomes such as the directive to move toward equity in women's sports, the improvement in the physical environment and services for students with disabilities, and the prohibiting of discrimination on the basis of race, color, or national origin if the institution is receiving federal funds. On the other hand, the implementation of these statutes and regulations has been costly and the contradictory language and practice has been problematic for institutions.

The passage of several federal statutes and regulations has improved the work environment for employees and the educational setting for students. They have directly contributed to the mission of teaching, research, service and diversity among students and staff. The problem, however, for institutions has been one of resources, understanding intent, and developing the expertise among staff to stay in compliance (Sandock, 1996). How will declining resources affect an institution's ability to stay in compliance? Will future regulations cause a shift in resources from student services and academic support programs? How can regulations be implemented without siphoning off resources and overburdening staff? How can a community based on principles of fair play and not litigation be developed? How can regulations be changed to meet the changing landscape of higher education without extensive legal costs and protracted battles?

Redefinition of Family and Home

During the 1960s and 1970s, pundits had a field day describing the demise of the family and the character and role of the emerging social structures that would replace the family. Toffler's (1970) epic book, *Future Shock*, describes a family neither headed for extinction nor stability but, rather, a family more likely to "break up, shatter, only to come together again in weird and novel ways" (p. 212). America's families have undergone many changes during the last three decades and these changes have profoundly changed our educational system. Hodgkinson (1989) in *The Same Client*, described some of the trends leading to Toffler's (1970) reconfigured family unit: "The 'Leave It to Beaver' household seems very atypical. Over one-third of all the marriages performed in 1988 were second marriages for at least one partner and over half of the marriages today end in divorce. And, the number of children living with one parent has risen dramatically during the last decade to over 15 million children living with one parent" (p. 3). Moreover, one out of four American children today under the age of 5 live in poverty and 40% of the poor are children (Hodgkinson, 1989, p. 3). Over half a million children are born to teenage mothers each year and an increasing number of children live among violence and exploitation (National Commission on Children, 1991, p. xviii).

At the other end of the human life-line are the generative Americans. Our older adult population, which is living longer, has given rise to an increasing number of four generation families and controls the wealth of this country. The wealth held by this graying population will make it more difficult for the Boomers and 13ers to achieve financial security and earn enough capital to invest in homes and retirement plans.

These demographic changes, coupled with the rapid changes in technology, have created very different family structures. Multiple marriages, single family households, domestic partners, and the effects of these changing arrangements on children will continue to challenge our educational institutions. Things that used to be done in the home, like caring for children, are done externally and things that were previously done externally, like banking and shopping, are now done at home (Komives & Woodard, 1996). What will be the family structure of the twenty-first century? Will there be an increasing trend for several generations to live together and pool resources? How will the changes in family structure impact higher education? Will families begin to view education as a commodity and shop for the best value on the Home Education Network?

Recycled Activism

The 1960s ushered in, and the 1970s ushered out, the last major progressive social activism in this century. Recently, much has been written describing student political ideology as liberal on some social issues and conservative on other issues. Some describe a resurgence in political activism (Williams & Malaney, 1996). Albach and Cohen contend "that regardless of the recent conservative protests, such as those against affirmative action, campuses will retain their potential as a source of progressive dissent in American society" (as cited in Williams & Malaney, 1996, p. 145). Others, however, have described a "trend of decreasing political activism—a willful unconcern" (Williams & Malaney, 1996, p. 146). The results of the Cooperative Institutional Research Program Survey (CIRP) data for Fall 1995 indicate that students interested in "keeping up to date with political affairs as an important goal dropped to an all-time low of 28.5 percent compared to 57.8 percent in 1966" (Higher Education Research Institute, 1996, p. 1). And it appears that the trend is away from activism—freshmen for the second straight year reported less interest in (1) "influencing social values;" (2) "influencing the political structure;" (3) "discussing politics;" (4) "cleaning of the environment;" and (5) "promoting racial understanding" (Higher Education Research Institute, 1996, p. 1). Hirsch (1993) captures this trend in describing students' attitudes about government and politicians—"they have little confidence in the political system and believe that social institutions are basically dishonest and self-serving" (p. 35).

This sentiment may not change as we move into the 21st century but it does seem likely that increasing tension over unresolved issues such as abortion, affirmative action, violence toward others, child neglect, drug profiteering, pollution, political corruptness, unscrupulous business practices, poverty, and racism will push students toward a level of activism similar to the 1960s and 1970s. However, the social activism of the early 21st century will be different from the 1960s in at least two ways. The first difference is that the new global generation will increasingly redefine social consciousness in a way that focuses on responding in a practical and rational way to current social issues (Hirsch, 1993). They are the reactive generation, according to Strauss and Howe (1991). They will be driven to fix the many problems facing the global community to avert another world-wide crisis.

The second difference is that the older population will continue to be involved and a strong force, thereby creating several distinct and entrenched factions. Alliances will be forged on issues like abortion, the environment, and affirmative action based more on the issue and not on an intractable commitment to political or ideological beliefs. Because of this alliance switching based on issues among and within different generations, it will be difficult for society to develop consensus on major issues.

Our institutions of higher learning will be expected to play a leadership role in the resolution of these issues. As Levine and Hirsch (1991) assert, higher education will have the opportunity "to lead, to use the current changes in student character as a basis for education, to prepare a generation of citizens who are socially engaged rather than socially estranged and institutionally alienated, as occurred in the 1960s" (p. 127). Will students develop the values and character that will be required for enlightened leadership in the twenty-first century? Will students become the fix-it generation and concentrate their efforts on practical solutions? Will a global economy reward students who prepare to work in multinational corporations; thus, discouraging students from pursuing practical and rational solutions to societal problems? Will campuses become human oases because of how technology will change the delivery of education, thereby, diluting any collective effort aimed at social reform?

THE THIRD MILLENNIUM: IMPLICATIONS FOR THE PRACTITIONER

In the colleges and universities of the 21st century, professors will do an increasing amount of their teaching and research from their homes, and students, likewise, will use both the work and home setting as learning conduits. Advances in computer technology and electronic retrieval of information will help professors to individualize teaching by selecting approaches most appropriate for their students (Wilson, 1994). Students will select courses from the World Wide Web Schedule of Classes and functions like advising, admission, registration, and career planning will be done electronically. And, faculty and students may have closer connections to colleagues and friends in other states and countries than to colleagues and friends in their department or college!

Most institutions will rely on revenue generated from tuition, contracts and grants, auxiliaries, and fund raising and less on state and federal support. This change in funding sources will lead to a reduction in the number of private liberal arts colleges and public colleges and universities and an increase in the number of for-profit corporations accredited for awarding both undergraduate and graduate degrees. The postmodern university will be closer to the marketplace, i.e. institutional activities will be directed at developing the curriculum and knowledge that have direct application to an international economy. The implications flowing from these changes will profoundly impact the student affairs profession. Some of these implications are described below as a way for the practitioner to frame the issues and contribute to purposeful change.

Restructuring

Most observers agree that the financial condition of higher education will not improve but rather will move closer to a market model (Breneman, 1993; Leslie, 1995). The increasing competition for dollars among other state and federal agencies will force higher education institutions to look elsewhere to fund program growth and infrastructure requirements, maintain facilities, and stay competitive technologically.

Student affairs professionals need to consider the role of the profession under these conditions and anticipate and prepare for significant role changes. Since student services is so labor intensive, how can practitioners take advantage of technology and, at the same time, reduce labor costs? Will outsourcing of functions further erode the value-added nature of these activities? What are some of the unlikely mergers that would result in savings but, at the same time, meet the emerging needs of a changing clientele? Are there new functions to be performed by student affairs professionals that will help institutions address the goals of improving learning and productivity? How do you decide what is central to the mission of the institutions and what activities/functions are falling away from centrality?

Technology

We know technology will be a major transformational influence for the postmodern university. It is not yet clear how technology will change the university; it is clear only that it will change. Wilson (1994) admonished us not to embrace technology with abandon but rather to make certain that it serves our needs and not the supplier's needs. We need to be a player in both the development and application of technology to teaching and learning. Student affairs professionals will increasingly take on responsibility for helping to design the learning environments in our postmodern universities. What knowledge base will be important for the practitioner in order to help design this future learning environment? What are the technological implications for basic student services such as admissions, financial aid, advising, etc.? How can we take advantage of technology in these areas while reducing costs to the institution and the student? How can we address some of the limitations of technology in terms of advancing higher order learning skills such as critical thinking, moral reasoning, and personal development?

Demographics

Changing demographics continue to influence how we think about education and how we need to organize our activities/programs to meet the needs of a changing population. As colleges and universities become more market driven, what does this change mean for access? Will higher education become a two-tiered system with one type of institution offering programs that are close to the market and that lead to the higher paying jobs and the other type of institution offering programs that lead to service positions? Will the students attending these different institutions sort themselves out by traditional socio-economic patterns? How will we take advantage of our knowledge of different learning styles and teaching approaches in order to meet the diverse interests and talents of our students? What role will the student affairs professional play in helping faculty understand these learning principles and the entering characteristics of their students?

Globalization

Perhaps the dominant force in restructuring our colleges and universities at the turn of the century will be globalization. The evidence is already present. Faculty currently work with colleagues all over the world and create consortia which lead to technology transfer and entrepreneurial arrangements. Many more students are taking advantage of courses offered electronically by other universities and colleges. Presidents are signing multinational agreements which embrace the internalization of education for the purpose of economic and technological development. The internationalization of education will redefine the role of the student affairs practitioner. Most other countries do not have well developed programs of student service/affairs. Will these countries look to the United States to assist in developing student affairs programs and preparation programs or will the influence of these countries lead to a profound change in student affairs in this country? What are some of the likely function and role changes? Will functions like admissions, financial aid, registration, and student accounts be contracted out to international service centers? Will advising and career planning be done using programs such as VideoPhone connecting the user to sites all over the world? Will the student affairs professional of the future become more of a technician than an educator? Or, will the future role be one of using knowledge about human development, learning, and individual needs to facilitate creating new learning environments that expand beyond the physical boundaries of today's campuses?

Societal Changes

In "Bowling Alone," Robert Putnam discusses a pattern of civic disengagement (Edgerton, 1995). He describes how there continues to be a lack of trust in public officials, an erosion of individuals participating in civic activities, a lessening of connections among people, and a movement away from teaching the virtues and skills necessary for democracy. Earlier, I described a similar trend for students based on the CIRP data. Others have described a similar trend among faculty. If this trend of civic disengagement continues on our campuses, how will student life be affected? Will students make career decisions based more on market trends than societal needs? Will a lack of civic training and engagement lead to an increasing escalation of the many problems confronting our society? What can student affairs practitioners do to reverse this trend?

New Roles and Models

New organizational roles and models are emerging in student affairs as a way to meet the challenges posed by a destabilized environment. Kuh, Whitt, and Shedd (1987) describe an emerging reality different from the mechanistic, objective, controlling reality so prevalent on many campuses. This new reality is one characterized by "conditions of uncertainty, mutual shaping, ambiguity, and multiple realities" (Bloland, Stamatakos, & Rogers, 1994, p. 49). Rhoads and Black (1995) describe this new reality for student affairs as a "critical cultural perspective" (p. 413). This approach addresses some of the criticism of the "grand theory" approach of student development by "considering the unique experiences of diverse social and cultural groups . . . the need for more localized understanding of human experience. This change in thinking about students and student life reflects a larger transformation in the social and behavioral sciences that places cultural understanding at the center of theorizing" (Rhoads & Black, 1995, p. 415). Garland and Grace (1993) discuss Rhoads and Black's theme of practitioners as transformative educators and suggest a new role for student affairs as the "integrator;" they describe this new role "as environmental scanner, milieu manager, market analyst, legal adviser, development officer, researcher, and quality assurance specialist" (p. 8).

The destabilization of higher education caused by societal changes and influences will result in new organizational models and roles for student affairs. We need to carefully examine how our role should change and be the initiator—not the recipient—of this change. We need to carefully think about organizational models that will reduce costs, increase efficiency, and lead to powerful learning environments.

CONCLUSION

These possible changes should be viewed as an opportunity to transform the academy into an institution which is accessible, embraces diversity, and focuses on learning and the connections among people. Student affairs practitioners need to take a leadership role in helping to restructure our colleges and universities based on student learning, "improving the quality and productivity of instruction" and "reinvent(ing) new social organizations, new ways of connecting, for the twenty-first century" (Edgerton, 1995, pp. 6-8). The remaining chapters will address in more detail the issues challenging higher education and the profession, the preparation and role of practitioners, and linkages between student affairs preparation and practice.

REFERENCES

Bloland, H. G. (1995). Postmodernism and higher education. *Journal of Higher Education, 66*(5), 521-559.

Bloland, P. A., Stamatakos, L. C., & Rogers, R. R. (1994). *Reform in student affairs: A critique of student development.* Greensboro, NC: ERIC Counseling and Student Services Clearinghouse.

Breneman, D. W. (1993). *Higher education: On a collision course with new realities.* (AGB Occasional Paper No. 22). Washington, DC: Association of Governing Boards of Universities and Colleges.

Cloud, R. C. (1992). The president and the law. *Educational Record, 73*(3), 8-14.

Cornish, E. (1996). *The cyber future: 96 ways our lives will change by the year 2005.* Bethesda, MD: World Future Society.

Coupland, D. (1992). *Shampoo planet.* New York: Simon & Schuster.

Edgerton, R. (1995). "Bowling alone": An interview with Robert Putnam about America's collapsing civic life. *AAHE Bulletin, 48*(1), 3-6.

El-Khawas, E. (1994a). *Restructuring initiatives to public higher education: Institutional response to financial constraints.* (ACE Research Briefs No. 8-5). Washington, DC: American Council on Education.

El-Khawas, E. (1994b). *Campus trends 1994: A time of reduction.* (Higher Education Panel Report No. 84). Washington, DC: American Council on Education.

Evangelauf, L. (1992, January 22). Enrollment projections revised upward in new government analysis. *The Chronicle of Higher Education,* p. A1.

Garland, P. H., & Grace, T. W. (1993). New perspectives for student affairs professionals: Evolving realities, responsibilities and roles. *ASHE-ERIC Higher Education Report No. 7.* Washington, DC: The George Washington University, School of Education and Human Development.

Guskin, A. E. (1994). Reducing student costs and enhancing student learning part II: Restructuring the role of faculty. *Change, 26*(5), 16-25.

Higher Education Research Institute. (1996). *The American freshman: National norms for fall 1995.* Los Angeles, CA: UCLA Graduate School of Education and Information Studies.

Hirsch, D. L. (1993). Politics through action: Student service and activism in the '90s. *Change, 25*(4), 32-36.

Hodgkinson, H. L. (1989). *The same client: The demographics of education and service delivery systems.* Washington, DC: Center for Demographic Policy.

Horton, N., & Andersen, C. (1994). *Linking the economy to the academy: Parallel trends.* (ACE Research Briefs No. 5-4). Washington, DC: American Council on Education.

Justiz, M. (1994). Demographic trends and the challenges to American higher education. In M. Justiz, R. Wilson, & L. Bjork (Eds.), *Minorities in higher education* (pp. 1-21). Washington, DC: American Council on Education.

Kaplin, W. A., & Lee, B. A. (1995). *The law of higher education: A comprehensive guide to the legal implications of administrative decision making* (3rd ed.). San Francisco: Jossey-Bass.

Komives, S. R., & Woodard, D. B. (1996). The profession: Building on the past, shaping the future. In S. R. Komives & D. B. Woodard (Eds.), *Student services: A handbook for the profession* (3rd ed., pp. 536-555). San Francisco: Jossey-Bass.

Kuh, G. D., Whitt, E. J., & Shedd, J. D. (1987). *Student affairs, 2001: A paradigmatic odyssey.* (ACPA Media Publication No. 42). Alexandria, VA: American College Personnel Association.

Leslie, L. L. (1995). *The changing nature of academic labor.* Baltimore, MD: Johns Hopkins Press.

Levin, H. (1989). *Raising productivity in higher education.* (Pew Higher Education Research Program). Philadelphia, PA: Trustees of the University of Pennsylvania.

Levine, A., & Hirsch, D. (1991). Undergraduates in transition: A new wave of activism on American college campus. *Higher Education, 22*(2), 119-128.

Loeb, P. R. (1994). *Generation at the crossroads: Apathy and action on the American campus.* New Brunswick, NJ: Rutgers University Press.

National Commission on Children. (1991). *Beyond rhetoric: A new American agenda for children and families.* (Final report of the National Commission on Children). Washington, DC: Author.

Rhoads, R. A., & Black, M. A. (1995). Student affairs practitioners as transformative educators: Advancing a critical cultural perspective. *Journal of College Student Development, 36*, 413-421.

Richard A. Harvill Conference on Higher Education. (1992, November). *The universities of the future: Roles in the changing world order.* Conference proceedings of The First Richard A. Harvill Conference on Higher Education, Tucson, AZ.

Robertson, R. (1992). *Globalization: Social theory and global culture.* New-bury Park, CA: Sage Publications.

Rossman, P. (1992). *The emerging worldwide electronic university: Information age global higher education.* Westport, CT: Greenwood Press.

Sandock, B. (1996). *Federal Regulatory Guidelines.* Unpublished paper.

Slaughter, S., & Leslie, L. (in press). *Academic capitalism: Politics, policies, and the entrepreneurial university.* Baltimore, MD: Johns Hopkins University Press.

Strauss, W., & Howe, N. (1991). *Generations: The history of America's future, 1584 to 2069.* New York: William Morrow.

Toffler, A. (1970). *Future shock.* New York: Random House.

Toffler, A. (1990). *Power shift: Knowledge, wealth, and violence at the edge of the 21st century.* New York: Bantam Books.

United Way of America's Strategic Institute. (1990, July/August). Nine forces reshaping America. *The Futurist,* 9-16.

Wexler, M., & Hulme, J. (Eds.). (1994). *Voices of the exiled: A generation speaks for itself.* New York: Doubleday.

Williams, E. A., & Malaney, G. D. (1996). Assessing the political ideology of college students: Reactions to the Persian Gulf war. *NASPA Journal, 33*, 145-159.

Wilson, B. J. (1994). Technology and higher education: In search of progress in human learning. *Educational Record, 75*(3), 8-16.

Chapter Two

Institutional Issues Facing Student Affairs

Carolyn R. Bair,
William M. Klepper, and
Christine E. Phelps Tobin

As one ponders the challenges presented by Woodard's "change-drivers" for the next millennium, there are many implications for the student affairs practitioner—so many implications that any well intended professional or practitioner-in-preparation could become frozen with fright. This deer-in-the-headlights response does not have to occur. A recall of our response to earlier challenges can prepare us for this oncoming traffic. Over a quarter century ago, the American College Personnel Association (ACPA) took "deliberate notice of the currents of change operating in higher education" in the implementation of Tomorrow's Higher Education (THE) Project (Butler, Ross, & Kubit, 1972, np). The first published report from the project was the monograph commissioned to Robert Brown entitled *Student Development in Tomorrow's Higher Education—A Return to the Academy* (Brown, 1972). Brown's projections can provide a perspective from which to examine the institutional issues facing student affairs. Furthermore, the comparison of Brown's work with the more recent ACPA (1994) *Student Learning Imperative: Implications for Student Affairs* reinforces his suggestions.

Addressing the most pressing issues, many of which were identified in Chapter 1, particularly within the context of current financial constraints, requires fundamental change. The premise of this chapter is that the overarching issue facing student affairs programs in the coming millennium is the development of organizational models that will reduce costs, increase efficiency, and lead to powerful learning environments; a necessity in marshaling the forces to face the "change-drivers" of the future. New theory is needed to guide our work with diverse student populations and diverse settings. New technology is changing the higher education landscape, the role of student affairs, and the traditional campus concept. Of the issues Woodard outlines in Chapter 1, six are most pressing to institutions of higher education and ultimately student affairs practice. These primary issues confronting student affairs practice are shifts in the American economy, changing national demographics, dwindling public confidence, increased legislative mandates, privatization, and emerging technology. These issues are interrelated and interconnected.

After a retrospective view, a revisiting of student affairs standards and guidelines for its practice will help us look to the future, while not forgetting the past. Knowing where student affairs has come from and where it has placed stakes in the ground to guide its future will allow for a strategic plan for the journey into the next millennium. Examination of the role of student affairs in the creation of a seamless learning environment, the facilitation of student learning, and the development of a community of scholars and learners will help frame student affairs' response to the institutional issues presented.

RETROSPECTIVE VIEW

Before presenting Brown's specific recommendations, a retrospective journey from the original academy to today's higher education may provide a path to the future. The first view, Plato's Academy in ancient Athens, would be a spacious park combined with an athletic establishment—"one could see Plato himself walking under the shade trees and expounding to a little trailing host of eager-eyed disciples the fundamental theories of his ideal Commonwealth" (Davis, 1914, p. 160). Note that there is no formal classroom. The learning environment appears outside the classroom; ". . . the youth of Athens complete their education after escaping from the rod of the schoolmaster. Here they have daily lessons on the mottos, which (did such a thing exist) should be blazoned on the coat of arms of Greece, as the summing up of all Hellenic wisdom: *Know thyself*, and again *Be moderate*" (Davis, 1914, p. 161).

As the academy emerged from the Middle Ages, learning centers became more defined by their settings. Bologna and Paris were the first universities where scholars banded together for protection and in order to set standards for teaching, pay, and tuition but gave little attention to building a permanent campus or supervising student life (Haskins, 1923). Oxford and Cambridge returned to the pastoral setting as the location for several residential colleges, combining living and learning within the English university structure (Thelin, 1996, p. 5). The American colonists built their colleges with the intent to "transplant and perfect the English idea of an undergraduate education as a civilizing experience that ensured a progression of responsible leaders" (Thelin, 1996, p. 6).

Once again, the viewer is reminded of the mottos of the original academy. Today these mottos are defined as developmental concepts, where "know thyself" becomes "establishing identity" and "be moderate" may be described as "managing emotions" (Chickering & Reisser, 1993). The focus is on the development of the individual within a learning environment that is a "just and disciplined community" (Boyer, 1990). Brown (1972) was cognizant of the interplay between the individual and the environment when he addressed future change. He believed that "the environmental factors that hold the most promise for affecting student developmental patterns include the peer group, the living unit, the faculty, and the classroom experience" (p. 34). Astin (1993) has confirmed, after studying the characteristics of the student's peer group and the teaching faculty, that these two factors are the most potent sources of influence on a student's growth and development during the undergraduate years. His findings go further to reaffirm the British "college" model of undergraduate education, which served as a prototype for many colleges in the United States—a residential setting that not only removes the student from the home but that also permits and encourages close student-student and student-faculty contact, smallness, and a sense of history and tradition that generates a sense of community (Astin, 1993).

From the ancient college past until today, higher education in America has prospered, differentiated and specialized within its component parts. Student affairs has been part of that development. A key indicator of its growth as a profession can be discovered in its codified standards.

STANDARDS OF THE PROFESSION

The profession has defined a set of standards that stake out student affairs boundaries within the higher education landscape. There is a ten-year history of development of these professional standards, beginning with the 1986 publication of the Council for the Advancement of Standards for Student Services/Development Programs (CAS). Over this decade of development, "the field of student affairs has established professional standards for many of its functional areas and has built a foundation for shaping the substance of its programs. Consequently, the various parts of student life are beginning to connect, each with a specific role in the learning community" (Mable, 1991, p. 9).

Using a broader historical perspective one could claim that standards for student services and development have been the concern of educators since the inception of American higher education (Mable, 1991, p. 6). Over time, these services have become more clearly defined and specialized so as to be distinguished, if not separated, from the formal curriculum of study. The development of the CAS standards was a natural outcome of this progression.

Student affairs can effectively face the issues of the future if it is guided by its standards and applies them in the context of the institutional mission that is unique to each college and university, and if it continues to develop these standards to anticipate and accommodate change. Even though the standards are used and hold great potential for student affairs programs and practices, there currently exists in them a limitation of scope with regard to the changedrivers, particularly in the areas of technology and changing demographics. Further, the current CAS (1986) General Standards "that govern the activities of all student services/development programs . . . (and) are integral to each functional area" do not include a tie to academic affairs (p. 5). Enlarging the scope of the CAS standards to address these limitations would help the profession by placing it in a better position from which to address the issues confronting higher education.

SEAMLESS LEARNING ENVIRONMENT

The best vantage point from which student affairs professionals can face the challenges of the future is one that encompasses the total learning environment in a seamless manner, where minimal distinction is made between where learning occurs (e.g., inside the classroom versus outside the classroom; curricular involvement versus co-curricular involvement; on-campus experiences versus off-campus learning centers or distance learning experiences). A major unrealized opportunity for student affairs professionals is to create lifelong learning opportunities, not only inside and outside the classroom in higher education (Kuh, 1996), but also a seamless system of education, including schools, training institutions, colleges and universities, emerging technologies, and distance learning techniques (Gee & Spikes, 1997). A recent survey conducted by the Social and Economic Services Research Center at Washington State University examined what the public wants from higher education. In essence, the findings indicate that higher education must change how it conducts business. Employees face obstacles to lifelong learning, namely the cost of education, the unavailability of courses offered in their geographical area, and courses offered at inconvenient times. Further, over 75 percent of the respondents think more courses should be offered using distance learning methods, while only 15 percent reported taking a course involving some form of distance learning (Social and Economic Sciences Research Center, 1997).

Student affairs' ties to the academic arena can be key in achieving total student development. The Student Learning Imperative (ACPA, 1994), highlighted research findings that indicate the more students are involved in a variety of activities inside and outside the classroom, the more they gain. Bridging organizational boundaries and forging collaborative partnerships help make learning experiences seamless. Working with faculty, campus organizations, and off-campus agencies offers rich opportunities for learning. Examples include instructional design centers, academic enrichment programs, faculty and staff development initiatives, community service opportunities, work settings, churches, and museums. Brown (1972) offered specific recommendations for the profession that are still useful and timely today:

(a) an academic department with student development staff teaching classes in human relations, values assessment, personal and group decision-making processes, human sexuality, service learning, leadership, and career planning;

(b) a consulting team that works with departments and individual professors to facilitate the structuring of curriculum and courses so that they might have the best chance for fostering student development;

(c) a student development staff that serves as administrators or program developers for special academic programs, such as experimental colleges, community-action programs, and work-study programs;

(d) out-of-class experiences designed for academic credit;

(e) curricular changes and innovations designed by a team with members from student affairs offering expertise in course content, learning and teaching, and student development.

Brown (1972) expanded the learning environment to address process as well as content, affective development as well as cognitive development, and competency attainment as well as knowledge learned; he thus defined the holistic development of a student. Howard Gardner (1993) extended the learning environment beyond the classroom when he defined intelligence as being verbal, musical, logical-mathematical, spatial, bodily, intrapersonal and interpersonal. Sternberg's (1996) triarchic theory of cognitive psychology—componential analytic intelligence, contextual practical intelligence and creative experiential intelligence—places further emphasis on a student-centered learning environment as a whole. Because of what we have come to know about the learner and the learning environment, it is apparent that the best vantage point from which student affairs professionals can face the challenges of the future is one that encompasses the total learning environment. There are many changes possible, even likely, in the delivery of educational services and practices. Student affairs professionals need to incorporate what we have learned about student learning and multiple modes of instruction in our quest to be on the forefront of the possible.

RESPONDING TO THE INSTITUTIONAL ISSUES

Shifts in American Economy

As a response to dramatic shifts in the American economy, organizations have moved to frequent practices of downsizing and budget cuts. The current state of diminished resources and increased expenses has led to critical budget problems, resulting in many changes on campuses, including program consolidation and elimination; privatization of services; a shift from quality to quantity; and an increase in external funding to support programs and services. Fundamental questions regarding funding allocation emerge when external funding is accepted, such as to what extent will the marketplace dictate which programs receive funding? For example, external funding is in place at Penn State University, where funding has been received by the career placement office for use in the development of interviewing facilities and by the student leadership office for a new program designed to develop the human relations skills of engineering students. When external funding is available for selected programs, the student affairs professional needs to be cognizant of the need for balance and to advocate for those programs still needing funding.

Changing National Demographics: Diversity as a Strength

Changing student demographics have occurred for a number of reasons, including the increasing enrollments of a more diverse student body. These changes present a greater challenge for achieving full participation of previously underrepresented groups in higher education (Nuss, 1994). Increased diversity has also led to moves to establish a greater sense of community on campus, and the development of a learning environment rooted in a critical cultural perspective, which is based on feminism, critical theory, postmodernism, and multiculturalism (Rhoads & Black, 1995).

One measure of diversity within a college or university is the degree to which the college-bound population of the geographical area served by the college or university is a mirror image of the enrolled population on the campus. Obviously this definition does not extend to historically black colleges and universities, nor to single gender institutions. However, as accessibility extends beyond selectivity, diversity extends beyond demographics. Therefore, an institution's commitment to diversity beyond numbers is a key indicator of its ultimate intent. To measure commitment is not easy. Commitment by definition requires an institution to mobilize the affective and rational behavior of its members. A committed community can only fill the gap between its intent and desired outcome through its actions. That action is delineated by the institution's goals.

A goal statement must contain measurable or verifiable results. Absent these results, the college cannot measure its progress. The Association of American Colleges and Universities (ACAS, 1995) in its exploration of the "new academy," defined diversity as follows:

> What is today called diversity is comprised of interrelated but distinct stands. At base, it involves the givens that each and every one of us is unique, at the same time as we are all nourished by cultures that both overlap and differ. But because human histories are marred

> by faulty thinking and injustices that have created vicious inequalities among these individual and cultural differences, our "common differences" too often rank and divide rather than simply distinguish us. In these "cauldrons of democracy," the new academy attempts to melt those invidious divisions, not the differences that make us all who we are. When access is not limited to the historically privileged few, democracy engages diversity. Framings of what diversity is and means begin to shift in recognition of the need to deal better than we have with the complexities of many kinds of human differences and similarities. (p. 3)

It is apparent from institutional case studies and current literature that the issue of diversity facing institutions has moved beyond demographics. The professional standards of the student affairs profession (CAS, 1986) reaffirm the institutional role in "giving voice" to its diverse population—"the institution must provide educational programs for minority students that identify their unique needs, prioritize those needs, and respond to the priorities . . ." (p. 6). Furthermore, Woodard's "demographic changes" forecast the "powerful influences in shaping students' attitudes, beliefs, behavior, and subsequent campus communities" these changes will engage. If the institution's diversity goal is to serve as the linchpin between an institution's intent to be accessible and its ability to enhance student learning while enriching its community of learners and scholars, these behavioral expectations must live and breathe in a person's day-to-day experiences on the campus or at a location other than the "campus." Student affairs by its intent and actions can bring strength to this linchpin, thereby enhancing student learning and development.

Student affairs practitioners must be dedicated to building multiracial colleges and universities and must continue to respond to these opportunities as enrollments of non-traditional students increase. The growing challenge of achieving full participation for previously underrepresented groups will continue to impact on our ability to establish community on campus and will influence our renewed emphasis on learning in a postmodern world.

Woodard concluded in his opening chapter that in facing the changedrivers of the future, these changes should be viewed as an opportunity to transform the academy into an institution which is accessible, embraces diversity, and focuses on learning and the connections among people. Each of these criteria should be applied to the process of generating alternatives and making choices. A clear delineation of the distinguishing elements of an institution's mission and educational purpose must precede the application of these criteria, because it is in the mission that boundaries are defined and in the purpose that outcomes are stated.

As an institutional example, The College of New Jersey's boundaries are clearly delineated in the closing portion of its mission statement—"primarily undergraduate, giving primacy to teaching, having an achievement oriented and diverse student body, medium sized, comprehensive, and residential" (The College of New Jersey, 1992, np). The issue for Woodard is whether these boundaries provide for accessibility, diversity, learning and connections among people. A closer scrutiny of the College's Purpose of Undergraduate Education is warranted to determine if these outcomes are delineated. In the introductory paragraph, it is stated that,

> The College of New Jersey is a highly-selective institution which provides students with an opportunity to participate in a unique community of learners. This community calls upon its members to recognize and strive for excellence, and to develop the objectivity and capacity for change which are marks of educated people. It also calls upon them to participate in service to others and exhibit a respect for and appreciation of diversity. (The College of New Jersey, 1990, np)

In a very different type of institution within the City Colleges of Chicago, the Kennedy-King College has in its mission "to accept all eligible students and to provide them with an education appropriate to their needs that will allow them to achieve the kind of economic, cultural, and social life they desire." The City Colleges of Chicago draw their students from and mirror the population of the city of Chicago, and the two-year Kennedy-King College is highly diverse. In terms of providing for accessibility, diversity, learning, and connections among people, Kennedy-King has adopted the following annual priorities for 1996-1997:

> Transfer education goals: 1) revitalize existing programs and implement viable new programs; 2) improve communication with four-year colleges on the performance of Kennedy-King alumni; and 3) implement a more coordinated and information-based marketing/outreach/recruitment system. Workforce preparation goals: 1) integrate school-to-work initiatives in credit and noncredit programs with accompanying faculty and staff development; 2) institute a collegewide system to improve employability of completers; and 3) continue to expand

and refine the structure of high school Tech Prep partnership programs to facilitate the enrollment and success of participants in the college. (Kennedy-King College, 1996)

These educational purpose statements define outcomes, and further, intent. Again, Woodard's accessibility, diversity, learning and community criteria when applied to the colleges' statements brings into focus the issues facing these institutions and their unique missions.

Dwindling Public Confidence

The American public's dwindling confidence in and, or disaffection with its colleges and universities has been an increasing cause for concern and a driving force for change. Dwindling public confidence has led to several quality assurance issues—academic competency and readiness of students, economic viability of programs and institutions, and the worth connected with students' collegiate experiences. The popular press has cited public dissatisfaction over many issues—not only academic and economic accountability, but also racial incidents, intercollegiate athletics, sexual harassment, and students themselves.

In addressing these issues, colleges and universities are increasing their internal and external assessments of programs, services, curricula and student outcomes in an effort to both set future directions and demonstrate effectiveness to the American public. Budgetary reviews have resulted in leaner, often more efficient organizations and in both program consolidation and elimination. A renewed emphasis on student learning has developed. Many new approaches have been initiated that engage students with others in community building and civic participation and that enhance students' skills in leadership and global understanding.

Student affairs professionals, working collaboratively with others across and outside their institutions, can assume a central role with respect to the rebuilding of public confidence and establishing directions for the future. A number of, if not all of, the areas in which public confidence needs to be rebuilt are certainly historically connected to student affairs. In responding to these issues, however, there is a pressing need for collaboration across the college or university community that can be fostered by student affairs professionals. Faith Gabelnick (1997), President at Pacific University in Oregon, stresses the importance of collaboration and of thinking in inclusive rather than exclusive terms: "If students are to change, then their teachers, mentors, and administrative leaders must adopt and model a different way of working and thinking. Roles and responsibilities for faculty and administrators will have to shift: the boundaries and historic tensions between these two groups will need to move toward a more collaborative perspective on university work and community responsibility" (p. 35). Reform is in the air partly because of the dwindling confidence of the public, and times of reform are often times of great opportunity regardless of the reasons necessitating the reform. Consequently, student affairs professionals now find themselves in a tremendous position to effect change not only for students but for colleges and universities, as well.

Increased Legislative Mandates

Tremendous financial constraints are present in higher education today. Resources were at an all-time high during the 1960s, but educators have experienced drastic reductions in recent years. As a consequence, organizational restructuring and program consolidation and elimination have occurred, and already-scarce fiscal and personnel resources are being utilized to address increased government regulation. These cut-backs leave many professionals in higher education wondering whether the human, technical and financial resources are available to continue to provide high quality services and programs for students.

Creative ideas and new approaches are needed, and student affairs professionals are again in a position to help their institutions. In addition to asking "how can I manage the increases needed in order to accommodate legislative mandates while still cutting back on expenditures?", student affairs professionals need to take a broad look at how to participate in restructuring and making transformations while keeping students' needs and programs positioned at the forefront of discussions. Marjorie Kelly (1993) addressed the need for creativity and change when making transformations in higher education:

> Transformation of any sort—whether human or chemical or corporate—is a perilous passage at best, calling for a radical letting go, and an openness to the unknown. It's hard to imagine anything more frightening. And it's hard to find a more likely route to progress—for in letting go of the old form, we create the space for a new form that will work even better. It comes down simply to this: that we can't advance as long as we're holding tight to what no longer works. And we have to break the mold before a new form can emerge. (p. 7)

Impact of Privatization

The decreases in federal and state monies, the limited resources available through private sources, and the reluctance to rely on tuition increases for added revenue have forced colleges and universities to be highly creative in developing strategies for balancing their budgets. Many higher education institutions have responded in part by moving to privatization, or outsourcing, of services. Privatization is used in many areas directly affecting students and historically connected to the student affairs administrative area. Examples are counseling services, health services, food services, residence hall management, and bookstore management. Although privatization may result in savings to the "bottom line," it is not without its disadvantages. In addition to questions as to whether or not monetary savings to the institution is the sole criteria for moving to privatization, Eddy, Spaulding, and Murphy (1996) raised several concerns:

> (a) Have all of the ways in which privatization will impact students and staff been identified . . . at each institution considering privatization;
>
> (b) How will privatization impact the student development philosophy and mission of higher education institutions;
>
> (c) Is the profit motive a healthy concept within the parameters of student development;
>
> (d) Will all of the personnel in the privatization structure be role models for students;
>
> (e) Will contractors or providers uphold the high professional and ethical standards expected of higher education personnel; and
>
> (f) How will student development professional organizations and associations interact with contractors and providers? (p. 2)

Other concerns include whether or not higher costs will simply be passed on to students by the contracting organization, and whether or not students will continue to have avenues for input and "voice" in matters affecting them.

Since so many of the moves toward privatization occur within areas historically housed in student affairs, it is important that student affairs administrators also take a strong role in the process of arranging for contracts with organizations that provide such services. Student affairs professionals are in the best position to establish in advance those contractual arrangements that will best ensure that the goals and missions of the institution are advanced and that student learning and development are taken into account.

Emerging Technology

According to Peter Drucker (Kenzer & Johnson, 1997),

> Thirty years from now the big university campuses will be relics. Universities won't survive. It's as large a change as when we first got the printed book . . . Higher education is in deep crisis. Already we are beginning to deliver more lectures and classes off campus via satellite or two-way video at a fraction of the cost. The college won't survive as a residential institution. (p. 162)

Student affairs must respond to the impact of emerging technology on teaching and learning, the impact of distance learning techniques on cognitive and personal development, and the development of community in the learning environment. There is a strong move toward competency-based instruction and assessment, competency certification rather than blanket course or program certification, and "self-instructional" multi-media packages. Distance learning does not automatically translate into disjointed learning, but rather, provides another tool to assist in the education of individuals (Wade, 1997).

There are many examples of student affairs areas that have moved in directions compatible with virtual campuses and technology-based distribution of learning in an effort to respond to the challenges of the future. In the area of career development the following activities can be found online: job listings; career planning guides, job search strategies, generic interviewing tips and other information; online resumes and resume development assistance; and interviews conducted through videoconferencing technology. In the area of counseling, the following initiatives are underway: Georgia College and State University is developing a desktop videoconferencing link between the Counseling Center on the main campus and remote campus locations, allowing "face-to-face" contact and assistance; practitioners are currently offering direct counseling services over the internet and self-help materials on web sites—perhaps the most comprehensive is the Virtual Pamphlet collection at the University of Chicago (Wade, 1997).

It is also interesting to illustrate how some distance learning focused institutions are defining student affairs work by extending programs and services beyond a "campus." Research conducted by Bair and Webster (1992) found consistent evidence suggesting that at many institutions traditional student affairs functions administered for the distance learning sites (as defined by having no institutional facility) were administered by the Academic Dean, while these same functions for on-campus programs were administered by student affairs. This pattern was found at institutions including Lewis University, College of St. Francis, Nova University, Brenau University, and Pepperdine University. This practice involved such areas as academic advising, career planning and placement, commuter student programs and services, counseling services, services for students with disabilities, judicial programs and services, learning assistance programs, minority student programs and services, recreational sports, student activities, and orientation. The opportunities are many. There is an immediate need for all student affairs professionals to become knowledgeable about and comfortable with the new technologies and to translate many of our current functions into these new media. We need to determine and define the role of student affairs in the virtual environment. The knowledge of and need for practices based on learning and student development theories will not disappear. We must be able to transmit that knowledge in new and different ways (Wade, 1997).

The above six areas outlined by Woodard are pressing issues and represent distinctive challenges to student affairs professionals. They are also opportunities for us to bring about change of a beneficial nature for our students and our colleges and universities. Because student affairs professionals are in a pivotal position to work collaboratively with students, administrators, faculty, and other stakeholders, we are in a position to act as agents of change in a positive way.

STUDENT LEARNING

Student affairs has historically viewed the academic experience (curriculum, the library, the classroom, and the laboratory) as preeminent (NASPA, 1987, pp. 9-10). In addition, the profession has asserted that feelings affect thinking and learning; student involvement enhances learning; personal circumstances affect learning; out-of-class environments affect learning, and a supportive and friendly community life helps students learn (NASPA, 1987, p. 11). These assertions are key to addressing the issue of student learning and personal development. *The Student Learning Imperative: Implications for Student Affairs* (ACPA, 1994) defines further the characteristics of the student affairs profession if it is be committed to student learning and personal development:

1. The student affairs division mission complements the institution's mission, with the enhancement of student learning and personal development being the primary goal of student affairs programs and services.
2. Resources are allocated to encourage student learning and personal development.
3. Student affairs professionals collaborate with other institutional agents and agencies to promote student learning and personal development.
4. The division of student affairs includes staff who are experts on students, their environments, and teaching and learning processes.
5. Student affairs policies and programs are based on promising practices from research on student learning and institution-specific assessment data.

In comparing Brown's (1972) proposed ties to academic affairs to the student learning imperatives, student affairs professionals are presented a seamless transition from one document to the other. Within these two ACPA publications, student affairs is reinforced in its efforts to join in the common purpose to advance student learning and development.

Student learning must be addressed as an issue in its totality within the learning environment. NASPA more recently assessed its role in the core teaching and learning activities of higher education (Whitt, 1996) and defined student learning outcomes to include cognitive competence (i.e., complex meaning-making, critical thinking, intellectual flexibility, reflective judgment, and ability to acquire and apply knowledge); intrapersonal competence (i.e., coherent integrated sense of identity); interpersonal competence (i.e., interdependence, collaboration, appreciation of diversity of people, communication skills, problem-solving and conflict-management skills, humanitarianism, and concern for community); and practical competence (e.g., accomplishing daily tasks, time management, career decision-making). Consequently, student affairs can only face the issue of student learning, as it is broadly defined, by starting with the general education of students.

The core curriculum of an institution's general education requirements can provide an educational foundation for building student affairs student learning strategies. Brown's original recommendations do not include this method of integrating student affairs into the teaching and learning activities of the institution. Over the last 25 years, the core curriculum has been reaffirmed as the essential ingredient in an undergraduate education, and therefore, is an ideal entry point for student affairs to build its ties.

For example, one institution requires every first year entering student to take six credit hours of interdisciplinary core courses, Understanding Humanity. The first of the sequence of courses is entitled Athens to New York. This course examines some of the ways in which philosophy, literature, art, and religion reflect and shape human culture in classical Athens, contemporary New York, and selected other times and places. Central questions include what it means to be human; to be a member of a community; to be moral, ethical, or just; and how individuals and communities respond to differences in race, class, gender and ethnicity. Attention is given to Western and non-Western cultures and to ways in which civilizations are mutually connected. The First-Year Experience student community service learning project is integrated into the course (College of New Jersey, 1996, p. 34).

This course was a starting point for developing strategies for student learning and personal development, and building ties to academic affairs. The most obvious tie between academic and student affairs was the integration of service learning into the course, based on the belief that the central questions of the course would come to life as students participated in community service. In other words, by integrating these academic and student life programs, the students could gain intellectual, intrapersonal, interpersonal and practical competence. Student reflections on their service learning experience have confirmed that these outcomes do result. For example,

> To me, in those moments, humanity never seemed more fragile and weak. My service experience opened my eyes to allow me to understand that we are weak and others are strong. But no matter what our circumstances, none of us has the right to stand in our safe, comfortable, and warm houses and pass judgment on those less fortunate. Until this experience these hungry souls were just nameless statistics in the paper and I had no real grasp of who they were. Now I do. I will never forget the man who came up to me with tears in his eyes and thanked me for being so kind to him. (Student volunteer at Trenton Area Soup Kitchen)
>
> I think that the most rewarding part of the community service was knowing that for a few hours a week, I brightened a few kids' days. It was a great feeling to walk into the crowded gym and literally have kids grabbing you and giving you giant hugs. It made me feel really special and I was glad to get a chance to do it. I discovered that I can

make a difference in someone's life. (Student volunteer at Ewing Community Center After School Program)

I learned that being human involves understanding that other people are human as well and that it is the true responsibility of the more fortunate to help the less fortunate. I learned that being a member of a community demands helping others in the community. The most rewarding aspect of my service has been knowing that I might have helped people in some way. I hope to continue serving my community in the future. (Student volunteer at New Jersey State Psychiatric Hospital)

In a much different setting, DePaul University's New Student Service Day is a program designed to bring DePaul University's newest students together as a first year class where they spend an afternoon assisting various community agencies at the beginning of the academic year. This program, developed by former Assistant Director of Student Life/New Student Programs K. K. Nielsen Cleland, was designed for DePaul to bring its mission to life—service to others and a commitment to the urban experience. A second objective of the program is to provide the opportunity to "process" and reflect on the importance of service work and one's responsibility to give back to the community. Faculty and staff team leaders facilitate a colloquium to process the experience immediately following the service component. The third objective of the program is to promote the community service opportunities that the institution offers throughout the year. The program is collaborative involving faculty, continuing students, new students, ministry, alumni affairs, and student affairs. In 1996, over 600 faculty, staff, alumni, and students participated in the event, serving 40 agencies, for a total of 2,400 hours of community service to the Chicago area in one day (DePaul University, 1997).

In yet another urban setting, the University of Louisville has a number of programs specifically designed for their many adult learners. The adult student orientation program includes a focus on a number of areas of special concern, such as child care, career planning, personal and academic support, and financial aid. The University also has a program called ACCESS (Adult Commuter Center and Evening Student Services) through which adult learners may use a service center containing a computer lab, copier, coffee, space for study group meetings, lunch area, and advising. This program, offered by student affairs, supports the academic mission and was designed following consultation with the faculty. A third program called SNAP (Saturday Night Alternative Program) is designed with the entire family of the adult learner in mind. Activities include movies, sports and recreation, games and events (B. King, personal communication, March 3, 1997).

COMMUNITY OF SCHOLARS AND LEARNERS

While campuses are often described as communities, the issue is whether a campus can really achieve this end. For a college or university to achieve community requires that all members be committed to a common set of expectations which define the community; and that they freely interact within and across the internal boundaries of the learning environment.

Arriving at a shared definition of community expectations is a difficult task. The first step is the development of a social contract (Crookston, 1974, p. 383). Over the years, colleges and universities have stated their expectations in catalogues either as a creed or beliefs statement. Widely differing institutional missions and vision statements highlight the contrast among institutions. For example,

> Loyola University Chicago is a Jesuit Catholic university dedicated to knowledge in the service of humanity. It is a comprehensive, independent, urban institution of higher education and health care. The university endeavors to develop in the lives of students, faculty, and staff, the spirit of searching for truth and living for others. . . . Loyola values freedom of inquiry, the pursuit of truth, and care for others, especially the young, the poor, and the sick. The university strives to develop in its community a capacity for critical and ethical judgment and a commitment to action in the service of faith and justice. . . . An urban institution, Loyola benefits from Chicago's exceptional cultural, economic, and human resources. In turn, the university affirms its long-standing commitment to urban life—and works to solve its problems—in Chicago, the nation, and the world. (Loyola University Chicago, 1997)

A contrasting example can be found from the College of DuPage, a community college located in a western suburb of Chicago. Surrounded by affluence and growth, this institution has grown in numbers to become one of the largest community colleges in the United States. The College of DuPage is guided by six philosophies, including (a) the power of teaching and learning; (b) a commitment to excellence; (c) valuing diversity; (d) embracing the call to remove barriers to educational opportunity; (e) supporting the full participation of the school in planning and decision making in the community as a whole; and (f) valuing service to students and the community (College of DuPage,

1996, p. 7). The College of DuPage is also guided by a mission that states:

> The mission of the College of DuPage is to be at the forefront of higher education, serving the needs of the community. The college will be the first place residents turn for the highest quality in educational and cultural opportunities. The college will serve as a model of distinction for community college education. (College of DuPage, 1995, p. 10)

Whatever the origin or form of the social contract, it must be articulated and disseminated as a guide for community members' actions. Wide participation in its creation will make it a community document and more inclusive of the values of the community. In its final form, a social contract is a statement of the behavioral expectations which the community willingly subscribes to for the common good. The original author of *The Social Contract*, Jean Jacques Rousseau wrote:

> Is a method of associating discoverable which will defend and protect, with all the collective might, the person and property of each associate, and in virtue of which each associate, though he becomes a member of the group, nevertheless obeys only himself, and remains as free as before? This is the problem, a basic one, for which the social contract provides the solution. If, then, we exclude from the social contract everything not essential to it, we shall find that it reduces itself to the following terms: Each of us puts into the common pool, and under the sovereign control of the general will, his person and all his power. And we, as a community, take each member unto ourselves as an indivisible part of the whole. (Rousseau, 1954/1762, pp. 18, 20)

The social contract allows for a broader definition of membership in the community. It provides a basis for community action, a statement of agreement as to the community's general purpose in the education of students. Thus, it can serve as a common behavioral guide for the college community.

Campus Life: In Search of Community (Boyer, 1990) called for campuses to return to certain principles in the form of a social compact. Although these principles assume primacy of the "campus" as we have known it, our challenge is to make them more visionary and apply them to learning environments of the future. Among the principles expressed as appropriate for campuses to hold were the following:

> First, a college or university is an educationally purposeful community, a place where faculty and students share academic goals and work together to strengthen teaching and learning on the campus. Second, a college or university is an open community, a place where freedom of expression is uncompromisingly protected and where civility is powerfully affirmed. Third, a college or university is a just community, a place where the sacredness of the person is honored and where diversity is aggressively pursued. Fourth, a college or university is a disciplined community, a place where individuals accept their obligations to the group and where well-defined governance procedures guide behavior for the common good. Fifth, a college or university is a caring community, a place where the well-being of each member is sensitively supported and where service to others is encouraged. Sixth, a college or university is a celebrative community, one in which the heritage of the institution is remembered and where rituals affirming both tradition and change are widely shared. (pp. 7-8)

The social contract or compact is then critical to the development of a sense of community on a campus or among a group of scholars and learners. Equally important are the social interactions of the community members. These interactions are determined in large part by the permeability of the internal educational boundaries that exist on a campus. In a recent assessment by a Mid-Atlantic think tank of student affairs professionals and educators, it was the conclusion that "the essence of community for higher education may have less to do with the changes in the composition of higher education than in our ability to redefine what it means to be educated for the 21st century" (Evans, Klepper, Walbert, & Bryan, 1995, np).

The classroom and campus present to students distinct learning environments and, therefore, boundaries for them to negotiate. If an institution seeks to optimize students' learning and personal development, interactions in the classroom, on the campus, and in the learning community must not be disjointed. The student should be able to distinguish but not separate the two.

Even though this partnership has been fruitful, student centered learning goes beyond the ties between academic and student affairs. Student learning and development flourishes best within a community of scholars and learners. Woodard concludes this point in his chapter when he raises the need to focus on the connections among people, the creating of a community, whether it be on a campus or not. To this point, Woodard and several colleagues are involved in the use of both videophone and videoconferencing as a way to deliver an international curriculum to doctoral students. In an effort to apply an international lens on issues in higher education and student affairs, The North American Consortium for Educational Restructuring (NACER) has been created to examine how higher education can be restructured to prepare for and contribute to a global society. Several institutions in Canada, Mexico, and the United States are participating. The use of new, and the application of existing technologies is essential in the development of this community of scholars and learners. In addition to the distance learning strategies, faculty will visit different campuses and offer courses, and students will visit different campuses and enroll in courses. Collectively, these efforts attempt to heighten interaction in the learning community and to develop a sense of community among the scholars and learners despite vast geographical distances and significant expense.

For several years institutions of higher education in the western United States have led the nation in providing distance-learning programs using technology. The region's geography and demography lend itself well to extensive telecommunications networks, with large stretches of land, and widely dispersed populations. The tremendous growth of distance-learning programs, along with the possibility of a new virtual university, has increased concerns about how to ensure that higher education programs delivered via telecommunications are of high quality. The effectiveness of technology itself is not in question. Research has consistently demonstrated that the achievement and satisfaction of students who learn via technology can equal those of students in regular classrooms. Rather, the focus is on surrounding issues of student isolation, how to provide effective advising and academic support services, and whether students in distance-learning degree programs have some assurance that an electronically delivered program will continue to be supported long enough to enable them to complete the degree. As a result, principles of good practice for electronically offered academic degree and certificate programs have been developed by a group representing the Western states' higher education regulating agencies, higher education institutions, and the regional accrediting community. These principles address several components of a learning environment including students and student affairs, and highlight the following practices:

a) The program provides students with clear, complete, and timely information on the curriculum, course and degree requirements, nature of faculty/student interaction, assumptions about technological competence and skills, technical equipment requirements, availability of academic support services and financial aid resources, and costs and payment policies;

b) Enrolled students have reasonable and adequate access to the range of student services appropriate to support their learning. Accepted students have the background, knowledge, and technical skills needed to undertake the program and

c) Advertising, recruiting, and admissions materials clearly and accurately represent the program and the services available. (Johnstone & Krauth, 1996, p. 40)

The quality of any learning community is measured by the degree to which the ideals of the institution continue to be reflected in the behavior of its members, and the boundaries of the classroom, the campus, and the learning environment remain permeable—thus providing a common foundation for student learning and personal development—a foundation built on ties between academic and student affairs.

CONCLUSION

There is no question we now face the most formidable challenges of our history: dramatically diminished resources coupled with public resistance to higher taxes and dwindling public confidence; demographic shifts resulting in increasing numbers of nontraditional students; increased legislative mandates; privatization; and emerging technology. We must shape our own destiny aggressively, or policymakers will do it for us, and that would be detrimental to the future and quality of higher education (Gee & Spikes, 1997).

Student affairs professionals have an essential role and responsibility to confront these changedrivers. They cannot be mere passengers in this journey to the next millennium. They must articulate their vision for the future, and strengthen their planning by the use and development of their professional standards.

Facing these critical institutional issues is not beyond the capabilities of the profession. There are institutions which have faced these challenges in this decade, and are stronger from their journey. Their success was gained by forming ties—educational partnerships—between academic and student affairs; partnerships borne out of a common commitment to student learning and personal development. We must make change an ongoing part of our institutional culture if we are to survive.

Student affairs professionals must also recognize the tremendous opportunity open to them in times of change. With that opportunity, we are in a position to design programs, environments, and practices that are advancements over anything ever offered before. Further, given new knowledge about the processes of change, we are in a position to engage with other stakeholders in the process of improving higher education.

REFERENCES

American Association of Colleges and Universities (1995). *Liberal learning and the arts of connection for the new academy.* Washington, DC: Author.

American College Personnel Association (1994). *The student learning imperative: Implications for student affairs.* Washington, DC: Author.

Astin, A. W. (1993). *What matters in college: Four critical years revisited.* San Francisco: Jossey-Bass.

Bair, C. R., & Webster, C. E. (1992). *Honoring commitments to diverse students and learning sites: A comparative study.* Paper presented at the annual meeting of the American College Personnel Association, Cincinnati, OH.

Boyer, E. L. (1990). *Campus life: In search of community.* Lawrenceville, NJ: Princeton University Press.

Brown, R. D. (1972). *Student development in tomorrow's higher education—A return to the academy.* Washington, DC: American College Personnel Association.

Butler, W. R., Ross, G. R., & Kubit, D. E. (1972). Foreword. In R. D. Brown, *Student development in tomorrow's higher education - A return to the academy.* Washington, DC: American College Personnel Association.

Chickering, A. W. & Reisser, L. (1993). *Education and identity* (2nd ed.). San Francisco: Jossey-Bass.

College of DuPage (1995). *College of DuPage 1995-1997 catalog: Reaching through teaching.*

College of DuPage (1996). *College of DuPage institutional planning 1995-1996: A year in review.*

College of New Jersey (1990). *College of New Jersey statement on purpose of undergraduate education.*

College of New Jersey (1992). *College of New Jersey vision statement.*

College of New Jersey (1996). *College of New Jersey student handbook 1996-1997.*

Council for the Advancement of Standards for Student Services/Development Programs. (1986). *Council for the Advancement of Standards: Standards and Guidelines for Student Services/Development Programs.* Washington, DC: Council for the Advancement of Standards for Student Services/Development Programs.

Crookston, B. B. (1974). The intentional democratic community in college residence halls. *Personnel and Guidance Journal, 52*, 382-389.

Davis, W. S. (1914). *A day in old Athens.* New York: Allyn and Bacon.

DePaul University (1996). *DePaul University new student service day '97.* Chicago: DePaul University, Office of Student Affairs.

Eddy, J. P. , Spaulding, D. J., & Murphy, S. (1996, Summer). Privatization of higher education services: Propositional pros and cons. *Education, 116*, 578-581.

Evans, N. J., Klepper, W. M., Walbert, J., & Bryan, J. T. (1995). Achieving community: Where are we in 1995? *NASPA Region II Newsletter, 15*(3), insert.

Gabelnick, F. (1997). Educating a committed citizenry. *Change, 29*(1), 30-35.

Gardner, H. (1993). *Multiple intelligences: The theory in practice.* New York: Basic Books.

Gee, E. G., & Spikes, D. R. (1997). Retooling America's public universities. *About Campus, 1*(6), 30-32.

Guskin, A. E. (1996, July-August). Facing the future: The change process in restructuring universities. *Change, 28*(4), 26-38.

Haskins, C. H. (1923). *The rise of universities.* New York: Holt.

Johnstone, S. M., & Krauth, B. (1996). Some principles of good practice for the virtual university. *Change, 28*(2), 38-41.

Kelly, M. (1993, July/August). Taming the demons of change. *Business Ethics, 7*(4), 6-7.

Kennedy-King College. (1996, September). *Priority statements of community colleges.* Presented annually to the Illinois Board of Higher Education.

Kenzner, R., & Johnson, S. S. (1997, March 10). Seeing things as they really are. *Forbes, 159*(5), 122-129.

Loyola University Chicago (1997). Loyola University Chicago mission statement.

Kuh, G. D. (1996). Guiding principles for creating seamless learning environments for undergraduates. *Journal of College Student Development, 37*, 135-148.

Mable, P. (1991). Professional standards: An introduction and historical perspective. In W. A. Bryan, R. B. Winston, & T. K. Miller (Eds.), *Using professional standards in student affairs* (New Directions for Student Services, no. 53, pp. 5-18). San Francisco: Jossey-Bass.

National Association of Student Personnel Administrators (1987). *A perspective on student affairs: A statement issued on the 50th anniversary of the student personnel point of view*. Washington, DC: Author.

North American Consortium for Educational Restructuring (1996). *The north American consortium for educational restructuring mission statement.*

Nuss, E. M. (1994). Leadership in higher education: Confronting realities of the 1990s. *NASPA Journal, 31*, 209-216.

Rhoads, R. A., & Black, M. A. (1995). Student affairs practitioners as transformative educators: Advancing a critical cultural perspective. *Journal of College Student Development, 36*, 413-421.

Rousseau, J. J. (1954). *The social contract.* (W. Kendall, Trans.). Chicago: Henry Regnery Company. (Original work published 1762)

Social and Ecomonic Sciences Research Center. (1997). *What the public wants from higher education.* Bellingham, WA: Washington State University Press.

Sternberg, R. J. (1996). *Cognitive psychology.* Fort Worth, TX: Harcourt Brace.

Thelin, J. R. (1996). Historical overview of American higher education. In S. R. Komives, D. B. Woodard, Jr. & Associates, *Student services: A handbook for the profession* (3rd ed., pp. 3-21). San Francisco: Jossey-Bass.

Wade, A. (1997). *The role of student affairs in the virtual university.* Paper presented at the annual meeting of the American College Personnel Association, Chicago.

Whitt, E. J. (Ed.). (1996). *Redefining the landscape: Student affairs workand student learning.* Washington, DC: National Association of Student Personnel Administrators.

Chapter Three

Issues Facing Student Affairs Professionals: The Four Realms of Professional Life

Joan B. Hirt and Don G. Creamer

Economic restructuring, emerging technology, demographic changes, and increased regulation are some of the global issues facing higher education that Woodard has discussed in the first chapter of this book. Bair, Klepper, and Phelps Tobin have examined those issues from an institutional perspective in Chapter 2. They suggest how the student affairs profession might address economic shifts, changing demographics, dwindling public confidence, increased legislative mandates, privatization, and emerging technology in ways that promote student learning and create communities of scholars and learners. Collectively, these authors describe the challenges confronting higher education in general and the student affairs profession in particular.

The impact that these critical changes have had on the daily lives of individual practitioners, however, has yet to be explored. How can the components of contemporary professional life be conceptualized? What demands do these various aspects place on professionals? What tensions do those demands create? How do those tensions influence the nature of the work professionals conduct on a daily basis? These questions form the focus of this chapter.

To conceptualize the nature of professional practice, it is useful to identify the four realms in which practitioners routinely operate: the personal, the institutional, the extra-institutional, and the professional. These realms represent very different, yet equally real, contexts which influence the day-to-day lives of professionals. Each creates a different set of demands and tensions which compete for the energy and attention of the practitioner. Understanding the nature of the realms and the different forces they impose will enable professionals to better understand the complexity of contemporary student affairs practice.

THE PERSONAL REALM

The personal realm includes those aspects of professional life most immediate to the daily lives of practitioners: career mobility and prospects; familial opportunities and obligations; and quality of life. Each creates a set of demands unique to the individual. Career aspirations, family circumstances, outside interests and lifestyles vary dramatically from person to person, yet they influence all student affairs professionals to some extent.

The balance between career and personal life is a difficult one for most student affairs staff. Estimates on attrition rates for the profession range from 39% (Burns, 1982) to 65% (Richmond & Sherman, 1991), and the most frequently cited reasons for that attrition relate to issues of limited career mobility. Given these rather striking statistics, it is interesting that current research on employment trends in the profession is very limited; only two studies have been conducted in the past six years.

Upward mobility is perhaps the most obvious issue for practitioners in this realm. The organizational structures for most student affairs arenas are relatively flat, offering large numbers of entry level positions, fewer mid-level opportunities, and dramatically limited senior-level opportunities. In 1990, 35% of all student affairs job announcements posted in the *Chronicle of Higher Education* were for entry-level jobs and an additional 28% offered positions one step above entry-level, while only 4% were for executive student affairs officers (Janasiewicz & Wright, 1993). Clearly, opportunities for upward mobility are limited.

Lateral mobility is a second career-related personal issue for many. The ability to move from one functional area of student affairs to another, for example from residence life to student activities, is seen by many as a legitimate form of career development. Yet opportunities for such transitions are relatively limited. Career opportunities in the housing arena continue to dominate the profession, representing 36% to 39% of all entry-level and 36% of all mid-level opportunities (Armstong, Campbell, & Ostroth, 1978; Janasiewicz & Wright, 1993).

In fact, the organizational structure and culture of the profession at the entry-level essentially constrains future lateral mobility. Young practitioners are urged to join and become active in the functionally-specific professional association most relevant to their positions (e.g., ACUHO-I, NODA, ACU-I, NACAS). Even when encouraged to affiliate with general professional associations like ACPA or NASPA, young professionals connect with the respective division or commission most related to their area of job responsibility. They become so firmly entrenched in the issues, trends and challenges confronting their functional arena that involvement in more than one area is virtually impossible. Without the knowledge of current issues or contacts with professionals in other areas, the possibilities of lateral movement to another area of student affairs are severely limited. It is almost as if the initial job in student affairs dictates the career opportunities one will have in the profession, rendering lateral mobility more a myth than a reality for most practitioners.

The third issue of career mobility entails movement between types of institutions. Increasingly, this mobility has been curtailed for practitioners. Community colleges seek professionals with prior community college experience. Liberal arts institutions call for professionals with a commitment to the heritage and tradition of the liberal arts education. Religiously-affiliated campuses list an appreciation for benefits of religiously-based education as a prerequisite for consideration. Large public institutions publicize that an understanding of the unique culture of land-grant institutions, for example, is essential in candidates. While there is no formal research to support the notion that institutionally-specific experience is becoming an increasingly important factor in career mobility, a close reading of the job announcements posted at conferences or published in professional newsletters will reveal this trend.

The combined impact of limited upward, horizontal, and inter-institutional mobility on the career aspirations of student affairs professionals cannot be understated. Entry-level professionals see their opportunities as limited; advancement is further curtailed after moving into mid-level positions; and nearly half of all professionals have reported dissatisfaction with career advancement potential in the field (Bender, 1980; Bossert, 1982; Solomon & Tierney, 1977).

The notion of occupational mobility cannot be explored without attending to the concomitant familial issues that arise when considering career advancement. The complexities of the contemporary family structure and life play an increasingly important role in the lives of student affairs professionals. Dual career couples, divorce and resulting child custodial issues, and care of aging parents are all factors that complicate professional life. While little research specific to student affairs has been conducted on these issues, it is reasonable to assume that trends in the general population are reflected in the profession.

For example, dual income families are rapidly emerging as the norm rather than the exception in American society, and there is an increasing reliance on two incomes to meet basic costs of living. Those in marriages or domestic partnerships must consider the career aspirations of their mates when contemplating any sort of occupational move. These considerations place severe limitations on career mobility.

Divorce and child custodial issues affect the professional lives of student affairs administrators. Parents who wish to retain an active role in their children's lives after a divorce want to remain in geographic proximity to those offspring. This competing demand severely curtails choices when considering career advancement.

An emerging social issue, care for aging parents, is a force likely to affect student affairs practitioners to a greater degree in the future. In 1980, the average age of a sample of NASPA members (mid- to top-level staff) was 43 years (Lawing, 1980), while the median age for those still in their first decade of post-graduate work was 28 years (Burns, 1982). Extrapolating those numbers to 1995, senior-level administrators are in their late-50s and mid-level professionals in their mid-40s. These data suggest that large numbers of professionals have parents who are senior citizens who may demand increasing care in the future, creating an additional tension in the personal realm of practitioners, both financially and in terms of time.

Finally, relatively sluggish salaries have affected both the satisfaction and quality of life for student affairs professionals. Sixteen percent of those who left the field cited salary limitations as a reason for accepting positions outside the field (Burns, 1982). Between languishing cost-of-living increases, severely curtailed merit increases, and increasing employee contributions for health care, expendable income for many professionals is lower than it was five years ago. The quality of life for many practitioners is stagnant, creating additional tensions when considering career aspirations.

The personal realm constitutes very real concerns that student affairs administrators confront on a daily basis in their lives. The cumulative effects of diminished career mobility, increased familial constraints and stagnating quality of life have serious implications for individual professionals. It is not surprising, then, that practitioners often feel underemployed, unchallenged, uncertain about future job plans, and limited in terms of advancement at their home institutions (Cox & Ivy, 1984; Jones, 1980; Roe, 1981).

THE INSTITUTIONAL REALM

The second context in which practitioners operate on a day-to-day basis, and in which significant professional issues exist, is the institutional realm. This milieu consists of those issues and demands that the campus places on individual professionals. Some are institutionally-specific while others are shared by many colleges and universities. Bair, Klepper, and Phelps Tobin identified a number of shared issues in Chapter 2 of this book (e.g., changing demographics, economic shifts), and several more come to light as this notion is explored more fully. What remains to be examined is the impact that these issues have on the nature of work performed and the role of individual professionals.

Changing demographics in higher education have led to the creation of new programs intended to serve populations heretofore not represented in colleges and universities. The most dramatic trend in the student affairs job market between 1980 and 1990 was the drastic increase in the number of positions that serve special populations (Janasiewicz & Wright, 1993). The emergence of centers for ethnic, women, non-traditional aged, learning disabled, physically challenged and other student populations, while enhancing services for students, has had some unintentional results for practitioners. Historically, professionals garnered expertise in a particular functional area of students affairs (e.g., student activities, career development). These recent additions to campus, however, introduce professionals into the field whose expertise is focused on a specific population (e.g., African-American or learning disabled students). This bifurcation has led to a sense of diminished common purpose for individuals in student affairs divisions (Hirt, 1992).

Trends in enrollment management create other impacts on the daily responsibilities of practitioners. Increasingly, campuses rely on the funds generated from enrollment figures to compensate for diminished revenues from other sources. This means that recruiting and retaining certain types of students are more valued than in the past. For many, this translates into an emphasis on quantity as opposed to quality. Where admissions counselors previously assessed the quality of preparation of transfer students, for example, contemporary practice focuses on meeting the targeted quota when admitting transfers. Housing officials who once considered the appropriateness of apartment-style accommodations for freshmen are now driven by occupancy goals when assigning students to facilities. Success for career placement specialists is no longer based on the optimal fit between a student and a job placement, but on the percentage of graduates placed. This shift in focus from quality to quantity changes the way in which professionals must perceive the nature of their jobs and the methods they employ to conduct their duties.

Downsizing has become one of the most pervasive management ploys in higher education in recent years, and over 60% of colleges and universities report major initiatives to restructure their organizations. While the procedures employed to examine reorganization may vary slightly from campus to campus, almost all are grounded in assumptions that emerge from the quality management literature. Essentially, campuses attempt to identify common values and goals for the organization. Once identified, individual units of the organization are required to demonstrate their relationship to those values and their contribution to the goals of the campus. Theoretically, organizational resources are then shifted to support the initiatives most crucial to organizational success, which leads to the consolidation and/or elimination of programs and services more distant from the core institutional values. The notion here is to allocate resources to promote collaboration among units to achieve common goals. In actuality, however, the process used to determine those resource allocations frequently pits one activity against another within the organization.

Translated into practice, today's student activities professionals are likely to spend as much time convincing top leadership that involvement is intimately related to the mission of the institution as they are in actually involving students in meaningful learning activities. Housing practitioners exert as much energy demonstrating to senior administrators that the residential experience is central to campus values as they do working with students to enhance that experience. Staff working with gay, lesbian, and bisexual programs spend as much of their time promoting the notion of the importance of that population to campus diversity as they do serving those students directly. This shift in the nature of daily activities has significantly affected the nature of professional work.

The increasing emphasis on technology has still other implications for student affairs professionals. Driven by the notion that increased use of technology leads to increased efficiency, campuses are developing hardware and software applications at an astounding rate. Tracking systems for judicial records enable campuses to report types of incidents, numbers of students involved, categories of sanctions, and percentages of recidivism, as well as to manage compliance deadlines with much greater accuracy. On-line advising in terms of academic interests and their relationships to careers is in use at most career centers. Even counseling centers are turning to software programs to assist students with assessing their needs and providing alternatives to conventional counseling sessions. Electronic mail and fax operations have changed the daily communication patterns among colleagues.

For practitioners, this shift toward greater use of electronics and technology has profound ramifications. For many, simply learning the skills to operate the necessary equipment is a challenge. For others, the time devoted to conceptualizing and designing the systems is a new experience. For most, however, the increased emphasis on technology has likely resulted in more time working with a computer screen and less time working with students. Professionals may feel that they know more facts about the students they serve, but are equally likely to feel they know fewer students.

Perhaps the most pervasive institutional impact on the student affairs professional, however, is increased competition for diminished resources. In fact, it could be argued that trends in enrollment management, quality management, and use of technology have all been driven by rapidly dwindling campus budgets. As fiscal constraints have become more widespread, program consolidation and elimination have led to increased concerns over not merely job advancement opportunities (Jones, 1980) but job stability. Positions vacated by professionals often are no longer filled immediately, and in many cases are eliminated permanently. Funds to attend professional conferences, participate in associations, even to subscribe to scholarly publications, have been eliminated at some institutions.

At first glance, these changes appear to impact mid- and senior level professionals most profoundly. More time is spent by those individuals estimating costs, calculating the effects of budget reductions, and documenting needs to compete for scarce resources. But more thorough consideration of the issue of diminishing resources leads to the recognition that practitioners at all levels are affected by these changes. Program planners are responsible for working with many more student groups than they did in the past. Counselors are compelled to refer students to group, rather than individual therapy and still cannot keep up with demand. All professionals are dealing with the issue of doing more with less, and those tensions change the nature of daily life on campus.

The cumulative effects of these institutional shifts are manifest in student affairs professional reports of inconsistencies between professional needs and organizational rewards, organizational barriers to promotion, and differentiated levels of professional development opportunities, as well as increased reports of job-related stress and diminished career satisfaction (Barnes & O'Donnell, 1985; Berwick, 1992; Bogenschutz & Sagaria, 1988; Hancock, 1988; Richmond & Sherman, 1991; Wood, Winston, & Polkosnik, 1985).

THE EXTRA-INSTITUTIONAL REALM

The third realm in which student affairs staff operate regularly is the extra-institutional realm, namely those demands and issues generated by bodies external to the campus including governing boards, state and federal agencies, and public sentiment. External constituencies have increasingly influenced the scope and nature of professional activity and cannot be ignored when considering the contemporary issues confronting practitioners.

In response to state mandates, governing boards are increasingly adopting policies that require more assessment and accountability from campuses. Some mandates are translated into campus practice through policies that change programs. Mandatory advising, required training for teaching assistants, and liability insurance for student organizations are examples of such impacts. Others are revealed at the campus level through policies that affect campus administration such as restrictions on travel, complicated purchasing systems, and complex hiring procedures.

For student affairs administrators, these policies have meant that more time is spent either operationalizing new requirements or responding to revised policies and procedures. While Resident Assistant training used to focus on team building, counseling techniques, and leadership development, current demands require sessions on sexual harassment, documenting incidents for liability protection, and legal implications of staff behavior. Recreation staff spend more time ensuring safety of equipment and facilities to prevent lawsuits and less time developing appreciation for healthy lifestyles. Orientation programs devote large amounts of time to testing students and explaining academic requirements and less time to issues like intellectual curiosity and love of learning. Senior-level staff are so inundated with forms requiring signatures and reports requiring compilation of data that less time and energy can be devoted to staff, let alone student needs.

Perhaps the most widespread influence on professional practice in recent years, however, emerges from federal legislation pertaining to higher education. Since compliance with such legislation is typically tied to continuing federal support which nearly all campuses receive in some form, professional staff have been forced to respond to these legislative mandates. Two examples serve to illustrate the impact of this issue on professional practice.

The Americans with Disabilities Act (ADA) was designed to ensure a lofty ideal: the right of all individuals, regardless of ability, to full participation in American society. Few would argue the importance of such a goal. The implications of the legislation, however, influence professional practice on college and university campuses (Rothstein, 1986; Jarrow, 1991). Most campuses needed to conduct a facilities audit to identify access and compliance issues for a wide variety of disabilities. Services for students with learning disabilities needed to be instituted or enhanced. Systems to identify, certify, and accommodate disabled students, faculty, and staff were required. Resources had to be diverted from other pressing campus issues to comply with the mandates of ADA. For practitioners, these requirements have entailed a shift in focus of some of their energies. More time must now be spent evaluating physical facilities when considering sites for programs or office relocation and reorganization. Arranging for interpreters and assistants at programs for students with disabilities shifts the balance from focusing on the content of the program to focusing on the process of the program. Responding to requests for reasonable accommodations demands more time from practitioners. At issue is not the value of engaging in such activities, but the demands compliance with this legislation creates for professional behavior.

A second example of an externally imposed mandate with serious implications for professionals is the Student Right To Know and Campus Security Act. Compliance has mandated that professionals publicize graduation rates and crime statistics, offer programs and services to victims, document legal and judicial consequences to perpetrators, and respond to public inquiries about matters related to these issues.

The list of areas where legislation in the past decade has intersected with higher education is extensive: student financial aid programs; educational facilities; migrant and disadvantaged programs; libraries; community development; continuing and cooperative education; institutional aid; international studies; minority recruitment; veterans education; and teacher education, to name but a few ("How house-passed legislation", 1985). In each instance, professionals engaged in those services have had to shift priorities, time, and attention. The result is that more time is spent documenting the existence of certain services than delivering them. Professional prestige and autonomy are more difficult to maintain when so much time and energy is expended conducting work dictated by external, rather than internal, mandates. The increased bureaucracy resulting from such legislation requires more time completing forms and paperwork which results in less time working with students and staff. The implications of such shifts for professional practice are profound.

THE PROFESSIONAL REALM

The fourth realm in which practitioners operate daily is the professional realm, consisting of the issues, activities and interests dictated by the student affairs profession. Certain developments within the profession have played an increasingly large role in the lives of administrators, and examining a few of the current trends illuminates the tensions the realm has produced.

Both functionalist (e.g., ACUHO-I, NODA, ACU-I) and generalist (e.g., ACPA, NASPA, NAWE) professional associations play an important role in the student affairs profession. However, these two types of associations place competing demands on practitioners. Each relies upon members to manage committees, provide services, disseminate information and sponsor regional and national conferences. As a result, membership in such organizations is considered a professional lifeline by many. But can participation in both functionalist and generalist associations be maintained?

Campuses have imposed very real constraints on time, money, and travel for most practitioners. These constraints have forced many student affairs staff to limit the extent of their involvement in associations. One may belong to both functionalist and generalist associations, but active involvement in more than one group is unlikely. The amount of time and energy required to serve on committees, present programs, and participate in conferences limits the number of organizations that the typical professional can support.

Even the services provided by associations can create stress for professionals. They bombard members with literature and research journals which describe emerging theory, current trends, and issues confronting their respective constituencies. Finding the time to read, digest, and operationalize so much information, however, is another matter for most practitioners. For many, the daily deluge of literature serves as a reminder of what they do not know and do not have time to learn.

Increased demands for doctoral level study represent another tension placed on practitioners by the profession. The terminal degree has become essentially a requirement for senior level professionals, 82% of whom have completed a terminal degree (Paul & Hoover, 1980). Yet, the conventional career pattern for the profession is to earn the masters degree and work for 5-8 years before considering post-masters study. The number of doctoral programs is finite, so those considering pursuit of the degree must usually relocate to an area where such a program is accessible. Curricula for the doctorate routinely require at least one year's full-time study, which translates for most professionals into a year of unpaid leave. The time, financial, and mobility constraints imposed upon many contemporary professionals prohibit them from considering pursuit of the doctorate.

Two current movements among the associations provide insights into future tensions the professional realm might impose. The first relates to the debate over accreditation versus self-regulation. As consumerism has permeated society, student affairs, like many professions, has sought to document to external constituencies the quality assurance controls it imposes upon its members. The emergence of the Council for the Advancement of Standards (CAS) during the 1980s is one example of this effort (Yerian & Miller, 1989). The latest dialogue focuses on whether student affairs divisions ought to adopt an accreditation process, or, at least, seek a registry status, rather than continuing to rely upon self-regulation to ensure standards of quality. If implemented in the conventional manner, accreditation—historically applied only to preparation programs—would likely require an extensive self-study of a division, followed by reviews conducted by a campus committee and a panel of outside experts. Self-studies are already required for institutional accreditation, and, for units like health and counseling centers, are required for professional accreditation. Moreover, the implementation of quality management principles has compelled most offices to conduct self-studies with respect to campus values and goals. The idea of conducting yet another self-study for purposes of divisional accreditation creates additional tensions. For practitioners, it suggests additional time and energy devoted to compiling data, analyzing procedures, and writing reports, all to serve the profession rather than to serve students directly.

The second emerging debate that may impact practitioners relates to the notion of credentialing and registry. A committee of CAS, representing leading professional associations, was formed in 1994 to explore the feasibility of creating a registry for preparation programs and for student affairs administrators. Registries for individual professionals typically require demonstration of certain competencies and skills, earned through educational credits, internships, and experiences. If student affairs moves in this direction as a means of assuring quality, it would likely entail professionals providing documentation of education and experience to earn initial registration with some sort of oversight board. Beyond that, however, it would likely entail requirements for continuing education credits. Just as teachers, medical specialists, and accountants are compelled to participate in ongoing educational endeavors to maintain credentials and licensure, student affairs professionals would be required to earn continuing education credits to maintain their registry status. A likely means to offer such continuing education would be through participation in specified sessions offered at regional and national conferences. Translated to practice, this means that continued participation in association activities would no longer be merely a professional development opportunity for practitioners, but in fact a requirement for continued employment. Another means for earning continuing professional education credits might be through some self-regulated education and training process coupled with a form of peer review. In either form, however, in an era where voluntary participation is constrained by financial and time limitations, the notion of mandatory, or even nonmandatory participation in continuing professional education might prove onerous for many.

The continuing demands for quality assurance in student affairs are not unreasonable in a society that has questioned the training and expertise of all kinds of professions. Implementation of such standards, however, has implications for practitioners whose finite human resources are already strained to the limit.

CONCLUSION

In summary, the four realms in which student affairs professionals operate on a daily basis create very different, yet equally powerful tensions. Limited career mobility, increased partner, child and parental responsibilities, and diminished quality of life all present dilemmas of a personal nature to administrators. Campus downsizing, the shift from quality to quantity, and technological innovations in the institutional setting have changed the nature of the work professionals conduct. Responding to outside constituencies and complying with increased legislative mandates are realities of the extra-institutional realm that change the way professionals spend their time and energy. Competing demands and calls for accreditation and registry suggest future tensions in the professional realm.

Hope should not be abandoned, however. Rather, the framework described herein is intended to provide readers with a way in which to conceptualize their profession. It is a method to analyze the influences that shape the work practitioners conduct on a daily basis. By comprehending the forces that influence professional life, student affairs administrators may be in a better position to analyze their individual situations and understand how those forces influence their daily lives.

Finally, the demands described in this chapter are not likely to dissipate in the near future. They are very real, very powerful, and very intrusive. Individual practitioners are the lifeline of student affairs, and the concerns that affect their daily lives must be considered if the profession is to thrive. By acknowledging and describing these tensions, individuals, institutions, and the profession may begin to remediate them in more practical, realistic ways.

REFERENCES

Armstrong, M. R., Campbell, T. J., & Ostroth, D. D. (1978). The employment situation in college and university student personnel. *NASPA Journal, 16,* 51-58.

Barnes, S. F., & O'Donnell, J. A. (1985, April). *Organizational vitality in student affairs.* Paper presented at the annual conference of the National Association of Student Personnel Administrators, Portland, OR.

Bender, B. E. (1980). Job satisfaction in student affairs. *NASPA Journal, 18,* 2-9.

Berwick, K. R. (1992). Stress among students affairs administrators: The relationship of personal characteristics and organizational variables to work-related stress. *Journal of College Student Development, 33,* 11-19.

Bogenschutz, M. H., & Sagaria, M. D. (1988, April). *Aspirations and career growth of mid-level administrators in higher education.* Paper presented at the annual meeting of the American Educational Research Association, New Orleans, LA.

Bossert, R. (1982). *Career mobility of mid-level administrators in higher education.* Unpublished doctoral dissertation, The Pennsylvania State University.

Burns, M. A. (1982). Who leaves the student affairs field? *NASPA Journal, 20,* 9-12.

Cox, D. W., & Ivy, W. A. (1984). Staff development needs of student affairs professionals. *NASPA Journal, 22,* 26-33.

Hancock, J. E. (1988). Needs and reinforcers in student affairs: Implications for attrition. *Journal of College Student Development, 29,* 25-30.

Hirt, J. B. (1992). Power, prestige and professionalism in student affairs. (Doctoral dissertation, The University of Arizona, 1992). *Dissertation Abstracts International, 53*(02), 420.

How house-passed legislation to extend the higher education act compares with the present law. (1985, December 18). *The Chronicle of Higher Education, 31*(16), pp. 12-14.

Janasiewicz, B. A., & Wright, D. L. (1993). Job market trends in student affairs: Ten years later. *NASPA Journal, 30,* 145-152.

Jarrow, J. (1991). Disability issues on campus and the road to ADA. *Educational Record, 72,* 26-31.

Jones, S. H. (1980). *Academic 8-to-5'ers: Student affairs staff at U.C. Davis.* Davis, CA: California University, Davis, Office of Student Affairs Research and Information.

Lawing, A. A. (1982). Enhancement and advancement: Professional development for student affairs staff. *NASPA Journal, 20,* 22-26.

Paul, W. L., & Hoover, R. E. (1980). Chief student personnel administrators: A decade of change. *NASPA Journal, 18,* 33-39.

Richmond, J., & Sherman, K. (1991). Student development preparation and placement: A longitudinal study of graduates students' and new professionals experiences. *Journal of College Student Development, 32,* 8-16.

Roe, B. B. (1981, March). *An analysis of career enrichment needs and programs for students affairs personnel.* Paper presented at the annual convention of the American Personnel and Guidance Association, Detroit, MI.

Rothstein, L. F. (1986). Section 504 of the rehabilitation act: Emerging issues for colleges and universities. *Journal of College and University Law, 13,* 229-265.

Solomon, L. C., & Tierney, M. (1977). Determinants of job satisfaction among college administrators. *Journal of Higher Education, 48,* 412-431.

Wood, L., Winston, R. B., & Polkosnik, M. C. (1985). Career orientations and professional development of young student affairs professionals. *Journal of College Student Personnel, 26,* 532-539.

Yerian, J. M., & Miller, T. K. (1989). *Putting the CAS standards to work.* College Park, MD: Council for the Advancement of Standards for Student Services/Development Programs.

Chapter Four

How Professional Associations are Addressing Issues in Student Affairs

Leila V. Moore and Carmen Guevara Neuberger

A review of the *Directory of National Trade and Professional Associations* reveals the names of approximately one hundred professional associations that have interests in student affairs. As with most professional associations, these student affairs-related organizations fulfill the general role of advancing the interests of the profession and the professional by providing continuing education experiences, standards for practice, advocacy for issues related to higher education, and journals, magazines and newsletters that transmit the knowledge of the field. Some associations also provide codes of ethics for their members. Student affairs professional associations offer both individual memberships and institutional memberships. And as the student affairs profession has grown more complex and specialized, some associations have focused on a particular functional area that can be found on a college campus, some are focused generally on student affairs as part of the institution, and still others are focused on the overall management and administration of the institution, including student affairs.

BRIEF OVERVIEW OF STUDENT AFFAIRS PROFESSIONAL ASSOCIATIONS

The three major generalist student affairs professional associations, the American College Personnel Association (ACPA), the National Association of Student Personnel Administrators (NASPA), and the National Association for Women in Education (NAWE), were established early in the twentieth century in response to concerns of various groups in the emerging student affairs profession. The Deans of Women were the first to organize as the National Association of Deans of Women (NADW) with a tightly defined target group of potential members in higher as well as lower and secondary education (Hanson, 1994, p. 31). Believing that linkages with other educational and women's organizations were essential to its vitality and growth, NADW became a department of the National Education Association in 1917 and was housed in the American Association of University Women headquarters building in Washington, DC. Acknowledging that deans of women had assumed wider educational roles and that other student affairs professionals had become members of the association, in 1956 NADW added a "C" (for counselors) to its name. In 1973, the name was expanded further to include administrators; it became NAWDAC for two decades. The association's name was again changed in 1991 to the National Association for Women in Education (NAWE) to reflect its expanded purpose to include individuals from diverse educational settings and endeavors beyond those in student affairs.

"The assumption that men and women occupied essentially separate spheres in the educational enterprise" (Hanson, 1994, p. 31) was reflected in the founding of both NAWE and NASPA, the National Association of Student Personnel Administrators, which began as the National Association of Deans and Advisers of Men (NADAM) in 1919. The focus of NADAM was on how young men should conduct themselves; consultation among members was the means for mutual education (Rhatigan, 1995, p. 5). The organization adopted NASPA as its name in 1951, broadening the base of the association to include other professionals beyond the deans and vice presidents of student affairs. The expanded purpose was to "discuss and study the most effective methods of aiding students in their intellectual, social, moral and personal development" (Rhatigan, 1995, p. 5). NASPA promoted itself as "the professional home for chief student affairs professionals and their principal assistants" (Rhatigan, 1995, p. 5).

The American College Personnel Association (ACPA) traces its beginnings to 1924 when the National Association of Appointment Secretaries (NAAS), composed of professionals who advised students on their careers, held an organizational meeting at the National Education Association (NEA) annual convention. They came as guests of NADW (Sheeley, 1991, Prologue). Changing its name from NAAS in 1931, ACPA, together with NADW, continued their founding relationship at annual conventions of NEA groups through 1942 when the conventions were discontinued due to World War II. No longer connected with NEA by 1947, reunification efforts led to the formation of the American Personnel and Guidance Association (APGA) which ACPA joined as Division #1 in 1952. ACPA became an autonomous association once again in 1992, 40 years later, and has expanded its professional programs and services for student affairs educators committed to the overall development of students in post-secondary education. Its focus is on new paradigms to improve and increase student learning (Neuberger, 1995, p. 4).

While ACPA, NAWE and NASPA are independent associations, several coordinated annual conventions have been held: ACPA and NAWDC (name changed in 1956) in 1973; ACPA, NASPA and NAWDAC (name changed again in 1973) in 1974; ACPA and NASPA in 1987. A joint ACPA/NASPA convention was held in 1997, a decade after the last one. Aiming to serve the entire student affairs profession, its theme was "Bridging History and Destiny."

Other functional associations have also been established to focus on specific areas in student affairs administration. For example, the Association of College Unions-International (ACU-I) was founded in 1914 to address the needs of college union and activities professional staff members (About the Association, 1995). In response to an unprecedented rise in college enrollment after World War II and subsequent concerns of housing and feeding this growing student population, the Association of College and University Housing Officers-International (ACUHO-I) was established in 1951. Its mission is to promote "quality residential living experiences at colleges, universities and other postsecondary institutions by providing programs, services, research and professional development experiences" (Sauter, 1994). The National Association for Campus Activities (NACA) was formally established in 1968 as the National Entertainment Conference (NEC). This association offers services such as cooperative buying, educational programs, talent showcases and trade publications (About your association, 1995, p. 167). A sample listing of 25 professional associations by year of founding provides an historical context for the development of these and other student affairs-related professional associations (Nuss, 1993, p. 366) (see Table 4-1). The professional association with

Table 4-1
A Sample Listing of Professional Associations by Year of Founding

Association	Year
Association of American Universities (AAU)	1900
Amer. Assoc. of Collegiate Registrars and Admissions Officers (AACRAO)	1910
Association of College Unions-International (ACU-I)	1914
National Association for Women in Education (NAWE)	1916
American Council on Education (ACE)	1918
Nat. Assoc. of Student Personnel Administrators (NASPA)	1919
American Association of Community and Junior Colleges (AACJC)	1920
American College Health Association (ACHA)	1920
Association of Governing Boards of Universities and Colleges (ABG)	1921
American College Personnel Association (ACPA)	1924
National Association of College Admissions Counselors (NACAC)	1937
National Orientation Directors Association (NODA)	1947
Association of International Educators (NAFSA)	1948
National Assoc. of College and University Business Officers (NACUBO)	1950
American Association of Counseling and Development (AACD)	1952
Assoc. of College and University Housing Officers-International (ACUHO-I)	1952
National Association of Personnel Workers (NAPW)	1954
American Association of State Colleges and Universities (AASCU)	1961
National Assoc. of State Universities and Land Grant Colleges (NASULGC)	1962
National Association of Independent Colleges and Universities (NAICU)	1967
National Association for Campus Activities (NACA)	1968
National Assoc. for Student Financial Aid Administrators (NASFAA)	1968
American Association of Higher Education (AAHE)	1969
Council for the Advancement and Support of Education (CASE)	1974
Association for Student Judicial Affairs (ASJA)	1987

Source: Table adapted by Dr. Elizabeth Nuss from material in *Encyclopedia of Associations.* Edited by D. M. Burek. Copyright 1992, Gale Research. Printed in the *Handbook of Student Affairs Administration.* Edited by M. J. Barr and Associates. Copyright 1993, Jossey-Bass Inc., Publishers. All rights reserved. Reproduced by permission.

the longest history on this list is the Association of American Universities (founded in 1900) and the most recent is the Association for Student Judicial Affairs (ASJA) founded in 1987.

THE CURRENT ROLE OF PROFESSIONAL ASSOCIATIONS

How Associations Respond to Societal Issues

In Chapters 1 and 2 societal influences and institutional issues facing student affairs practitioners have been described. Professional associations strive to remain current with these issues and develop responses in a timely fashion. Issues that impact on the profession are sometimes communicated to members or their institutions first by their professional associations, but other times it is association members who identify issues first for which they require further information, analysis, or suggestions for responding. The more critical the issue is to the survival of the institutional or individual member, the more important the role of the professional association becomes in responding to the member. Internal and process matters such as the organization of the association, provision of member services, and financial stability of the association can significantly affect the quality and effectiveness of the association's response to issues. In times when the issues are related to the very survival of the member, members may be particularly dependent on and critical of their professional association's effectiveness, especially if they perceive that the organization is preoccupied with internal rather than external matters.

Thus, in recent years, professional associations have become increasingly involved with issues facing higher education. Associations with a specialized focus, such as the Association of College Unions - International, as well as those with a broader interest, such as the American Association of University Administrators, have responded to higher education issues. There is also an apparent trend away from any one professional association staking a claim in response to an issue. Occasionally, a professional association will choose to focus its attention on a relevant topic whether or not its competitors are focused on the same issue. However, the more central the issue to the future of higher education, the greater the number of professional associations that seem to focus on contributing their responses along with those of other professional associations.

These responses to issues range in format from planning convention themes related to these issues, through production of written materials or white papers, to participation in distance learning ventures such as teleconferencing and listserv discussions. As institutions and members have responded to the issues of the day, professional associations have also provided analyses of these responses by developing case study materials and adding opportunities at national and regional meetings for members to discuss and evaluate the effectiveness of diverse responses to campus issues. In addition to these analyses of issues, some professional associations have also turned their energies toward improving standards of practice in the field. One example of this focus on improved standards is the effort of the American College Personnel Association (ACPA) and the National Association of Student Personnel Administrators (NASPA) to develop a statement outlining "Principles of Good Practice" for their 1997 joint convention.

Responses of professional associations to four recent issues in higher education raised in Chapters 1 and 2 will be discussed in this chapter. These issues are (a) identification and assessment of student outcomes; (b) increased attention to the learning process; (c) economic constraints and (d) technological advances for managing information. An analysis of these responses suggests a new role assumed by professional associations with respect to the issues, and it also points to new concerns for these associations. Following a discussion of the responses to each issue and the roles suggested by these responses is an analysis of the responses as they affect the future role of professional associations in higher education.

Institutional Responsibility for Outcomes

As described in Chapter 2, a focus on student outcomes has become the means by which institutions are expected to hold themselves accountable for the quality and content of a college education. Students and their families, the work force which students will enter, funding sources and policy makers all look for evidence that an institution has delivered on its specific promises relative to the education of its students.

Institutions have articulated outcomes which they publicly state as their expectations for the growth or development of students based on the campus experience offered at that institution. However, other outcomes have been added to those stated by the institution. Some state legislators have successfully introduced state-wide basic knowledge examinations for all students and have established acceptable levels of mastery as an expectation for knowledge acquisition (Griffith, 1995; Mitchell, 1995). Recruiters have stated their expectations that college graduates will be able to function as team players, be capable communicators, both verbally and in writing, and be able to oversee and motivate the work of others (Bretz, Rynes, & Gerhart, 1993; Ferren, 1990). Students have also stated their expectations for outcomes of their education, including graduating without significant indebtedness, access to job opportunities that have salaries equivalent to their investment of time and money, and ability to graduate in a reasonable period of time (Burd, 1996; Dey, Astin, Korn, & Riggs, 1992; Moore, 1995).

The idea that there might be multiple expectations of outcomes for students also implies that some outcomes may contradict others, or that an institution may not be able to deliver on the multiple expectations. Whether outcomes are multiple or singular, consistent or contradictory, there seems to be no disagreement that successful achievement of outcomes is a very important way for campus administrators to explain the process of higher education and hold themselves accountable for certain results.

Professional associations have supported institutions in responding to this issue by providing information, opportunities for discussion and examples of best practice. Assessment, one approach to the description and evaluation of outcomes, has been the major focus for the last several years of the American Association of Higher Education (AAHE), whose conferences and publications are among the most visible evidence of a professional association response to this issue. Another response is the focus on Total Quality Management (TQM) and Continuous Quality Improvement (CQI) which, again, are topics that seem to proliferate in the writings and conference themes of AAHE. Other professional associations with a generalized membership, such as the American College Personnel Association (ACPA) and the National Association of Student Personnel Administrators (NASPA), have certainly added to the literature base on outcomes, assessment and TQM. The tables of contents of ACPA's *Journal of College Student Development* and the *NASPA Journal* reflect the contributions of these two associations. Professional associations have also been instrumental in providing various forums for discussion among practitioners. Some examples of diverse forums include teleconferencing, listserv, single-topic regional drive-in seminars and roundtables at annual conventions. Professional associations have also taken leadership in stressing the urgency of the issue and its relevance to student affairs by featuring in their journals and magazines articles, dialogues between practitioners and those who state expectations.

Focus on the Learning Process

Student affairs professionals realize that the interaction between faculty and students is a keystone to the successful experience of the student. This interaction can be a rich mentoring experience, an opportunity for the student to become familiar with or participate in the research of the faculty member, a tutorial experience for students, and, when the faculty member meets students in small groups, a chance for collaborative learning to take place.

Student affairs professionals are coming to an awareness of the role they may play both in fostering such interactions between professors and students and motivating students to take advantage of them, and in providing similar interactions between themselves and students. While community college and "college without walls" staff and faculty have long been aware of the importance of helping students learn how to learn and fostering lifelong learning, four-year residential institutions seem to be slower in recognizing that learning and learning how to learn is a central unifying mission of higher education. An analysis of the conference themes and journal topics of those professional associations that focus on two-year college concerns reveals the clear advantage enjoyed by two-year staff and faculty when it comes to understanding the central role of learning as both a process and an outcome.

While other professional associations have certainly contributed to the education of faculty about learning, the associations more directly related to student affairs have not made a similar contribution until quite recently. The work of the American College Personnel Association in presenting a position paper entitled the Student Learning Imperative and that of the National Association of Student Personnel Administrators on their Reasonable Expectations Project represents a new direction for student affairs professional associations in placing a priority on understanding and studying this issue. ACPA's March/April 1996 edition of the *Journal of College Student Development* was a special issue on the Student Learning Imperative that provides an important and useful dialogue for understanding better the role of student affairs organizations in promoting student learning.

Economic Constraints

As federal and state aid to education dwindles even further, the role of the development office and the alumni association has become far more central to the survival of more and more institutions. Efforts have been made on many campuses to diversify the income sources that support their institution, including greater consideration of corporate sponsorships, increased alumni fund-raising, separate fee structures to create more stand-alone functions that do not rely on institutional dollars, and, of course, tuition increases (Dostart & Olsen, 1995; Kendrick, 1996). For institutions relying mainly on tuition increases as a way to offset costs, there have been some surprises. On many campuses, the rise in tuition has produced a shift in the kinds of students who attend their college, with students who had formerly been able to attend the institution opting instead for a less expensive college or university. When tuition hikes are not accompanied by an increase in financial aid in the form of scholarships and grants in particular, campuses may see an even more dramatic shift in the student body. Intent on avoiding greater debt, these students will seek accommodations for necessary work schedules, including reduced course loads, which has often resulted in extending the time to degree ("Correspondence," 1991).

The idea of moving to purchased services to cut costs has taken hold and, because more services are located in student affairs, this trend often affects student affairs disproportionately to the rest of the institution. There is probably no institution of higher education that would not be vulnerable to the idea of purchased services, but at this time the concept seems to be more seriously under consideration in small four-year private institutions that might be the group of institutions most profoundly affected by financial concerns. In terms of the response of professional associations to this matter, the Association of College Unions-International (ACU-I), the Association of College and University Housing Officers-International (ACUHO-I), and the American College Health Association are three examples of associations fully aware of the trend toward privatization which have devoted conference themes or theme tracks, special task forces, and special publications to this issue. In the matter of finances, this issue seems to produce the need for an immediate response both by professional associations and by institutions. Plans to trim budgets are being developed quickly on many campuses, and decisions are being made based on whatever knowledge is available to the staff and faculty at the institution at the time of their decision. The urgency of this issue has produced needs from campus administrators to have immediate information about reports of the impact of various ideas on the mission and attractiveness of the institution to students. The National Association of College and University Business Officers (NACUBO) has historically provided such information to its members and student affairs organizations that belong to the Council of Higher Educational Management Associations, sponsored by NACUBO, now contribute to these publications, express their views, and assume a role in presentations on this topic at NACUBO conferences.

Managing Information

We have become an information-based society and as Woodard notes, cyberspace and all that it infers is now present on most campuses. Those who have difficulty affording a connection to the Internet or their own World Wide Web site are already feeling the effects of not being "in the loop." Most institutions are studying ways to bring themselves into cyberspace. The effect of the Internet on where and how learning takes place is already felt, and institutions have placed a high priority on the search for the means to move entire campuses into this new arena for providing information and fostering learning. Many institutions have begun to see the effect on staff, faculty, and students as computer networking is made available to all on their campuses (see Chapter 1).

Distance learning is also exploding in popularity (see Chapter 2). So far, the effect of distance learning has been seen primarily in the area of continuing education (see Chapter 1), but as part-time study becomes a reality for more campuses and as budget cuts affect the availability of faculty and lead institutions toward consortia of faculty who teach via downlink, the effect of distance learning on all aspects of the curriculum is not far away. Distance learning, facilitated by computer links, transmits learning electronically, eliminating or greatly reducing the face-to-face personal contact between and among learners and faculty members.

Student affairs professional associations have sponsored some programs and services that help student affairs staff learn more about cyberspace. However, communication about rapid innovations in hardware and software and the ways some campuses have discovered use of the Internet and information management systems seems to be coming mostly from the private sector. The "Coming Events" and "Infotech Services" sections of the *Chronicle of Higher Education* routinely include sponsorship of meetings and workshops and marketing of training programs on information technology by such groups as Microsoft Corporation, IBM, Micromedium Inc., Datatel, Peoplesoft, and CARS Information Systems Corporation. Most professional associations seem to have lagged behind in educating their members in this important area. In many cases, professional associations have just begun to use electronic mail as a way to communicate with members. Until very recently there has been little beyond the provision of listservs and inclusion of a home page on the World Wide Web that appears to distinguish student affairs professional associations in their responsiveness to this issue. ACPA commissions and state divisions and NASPA regions are now sponsoring workshops revolving around technology, student misuse of the computer, and student development issues related to computers.

CONTINUING EDUCATION AND THE CHANGING ROLE OF PROFESSIONAL ASSOCIATIONS

Associations have provided important continuing professional education both to their members through their responsiveness to issues of concern to the membership and to higher education in general. Depending on the issue, however, the quality, timeliness and relevance of their response has varied. Recent issues have also pointed to the need for student affairs professional associations to rely more heavily for information on associations that do not typically attract their members. Provision of continuing professional education may be shifting from associations developing and transmitting their own information to the role of brokering with other associations to provide such information. The example of efforts of CHEMA in educating student affairs leaders on privatization described under the *Economic Constraints* section of this chapter and a new collaborative effort initiated by NACUBO and NASPA on benchmarking in student affairs are good examples.

Until quite recently, professional associations have also been the primary locus of a measure of perspective and objectivity on issues that affect higher education more broadly. Certainly there have been any number of outstanding efforts in recent years by associations to provide leadership in developing a broader view of such issues and their impact on higher education in general. The American Council on Education (ACE) produced and distributed white papers on fraternity and sorority liability issues, AIDS on campus, alcohol policies, the Campus Security Act and the most recent Telecommunications Act of 1996 with its Exon Amendment or Communications Decency Act. In addition, several specialized associations have focused on the year 2000 in producing thoughtful papers that reflect on the future of their particular function in higher education.

Associations are particularly well suited to respond to the broad societal and institutional issues described in Chapters 1 and 2 through consortia groups such as the Higher Education Secretariat (HES), a growing group of more that 30 national associations convened monthly by the American Council on Education (ACE) and the Council of Higher Education Management Associations (CHEMA), a group of equivalent number with some overlapping membership, convened twice a year by the National Association of College and University Business Officers (NACUBO). The meetings of these groups are focused on how collaboration can occur in responding to issues affecting higher education in general. Individual student affairs practitioners' issues as well as those related to academic preparation program curriculum, faculty, recruitment and retention are addressed through professional development programs sponsored by ACPA and NASPA. These include national, regional and state conferences and association publications that draw authors active in either or both associations who are interested in making contributions to the field at large.

Through the years, various association leaders have called for the union of the major student affairs associations. Reflecting the differences which characterize higher education in general and justify the existence of a variety of colleges and universities, members of these professional associations have chosen to preserve their own identity by remaining autonomous. "Like other organizations, associations are distinctive for many reasons, including those attributable to organizational culture" (Nuss, 1993, p. 368). Those cultures are constantly evolving, incorporating changes in the beliefs, values and attitudes of society as well as those of the members (Kuh, Schuh, & Whitt, 1991).

The primary purpose of each association as well as its major clientele in the student affairs field determine the membership it attracts; for example, the advancement of women has always been a primary focus for NAWE; institutional membership with voting delegate designation and issues of concern to the chief student affairs officer has been traditional for NASPA; and counseling-centered, functional area programs developed and executed by senior-level, mid-level and entry-level practitioners and faculty members have characterized ACPA through the years.

Administrative concerns of the generalist such as downsizing and organizational structure are now a common focus and diversity in membership and programs has been expressed as a priority by all. All three associations have small office staffs (nine full-time equivalents for NASPA, six for ACPA, and four for NAWE) and are located in the Dupont Circle area of Washington, DC. Thus, governmental relations and liaison with other associations are primary activities in addition to membership recruitment, administrative support and assistance to the volunteer members who plan regional, state and national professional development and placement programs.

Students are the heart of the student affairs profession and are featured in all association mission statements. As published in its Bylaws, ACPA's mission is "to serve students by means of the Association's programs for educators who are committed to the overall development of students in post-secondary education" (American College Personnel Association, 1996-97, p. 4). NAWE's mission statement, as included in its Bylaws, states among other things, that NAWE "is committed to life-long learning and to furthering educational opportunities for women students and professionals at all levels of learning, growth and development" (National Association for Women in Education, 1995-96, p. 118). The National Association of Student Personnel Administrator's 1995-96 Annual Report states, "Its mission is to serve student affairs administrators who bring an institutional perspective to their work with students in higher education" (frontispiece).

Leadership opportunities in these associations are important to faculty and graduate students in preparation programs as well as to practitioners invited to participate in governance to varying degrees, depending on the respective structure of each association.

Other important roles of professional associations are reflected in the work they sponsor in setting standards for practice in the field. The Council for the Advancement of Standards in Higher Education (CAS), composed of close to 30 student affairs and academic support professional associations, represents the most visible effort of professional associations to focus on standards. CAS is both an example of the role of professional associations in collaborating with one another and of the need to combine areas of expertise to serve a purpose broader than what any one association could serve. The CAS standards (Council for the Advancement of Standards, 1992) have been used by many colleges and universities for self studies, by accreditation teams making site visits, and they are under consideration for use in benchmarking efforts. Concern for standards to use in educating new professionals is also part of the current role of professional associations and CAS. Issues facing higher education often produce new needs and advocacy for modifications reflecting changing needs of the field often emanate from professional associations.

The strengths of professional associations lie in their familiarity with issues that have been part of their history, their ability to link with other similar professional associations, their ability to take advantage of their members' overlapping affiliations with other associations to strengthen existing programs, and their willingness to find common ground and respond to issues broader than student affairs. The strength of these associations can also be their weakness, as they may remain reluctant to seek new alliances with less obviously related professional associations or place greater priorities of time and resources in anticipating member needs for information and programs related to emerging issues in the field. Cyberspace in particular has already had an enormous effect on professional associations. Before information and links with other professionals could be accessed as easily as they can now, professional associations enjoyed the role of being the best provider of such links via their annual meetings, their other face-to-face professional education opportunities, and array of publications. With cyberspace, professional associations have become one of many ways to establish such links. What this competition will do for professional associations remains to be seen.

A LOOK TO THE FUTURE FOR PROFESSIONAL ASSOCIATIONS

A "state of the art" publication is often used by interested readers to take a measure of the future, based on what is now current in the field. In this case, however, the changes just on the horizon for higher education may not be reflected in our best practice to date.

For example, issues facing higher education now and for the foreseeable future seem to be more overpowering and overwhelming than others, particularly since there seems to be an increase in the number of issues faced by college campuses that have impact on the very survival of an institution. The necessity to survive prompts a willingness to rethink old assumptions and old practices. New organizational structures are emerging and may replace the way we organize our campuses. The sweeping nature of our current issues forces functional specializations on campus to find new ways of working with other areas if they are to survive at all. Student affairs professional associations have recently focused on how these broad issues of survival have fragmented or transformed what we have historically thought of as student affairs divisions. As structures change, professional associations must address the demands of their members for ways to respond to these changes.

The more widespread nature of the issues that have recently emerged for higher education, such as greater ease of access to information, place into question the matter of who professional associations serve. Until now, professional associations have sought members by providing "members only" services or reduced rates for members when programs are provided for nonmembers as well. Will more ready access to information lead to a demand for professional associations to serve all of higher education? The World Wide Web already provides us with one vehicle to do so.

The concept of re-engineering, which includes radical rethinking of processes to produce quality, has already been introduced on some campuses. It has resulted in new ways of thinking about how a campus finds the money to open its doors, how it holds itself accountable to the many clients and customers who are served by higher education, how it learns to work smarter, and how it rethinks its educational offerings. Professional associations will be affected by the rethinking of these concerns. For example, what would be the effect on student affairs professional associations if campus representatives and marketing specialists such as those for IBM and Apple that currently join as associate members actually become active participants in the association? What might happen to professional associations in student affairs if campuses restructure themselves and form one functional area that includes areas separately known as student affairs and academic support programs?

Associations that focus on a specialized area of student affairs will be particularly vulnerable in the future. As programs and services are transformed, professional associations representing the status quo, or the way things were, will need to see how to transform their own purposes to respond. As offices on campus are increasingly staffed with people who are not familiar with the knowledge base, skills and attitudes of a function such as counseling or advising, continuing professional education becomes even more critical. Recent developments in distance learning provide strong opportunities for specialized associations to reach their clientele and associations are responding by revising their internal structure and their program and funding priorities to provide for this critical function. Teleconferencing is increasingly utilized as a vehicle for professional development and as interactive media are developed further, there is no doubt that professional associations will be active participants.

In the past, professional associations have relied on academic preparation program faculty and current members to recruit new members. Will future trends allow professional associations, in their recruitment efforts, to rely solely on those who already see the value of professional associations? Who will be able to convince those who have entered the field without student affairs graduate education or access to a knowledgeable student affairs staff member to join a professional association?

How will the role and delivery of continuing professional education look in the future? Perhaps professional associations will become service providers to higher education in general by offering institutional memberships and rate reductions to members for special programs that can be delivered via distance learning technology. Perhaps associations will continue to use a teleconferencing service provider to deliver such programs, turning their attention to brokering with a variety of delivery services and to a variety of content programs developed by other continuing professional education providers to serve their members.

CONCLUSION

The enormity of the changes now facing higher education will most surely result in the transformation of programs and services on campus. Old definitions of programs and services will be replaced by definitions that deal with the relevance of a function to the overall mission of the institution, and in the process, the traditional office of career development or of academic advising may not be physically discernable. Instead, we may find these functions imbedded in many places on campus depending on the need for the function by a community of students within the institution. These functions may be provided by off-campus agents, by faculty on a reduced load, by other undergraduate students or by student affairs staff. Professional associations have the unique opportunity to provide a "big picture" perspective on these changes. Utilizing their continuing professional education role, associations can become education providers for staff who need the knowledge to fulfill their responsibilities. They can also become collaborators as they join with other associations in providing this education.

Professional associations have an opportunity to assess the common outcomes of higher education, possibly providing supplemental information on a regional basis to colleges and universities interested in how others achieve these outcomes. As a potential clearing house for "best practice" in fulfilling certain functions, professional associations can provide access to information about these "best practices" to others, as ACPA and NASPA did at their 1997 joint convention. They could become valuable contributors to the principles associated with Continuous Quality Improvement and Total Quality Management. As they know their own members and their talents, they can become a referral agent for campuses wishing to take advantage of the expertise of others in solving local problems.

As campuses reconfigure their offices and staffing patterns, professional associations are in the unique position of anticipating common new staffing patterns, of seeking linkages between existing professional associations that would support the new pattern, and of even considering a merger of associations to maximize effectiveness in meeting the needs of staff in these new patterns. As a contract provider themselves for continuing professional education, professional associations might join together in funding the delivery systems and in finding the educators to respond to the continuing learning needs of campus staff.

These new or expanded roles for professional associations also suggest a transformation of the infrastructure and assumptions of the professional association. As members of professional associations, we have often thought of our work as a series of processes taking place in a certain part of the organization, and carried out only or primarily by people like us. We join professional associations to network with and learn from people like us. Suppose that our work is done by people like us *and* faculty members *and* students? If our professional associations fail to include all who do our work and do not respond to the diverse needs of a more diverse membership, those professional associations will exist for a smaller proportion of the staff of a college campus. Their relevance to "real" campus needs will be questioned, and they may soon find themselves out of existence.

Potential new memberships produce the need to rethink assumptions about levels and types of continuing professional education, about what a campus can realistically provide for itself without relying on professional associations for such education, how to subdivide delivery systems for continuing professional education in order to make them accessible, what types of member benefits should be provided, what new income streams in addition to membership dues must be in place, and who the association serves beyond the individual member. With these questions emerging and the issues of higher education being as pervasive as they have been in recent years, the primary issue then facing professional associations in the future will be how to find and use new approaches to the design and delivery of programs and services that are relevant to that future.

REFERENCES

About the Association. (1995). In *Association of College Unions-International membership directory and sourcebook.* Bloomington: ACU-I.

About your association. (1995). In *National Association for Campus Activities membership directory.* Columbia: NACA.

American College Personnel Association member resource directory. (1996-97). Washington, DC: ACPA.

Bretz, R. D., Jr., Rynes, S. L., & Gerhart, B. (1993). Recruiter perceptions of applicant fit: Implications for individual career preparation and job search behavior. *Journal of Vocational Behavior, 43*, 310-327.

Burd, S. (1996, May 3). Republicans in congress start examination of college costs. *Chronicle of Higher Education, 42*(34), A27.

Burek, D. M. (1992). *Encyclopedia of associations.* Detroit: Gale Research.

Correspondence. (1994, Fall). A publication of Student Affairs and Student Services, Cincinnati, OH: University of Cincinnati.

Council for the Advancement of Standards in Higher Education. (1992). *Preparation standards and guidelines at the master's degree level for student affairs professionals in higher education.* College Park, MD: Author.

Dey, E. L., Astin, A. W., Korn, W. S., & Riggs, E. R. (1992). *The American freshman: National norms for Fall 1992.* Los Angeles: Higher Education Research Institute, UCLA.

Dostart, P. J., & Olsen, O. P. (1995, Winter). Cost centers to profit centers. *Higher Education Law Bulletin, 4*(4), p. 3ff.

Ferren, A. (Ed.) (1990). Curricular reform: The personal dimensions. *Liberal Education, 76*(3), 36-38.

Griffith, F. A. (1995, October). How standards-based K-12 reforms affect higher education. *AAHE Bulletin, 48*(2), 12-15.

Hanson, G. S. (1995). The organizational evolution of NAWE. *Initiatives, 56*(4), 29-36.

Kendrick, A. (Ed.). (1996). *Organizational paradigm shifts.* Washington, DC: National Association of College and University Business Officers.

Kuh, G. D., Schuh, J. H., Whitt, E. J., & Associates. (1991). *Involving colleges: Successful approaches to fostering student learning and development outside the classroom.* San Francisco: Jossey-Bass.

Mitchell, R. (1995, October). Front-end alignment: An introduction to the standards movement. *AAHE Bulletin, 48*(2), 7-11.

Moore, L. (1995, February). *What students want.* Paper presented at the Delaware Valley Student Affairs Conference, Philadelphia, PA.

National Association for Women in Education member handbook. (1995-96). Washington, DC: NAWE.

National Association of Student Personnel Administrators annual report. (1995-96). Washington, DC: NASPA.

Neuberger, C. (1995). Brief history of ACPA. In *American College Personnel Association member resource directory* (pp. 3-4). Washington, DC: ACPA.

Nuss, E. (1993). The role of professional associations. In M. J. Barr & Associates, *The handbook of student affairs administration* (pp. 374-377). San Francisco: Jossey-Bass.

Rhatigan, J. J. (1995). NASPA history. In *National Association of Student Personnel Administrators 1995-96 member handbook* (pp. 5-6). Washington, DC: NASPA.

Sauter, J. (1994). *Association of College and University Housing Officers - International report.* Columbus: ACUHO-I.

Sheeley, V. L. (1991). *Fulfilling visions: Emerging leaders of ACPA.* Washington, DC: ACPA.

Part Two

Preparation of Student Affairs Professionals

In Part Two, the focus of the monograph shifts to the preparation of student affairs practitioners to meet the challenges outlined in the first section. The three chapters in this section focus on the students in student affairs preparation programs, the faculty, and the curriculum in our student affairs preparation programs. In Chapter 5, Christine Phelps Tobin addresses the recruitment, selection, and retention of well qualified, committed graduate students. Recommendations for faculty, practitioners, institutions, and professional associations are provided. Phelps Tobin highlights three current challenges facing the profession: the recruitment of highly qualified graduate students who are underrepresented in our preparation programs and in the field; the improvement of the recruitment and training process to better ensure that those who graduate from preparation programs will be retained in the field; and the expectation that those who are being considered for entry-level positions in the student affairs field have the appropriate educational training and background necessary to assume such positions.

In Chapter 6, Nancy Evans and Terry Williams present data from a recent national survey to provide a profile of current student affairs faculty. Characteristics and qualifications essential to prepare faculty members for a rapidly changing and challenging academic climate are identified, along with information about the environment in which they work. Recommendations are made regarding the necessary qualifications of faculty with regard to knowledge, values, skills, and behaviors. In conclusion, suggestions are made for the preparation of future student affairs faculty.

Marylu McEwen and Donna Talbot address the design of the student affairs curriculum in Chapter 7. This chapter focuses on the formal curriculum in student affairs, its history, professional standards, and specific components of the curriculum. The majority of attention in the literature has been given to the master's degree curriculum, while greater variation and less consensus exist for doctoral-level education. Current, emerging, and future curricular issues are discussed.

The preparation of student affairs professionals is critical if student affairs is to continue to be a healthy, responsive profession. Three components are necessary to ensure success in this area: recruiting, selecting, and retaining qualified graduate students; hiring faculty with appropriate and necessary characteristics and qualifications; and designing and continuously developing the curricula of student affairs preparation programs so that graduates will be well prepared to serve their institutions and their constituents.

Chapter Five

Recruiting and Retaining Qualified Graduate Students

Christine E. Phelps Tobin

The influence of a professional field of practice is determined by the quality of its human resources. In the coming millennium, student affairs will be shaped by those who enter the field today. Attracting and retaining high quality individuals to the student affairs field will directly effect the contributions made by student affairs professionals on campuses across the nation and throughout the world for decades to come. Given the increased numbers of nontraditional students, students of color, and students from other underrepresented groups entering colleges and universities, student affairs is faced with a significant and demanding challenge that must be responded to with vision, commitment, and enthusiasm, and supported by human and fiscal resources and viable strategies to ensure the health of professional preparation and practice.

The purpose of this chapter is to identify and describe the issues and practices surrounding the recruitment, selection, and retention of qualified graduate students in student affairs preparation programs. Recommendations are directed to faculty, practitioners, institutions, and professional associations about how to improve recruitment, selection, and retention practices to insure the continued flow of committed, capable, and highly qualified individuals into the field.

RECRUITMENT

Widespread interest in graduate student recruitment, across all disciplines, began to surface in the mid 1980s. This heightened interest seems to have begun when the effect of the nation's demographic shift on undergraduate enrollment reached the graduate ranks. Much of the literature on this topic involves the recruitment of women and minorities and focuses on specific academic programs (Arns, 1983; Malaney, 1984; 1985).

Since the publication of the previous edition of this monograph in 1988, increased interest has been placed on the recruitment and preparation of the student affairs professional. An increase in publications, programming efforts, and membership in ACPA's Commission XII: Professional Preparation, are indicators of this increased interest. Concern about declining enrollments in student affairs preparation programs and corresponding reductions in faculty members and other resources devoted to these programs during the 1970s and the 1980s provided the backdrop for the previous edition of this chapter (Komives & Kuh, 1988). In response to these same concerns, the American College Personnel Association (ACPA) and the National Association for Student Personnel Administrators (NASPA) formed an interassociational task force in 1987 to address these issues. The ACPA-NASPA Task Force, comprised of faculty and practitioners, published a report in 1989 addressing the issues of recruiting, preparing, and nurturing the student affairs professional (Task Force, 1989).

Traditionally passive recruitment practices, combined with an increased emphasis on the recruitment of highly qualified graduate students representative of campus diversity, has heightened the recruitment challenge (Komives, 1993; Komives & Kuh, 1988; Sagaria & Johnsrud, 1991; Task Force, 1989). Part of this challenge is to determine who to recruit, and where to commit very limited resources. Enrollment demographics, recruitment practices, and recruitment constraints will be discussed.

Enrollment Demographics

Much has been written about who enters student affairs preparation programs and the field, and how they enter (e.g., "by accident," because of role models, as a result of recruitment efforts, as a natural extension of undergraduate experiences, etc.) (Coomes, Belch, & Sadlemire, 1991; Hunter, 1992; Keim, 1991; Komives, 1993; Komives & Kuh, 1988; Richmond & Sherman, 1991; Task Force, 1989). This information is helpful in analyzing the effectiveness of recruitment practices, and ways to improve them.

Over 2,100 students were enrolled in preparation programs in 1973. This figure declined steadily until 1987 to a low of 1,640, at which time enrollment figures jumped dramatically, with over 3,200 students enrolled in 1990 and nearly 3,500 students enrolled in 1994. At the same time, the number of programs has increased from 41 masters programs and 28 doctoral programs in 1973 to 74 masters programs and 41 doctoral programs in 1994 (Keim, 1985; Keim & Graham, 1994). This information is included in Table 5-1. Possible explanations for the dramatic increase in enrollment since 1987 include the increased number of programs available to students; increased numbers of students pursuing graduate and professional study; greater visibility of the student affairs profession and student affairs preparation programs stemming from the heightened focus on recruitment efforts as outlined by publications in the late 1980s such as the previous edition of this monograph (Young & Moore, 1988) and the report published by ACPA-NASPA (Task Force, 1989).

During 1993-94, the last year for which figures are available, approximately 3,548 people were enrolled in graduate study in student affairs programs. Of this number, 632 were doctoral students, and 2,816 were masters students. According to these figures, women make up 55 percent of all doctoral students and 66 percent of all masters students. Students of color make up 18 percent of all graduates (Keim & Graham, 1994). After a period of decline in the enrollment of graduate students of color in the 1980s (Pruitt & Isaac, 1985), enrollment rates for this population have remained unchanged over the last decade (Cheatham & Phelps, 1995). The majority of doctoral students are between the ages of 31 and 35, with few (2%) students younger than 25, or older than 45 (5%) (Coomes, et al., 1991). Comparable figures for masters students are not available.

Students enter preparation programs with a variety of undergraduate majors including: (a) social sciences (54%); (b) humanities (18%); (c) education (12%); (d) science and math (11%); and (e) business (9%) (Hunter, 1992). Five factors are important in choosing a student affairs career for currently enrolled, as well as prospective students: (a) role models (Blackburn, Chapman, & Cameron, 1981; Daloz, 1986; Richmond & Sherman, 1991; Young, 1985); (b) critical incidents, such as undergraduate experiences in student life and residence life (Carpenter, 1983; Hunter, 1992; Holmes, Verrier, & Chisholm, 1983; Komives, 1993; Richmond & Sherman, 1991); (c) others' support (Komives &

Table 5-1
Student Enrollment in Student Affairs Preparation Programs

Doctoral

Year	N Stud	N Prgms	Mean	% Men	% Min	% Wmn	% Min
1972-73	500	28	17.9	76		24	
1976-77	507	30	16.9	66		34	
1979-80	513	27	19.0	57		43	
1983-84	493	32	15.4	51		49	
1986-87	499	30	16.6	53		47	
1989-90	842	43	19.6	47	19	53	20
1993-94	632	41	15.4	45	18	55	18

Specialist

Year	N Stud	N Prgms	Mean	% Men	% Wmn
1972-73	115	17	6.8	62	38
1979-80	79	14	5.6	59	41
1983-84	55	11	5.0	41	59
1989-90	52	10	5.2	40	60
1993-94	43	9	4.8	32	68

Masters

Year	N Stud	N Prgms	Mean	% Men	% Min	% Women	% Min
1972-73	1548	41	37.8	55		45	
1976-77	1480	43	34.4	43		57	
1979-80	1186	41	28.9	41		59	
1983-84	1123	45	25.0	35		65	
1986-87	1098	43	25.5	35		65	
1989-90	2402	87	27.6	33	14	67	12
1993-94	2816	74	38.0	34	18	66	18

Sources: Keim (1985); Keim & Graham (1994)

Kuh, 1988); (d) shared values (Canon, 1989; Hunter, 1992; Komives, 1993); and (e) current student affairs professionals. Of these five factors, current practitioners exert the greatest influence in the decision to pursue a career in student affairs (Hunter, 1992; Komives, 1993). Location, availability of assistantships, reputation, and proximity to home are the most important reasons for entry into specific preparation programs (Richmond & Sherman, 1991).

Recruitment Practices

A comprehensive study of graduate student recruitment practices across disciplines found that the most cost effective and most widely used recruitment strategies were (a) personal contact, (b) program-specific publications, and (c) financial assistance. Furthermore, a significant relationship was found between the effectiveness of a recruitment program and the presence of professional recruitment personnel (Baron, 1987).

The words passive, unsystematic, and unintentional characterize the recruitment practices that have typically been used throughout the student affairs field to attract prospective graduate students into preparation programs (Andreas, et al., 1993). Limited recruitment materials and programs have been developed over the years; however, they have not been distributed or implemented on a wide scale basis (Komives, 1993). The recruitment materials that have been developed are designed to assist prospective masters students to explore student affairs as a career field (Kirby & Woodard, 1983; Komives, 1990; NASPA, 1990; Rentz & Knock, 1990; Rentz & Saddlemire, 1987; Trimble, Allen & Vidoni, 1991) and to identify graduate programs (Keim & Graham, 1994).

In addition to recruitment materials, professional associations have developed programs on the regional and national levels to inform individuals about career opportunities and graduate study in student affairs. The annual National Week for Careers in Student Affairs project, sponsored jointly by ACPA and NASPA, which includes three regional forums throughout the country, and NASPA's Minority Undergraduate Fellowship Program are examples of two such efforts. These programs suffer from low numbers of participants, however, and their effectiveness in influencing the matriculation of graduate students is unclear.

A model of graduate student recruitment suggests five steps: (a) conduct assessment (analysis of the institution, the students, the "competition," the job market); (b) develop recruitment and enrollment objectives, (c) develop a recruitment plan and recruitment strategies to meet the above objectives; (d) implement the recruitment program; and (e) monitor and evaluate the recruitment program (Baron, 1987). This model can provide a useful framework for our efforts, at each level, in the recruitment of qualified graduate students in student preparation programs.

In addition, Malaney (1985) offers five recruitment strategies useful to institutions, departments, and programs seeking high quality graduate students, or specific types of students. The first recruitment strategy is the *competitive strategy*, which is based on the notion that even the most prestigious institutions and programs in the country want to recruit the finest students; therefore, recruitment remains an important issue at these institutions. Gaining prestige is recommended by having outstanding faculty members and emphasizing the outstanding characteristics of a particular institution, department, program, and area (Malaney, 1985).

The second recruitment strategy is *maintaining alternatives* which suggests that a program make attempts to tap as many potential sources of undergraduate students as possible. International institutions as well as sources other than undergraduates approaching graduation should be considered.

The third recruitment strategy is a cooperative strategy termed *contracting* in which lists of graduating seniors from related programs are sent to graduate programs at other institutions (Malaney, 1984).

Coalescing is the fourth recruitment strategy, and is similar to contracting, but tends to be more formal in structure and operational goals. An example of coalescing is illustrated by the Committee on Institutional Cooperation (CIC), which is made up of representatives from each university in the Big Ten Conference plus the University of Chicago. One of the goals of the CIC is the recruitment of minority undergraduate degree recipients of CIC institutions to pursue graduate education at CIC institutions. In support of this goal, each year the CIC sponsors a name-exchange program, where CIC institutions share lists of minority undergraduates who are interested in pursuing graduate study.

The final recruitment strategy is *coopting* which includes the addition of individuals or groups outside the organization (program) to the policy-making structure of an organization. The addition of practitioners as adjunct faculty has long been a practice in student affairs preparation programs. Other student affairs programs find it helpful to form an alumni or practitioner advisory committee, which could provide input regarding many issues, including those related to recruitment and retention. Malaney (1985) suggested that these strategies should be pursued simultaneously.

Recruitment Constraints

Attracting diverse and highly qualified graduate students to preparation programs is a challenge constrained by many factors, including enrollment issues. These constraints were outlined in the report by ACPA-NASPA (Task Force, 1989). Despite greater numbers of students enrolled in programs today, these constraints remain unchanged.

1. A lack of awareness of the profession by undergraduate students who represent the major market for new student affairs professionals.
2. Low-paying, low-status positions at the entry level which make it difficult to attract undergraduate students and educational practitioners.
3. The perception of limited career mobility, especially as viewed by undergraduate resident assistants, who may see student affairs narrowly as only residence hall administration.
4. The absence of a parallel undergraduate program. Even though liberal arts, general education, and behavioral science majors are the most similar to college student affairs in values and learning objectives, the field is rarely perceived by individuals in such undergraduate majors as a natural extension of their studies.
5. Inadequate explanations of student affairs professionals' responsibilities by practitioners which leave potential graduate students confused and uninformed and less interested in pursuing this field of study.
6. The failure of student affairs practitioners to encourage current students to consider the field. Some practitioners even discourage students with whom they work from entering the field by openly expressing dissatisfactions with their jobs.
7. Absence of information about the student affairs profession in university placement and career development offices.

Obviously, recruiting increased *numbers* of qualified graduate students into our preparation programs may not be realistic given the continued limited resources facing higher education in general, and colleges of education in particular. Without additional faculty, graduate student funding, and other resources, increasing enrollment is not recommended, particularly when fewer positions are available. Many programs are directing their efforts toward recruiting the finest and most diverse graduate students available.

Fifteen years ago, roughly 50 percent of the individuals annually employed in entry level positions presented academic credentials from student affairs preparation programs (Stamatakos, 1981). More recent data indicate that approximately 36-57 percent of entry level positions advertised in *The Chronicle of Higher Education* during selected periods in 1992 and 1993 prefer or require a graduate degree from a student affairs preparation program (Erwin, 1992; 1993). Furthermore, placement data from the last few years of ACPA and NASPA conventions indicates that candidates outnumber job listings by a ratio of more than 2.4 to 1.0. Based on this recent data, additional challenges have appeared. Careful follow-up with graduating students as they enter the marketplace will help to clarify hiring trends. Also, on-going follow-up with graduates of programs will provide necessary information to better understand what happens throughout their careers. A better understanding of martketplace opportunities may ultimately influence our recruitment and admissions efforts, program design, and program offerings. Graduate preparation programs must pay attention to numbers of students entering our programs, and ultimately the profession, as well as to student demographics. Specific recommendations include:

1. Recruit highly qualified graduate students who are clearly underrepresented in our preparation programs and in the field, not more students. This goal includes more men in masters programs, more students of color, and a broader range of student ages and ableness.
2. Improve the recruitment process to better ensure that those who graduate from preparation programs are likely to remain in the field beyond the first five to six years, which is when a significant number of practitioners tend to leave the field (Komives & Kuh, 1988).
3. Continue to work within our profession to encourage those who hire to require formal education in student affairs.

Recruitment recommendations will be provided at the end of this chapter.

SELECTION

Admissions requirements and the admissions process lead to the selection of graduate students in preparation programs. Recommendations will be provided for modifications and improvements in these areas at the end of this chapter.

Admissions Requirements

Since the 1960s, ACPA's Commission XII (Professional Preparation) has collected information about admissions requirements from preparation programs nationwide. Analysis of data included in the 1994 edition of the *Directory of Graduate Preparation Programs in College Student Personnel* (Keim & Graham, 1994) indicates that admissions requirements, for doctoral and masters programs respectively, include the following: (a) a stated minimum GPA (93%, 96%); (b) GRE or other standardized exam (98%, 52%); (c) interview (65%, 41%); (d) recommendations (100%, 95%); and (e) prior years of experience (77%, 11%).

Many students apply to two or more preparation programs, and in recent years this process has become highly competitive and sophisticated. Whereas several years ago the publication of admission standards allowed interested students to determine for themselves the likelihood of admission, programs are now conducting interviews with greater frequency to make selections from a larger, much more qualified, experienced, and increasingly diverse candidate pool (Keim & Graham, 1994).

No longer are virtually all applicants admissible (Komives & Kuh, 1988). Calls for more flexible and inclusive admissions requirements have been made in an effort to remain focused on the goals of recruiting more diverse candidates. This change raises concerns about the appropriateness of publishing minimum admissions standards. Individuals who do not meet the standards typically do not apply, while, alternatively, those with potential for success may be discouraged from applying altogether. In effect, publishing admissions standards may eliminate some of the more diverse and underrepresented populations that are targets of recruitment efforts. Somehow, the biases and expectations that influence faculty when evaluating the performance of underrepresented persons must be set aside or neutralized (Komives & Kuh, 1988). Sedlacek's noncognitive factors to predict academic achievement (Tracy & Sedlacek, 1985) have become very useful for effective consideration of racial and ethnic minorities, as well as other students whose undergraduate leadership experiences and motivation signal a better prognosis of success than their test scores or undergraduate grades. Sedlacek and Brooks (1976) proposed seven non-cognitive variables that are related to academic success: (a) positive self-concept; (b) realistic self-appraisal, (c) understanding of and an ability to deal with racism; (d) preference for long-term goals over more immediate, short-term needs, (e) availability of a strong support person, (f) successful leadership experience, and (g) demonstrated community service. Students who do not meet minimal academic standards should be encouraged to assertively build their case around these indicators and request an exception to stated minimums (Komives, 1993).

The case to utilize more flexible admissions requirements is strengthened not only by our rich experiences, but by empirical evidence that runs counter to institutionalized admissions practices. Undergraduate grade point average (GPA) is not correlated with any measure of success after college including income, involvement in community affairs, personal and physical well-being, happiness, or professional accomplishments (Cohen, 1983; Hoyt, 1966; Komives & Kuh, 1988; Samson, Graue, Weinstein, & Walberg, 1984). A similar argument has been made concerning the utility of graduate admission test scores. Young (1986) found that undergraduate GPA was negatively related to letters of recommendation and performance as a graduate student, and GRE scores were not linked to undergraduate GPA.

Quantifiable information, such as GPA and GRE scores, can remain useful, however, as students compete for centrally allocated scholarships and other awards. This type of information will continue to be important across the campus community so that we can maintain comparable levels of recognition with other disciplines. Non-academic variables, such as racial prejudice and taciturn affect, may become apparent during the selection process, and the quantifiable requirements may allow for an easier rationalization of the rejection of such applicants (Komives & Kuh, 1988); however, in an effort to maintain ethical practice, candidates should receive direct feedback regarding these admission variables as well.

With the increased use of interviews in the selection process, non-academic variables such as the ability to apply basic counseling and listening skills; empathy; respect for individual differences; positive regard for thoughts and feelings of others; flexibility to face a variety of issues; and the ability to demonstrate understanding of and sensitivity to multicultural issues; and/or personal traits, can be weighted more heavily. Desirable personal traits have been consistently described and include the capacity for introspection, a sense of personal well being, confidence, humor, tolerance, respect and understanding for persons different from oneself, sensitivity, integrity, acceptance and application of criticism, resilience, and versatility (Andreas, et al., 1993; Appleton, Briggs, & Rhatigan, 1978; Saddlemire, 1974). These are characteristics of mature, self-directed people. Assessment of personal traits is very subjective, and selection committees must rely on reference letters/conversations and their own clinical skills. Potential for graduate study, as described in letters of recommendation, may be an adequate predictor of successful performance. A strong academic record, combined with personal characteristics that have been linked to successful practice, may predict leadership in the field, an important consideration in evaluating applicants (Komives & Kuh, 1988). Recruitment and selection procedures are among the least constrained activities engaged in by virtually all universities. As a result, a commitment to enroll and graduate more diverse students must be the responsibility of each department and each program (Pruitt & Isaac, 1985). More flexible and inclusive admissions criteria, along with greater emphasis on non-cognitive variables, will allow increased opportunities to admit historically underrepresented students.

Admissions Process

Approximately two-thirds (61%) of the 53 institutions including this data in the 1994 *Directory of Graduate Preparation Programs in College Student Personnel* (Keim & Graham, 1994) reported using a rolling admissions deadline, and/or admission to the program 60 days prior to the start of the semester. Institutions with set application deadlines indicated a preference for early Spring semester dates, primarily during January, February, March, and April. Since the majority (65%) of doctoral programs and a significant number (41%) of masters programs require an admissions interview, this opportunity should be used to attempt to identify some of the non-cognitive and interpersonal variables important to success in the student affairs field. Identification of unacceptable attitudes (overt racism, sexism, homophobia, inability to respect individual differences, lack of positive regard for the thoughts and feelings of others, negative attitude as learner, and emotional difficulties), along with inflexibility, should be a part of the screening process.

Since increasing numbers of potential students are applying to multiple programs, greater uniformity in the admissions process between programs, coupled with the cooperation of national and regional recruitment and placement events and the hiring of graduate assistants/interns, will strengthen the admissions process. Consistent and compatible screening procedures and standardized candidate reply dates have been suggested (Komives & Kuh, 1988). Faculty must work closely with graduate colleges, colleagues on other campuses, and practitioners to develop and maintain an effective admissions process.

RETENTION

High quality recruitment practices will greatly enhance retention efforts. Although retention in student affairs preparation programs tends to be strong due to the type, quality, and number of activities in which students participate beyond the formal curriculum, several retention issues are of concern on both the doctoral and masters level. In addition, several models have been developed which attempt to address the issue of student retention, and lend support to retention efforts. At the end of this chapter, recommendations to improve the retention of graduate students will be made.

Even though overall retention of graduate students in student affairs preparation programs is high, these students are not exempt from retention issues which seem to plague many graduate students. Some of these issues may be more serious for doctoral students rather than masters students, but in general, several concerns must be addressed including (a) funding, (b) involuntary attrition, (c) psychological fit/social adjustment, (d) personal and professional challenges, (e) program requirements, and (f) unique issues of concern in the retention of graduate students of color.

The fact that financial aid facilitates both entry and persistence is well known. Less obvious is the fact that the form of aid is equally as important. Assistantships, especially those in a student affairs area, are preferred over loans. Not only do these opportunities provide necessary financial compensation, they quite often provide invaluable professional experience that enhances the more theoretical classroom curriculum. Many students, including students of color, are heavily in debt from undergraduate study and are not well-positioned to acquire additional debt. Earmarking special funds for minority students may be necessary for retention as well as for recruitment (Pruitt & Isaac, 1985). Faculty, practitioners, and graduate schools must work together to maximize any and all funding opportunities.

While it is possible that some unacceptable attitudes and interpersonal skills will be identified during the screening process, it is more likely that such problems will surface later, through classroom interactions, or observations by internship or practicum supervisors. Involuntary attrition warrants decisive, fair treatment. Advising students out of programs for non-academic reasons is fraught with potential problems; therefore, proactive steps should be taken when possible. Reviewing professional ethics statements early in a graduate program might influence some students to voluntarily withdraw after learning that particular attitudes are not valued in student affairs. Unfortunately, because of ambiguously defined criteria for professional "success" and fear of litigation, some programs allow students who exhibit unacceptable attitudes or behavior to earn advanced degrees (Komives & Kuh, 1988).

The psychological fit and social adjustment of graduate students is critical in their decision to persist in a program. Adequate opportunities should be made available to students to make connections throughout the campus community so that a sense of belonging can be developed as soon as possible. Active involvement with assistantships and student organizations helps to integrate students both academically and socially on campus. Quality orientation and mentoring programs can assist in this process as well.

Attention should be paid to helping students learn to balance multiple responsibilities and commitments. Personal and professional challenges are often heightened in graduate school and early in one's career. Students must be encouraged and supported in their struggle to understand and learn how to balance competing personal and professional demands. The curriculum may be used as a more formal avenue to address some of these critical retention issues. Information about time management, expectations of graduate students, career opportunities, career development, and professional health and on-going professional development can be incorporated throughout the curriculum. Career information must be particularly directed toward women and minorities because they are at greater risk of leaving the field (Komives & Kuh, 1988). Faculty and practitioners must provide superior educational preparation that links theory with practice (Task Force, 1989).

Unreasonable or out-dated degree requirements may interfere with the persistence of graduate students. For example, the high level (84%) of doctoral programs requiring residency may work at cross-purposes to students who desire, or are required because of financial necessity, to attend part-time (63%). Careful evaluation of the mandatory residency requirement must be considered in an effort to provide greater flexibility for part-time students (Coomes et al., 1991).

Often, the attrition rate for graduate students of color is attributed to the failure of the department, or more specifically, individuals in the student's program, to encourage and enable them to become an integral part of the program, department, and university (DeFour & Hirsch, 1990). Because most graduate programs have low enrollments of students of color, and few, if any, faculty members and practitioners of color, students of color are more likely to find themselves isolated in situations that lack both formal and informal support systems (Pruitt & Isaac, 1985). Support programs and services geared toward all graduate students, yet with particular attention and sensitivity directed toward graduate students of color, are recommended. Supportive efforts include the following: (a) making available counseling and peer support groups for students, their families, spouses, and partners; (b) providing career development and placement services; (c) making available academic support services which focus on writing, computing, and research design and analysis; (d) providing options for housing and day care facilities; (e) designing programs to address personal and academic concerns involving graduate school life; (f) educating the campus community about the special interests and developmental needs of this population; (g) committing to changes in institutional policy and practices, including the adoption of inclusive curricula and demonstrating an appreciation for how students of color respond and adjust to the graduate school environment; (h) providing more opportunities for graduate students of color to be drawn into campus life; and (i) providing quality advising (Beeler, 1991; Cheatham & Phelps, 1995; Cowell, 1985).

RECOMMENDATIONS

Given the current enrollment demographics, enrollment issues and needs, and recruitment practices and constraints, several recommendations can be directed to faculty, practitioners, institutions, and professional associations. Strengthened collaboration and cooperation between these groups will greatly enhance the success of all recruitment efforts. Integration and coordination is required. Across the board, extraordinary efforts must be made in recruiting students from underrepresented groups (Komives, 1993; Komives & Kuh, 1988; Sagaria & Johnsrud, 1991). It is important to examine what biases determine who is encouraged to enter the field and who is not. Given the importance of role models and critical incidents at the undergraduate level, the opportunity to enhance diversity within students affairs may be improved by diversifying the ranks of those nurtured and selected for undergraduate student leadership roles (Hunter, 1992).

Stable and traditional recruitment channels, such as the "old boy network" and alumni, offer both advantages and disadvantages. Advantages include greater access, communication, and familiarity with the program, campus, faculty, and student affairs field. A major disadvantage to traditional recruitment channels is that they tend to perpetuate biased enrollment patterns. As a result, multiple forms of recruitment strategies should be used. Efforts must be made to break out of these passive channels, and actively focus recruitment efforts to select groups of undergraduate colleges and targeted advertising media (Pruitt & Isaac, 1985). In addition, we must look beyond the traditional undergraduate pools, and consider returning adults as potential students, as well as individuals who currently work on campus and throughout the community. Affiliation with an academic community; quality of life benefits; challenging assignments; rewarding work; and involvement with research and development activities and professional associations, are useful markers to incorporate into recruitment efforts (Task Force, 1989).

According to analysis of data from the recent *Directory of Graduate Preparation Programs in College Student Personnel* (Keim & Graham, 1994), 39 percent of doctoral programs, and 26 percent of masters programs offer funding to less than half of their students. Clearly there is a critical need to develop additional funding, tied to professional experience, for our prospective students. Funding will assist not only in the recruitment process, but in retention, as well as the overall quality of the educational experience.

Faculty, practitioners, institutions, and professional associations all play an important role in the recruitment, selection, and retention of qualified graduate students. Several recommendations are directed to each group in the sections below.

Faculty

Because faculty play a critical role in the recruitment and retention of qualified graduate students, several recommendations follow that are directed specifically at them. Several recommendations for faculty were included in the ACPA-NASPA report (Task Force, 1989) that continue to be valuable. Those recommendations include informing undergraduate advisors and faculty, especially in liberal arts, education, and behavioral science fields, about the importance of college student affairs to the quality of the undergraduate experience. In addition, faculty should ensure that career centers on campus include sufficient information about student affairs as a career option and encourage them to inform the general public about the field. In addition, faculty should actively and persistently seek nominations of prospective students from alumni and current students (Cowell, 1985; Task Force, 1989), while trying to avoid biased enrollment patterns.

Other recommendations for faculty include forming alumni advisory committees to assist in the recruitment process, as well as working closely with practitioners to develop meaningful assistantship opportunities and supervisory relationships, recruitment materials, and open lines of communication. In collaboration with student affairs practitioners on campus, faculty must utilize opportunities in any related undergraduate courses (e.g., leadership, resident assistant training, career decision making, orientation to college, etc.) to discuss career opportunities and graduate study in student affairs. Faculty must expand the awareness on campus of the student affairs field and their specific program and actively involve practitioners, alumni, and current students in any and all recruitment efforts. Faculty are encouraged to examine and evaluate all materials pertinent to a specific program for their accuracy, inclusiveness, and distribution. Materials must be developed that are appropriate to a wide diversity of groups and individuals, free of concepts, graphics, language, or distribution that might tend to communicate only with traditional groups and majority individuals. Faculty can also develop opportunities for formal learning and informal socialization experiences for individuals who wish to investigate the field. Faculty are encouraged to work with academic departments, colleges, and graduate schools to utilize provisional status policies for graduate students who may not be eligible for regular admission (Komives & Kuh, 1988). Faculty are highly encouraged to reexamine mandatory residency requirements in an effort to determine whether programs are most effectively meeting the needs of students, programs, and the educational process. While 84 percent of doctoral level preparation programs have a mandatory residency requirement, only 37 percent of doctoral students enroll on a full-time basis (Coomes et al., 1991). More creative and flexible strategies may be in order to better accommodate this population. Faculty must also carefully follow up student inquiries, applications, and acceptances. Attention to those details can increase both the applicant pool and the number of students who actually enroll (Cowell, 1985).

Practitioners

Since the most effective recruitment practice is personal contact between a current practitioner and a prospective student recruitment activities should be considered a basic function for all practitioners and every student affairs division. Increased efforts must be made by all professionals in all functional areas across institutional type to develop multiple and intentional experiences for prospective graduate students. Practitioners must be willing to be involved with and supportive of career days, career development programs, orientations, and campus organizations. Practitioners must be assertive and intrusive in the identification of students with the academic, interpersonal, and organizational skills and temperament to be successful in the field and consult with them individually about their career choice. Involved students tend to seek employment in the areas they have already experienced, which leads to compelling interventions for functional areas that need to "grow their own" prospects. Functional areas and areas which focus on special populations should consider such support systems as student advisory boards and a system of student peer helpers to bring interested students into the profession. To ensure enhanced breadth and depth of student talent in the field, professionals who work with student leaders (e.g., residence life and student activities) must engage in planned recruitment and career mentoring activities. Student leaders, such as resident assistants, need early exposure to the breadth of student affairs functions beyond any narrow view of traditional roles (Komives, 1993; Task Force, 1989). Practitioners should also advocate for the expansion of graduate assistantship positions beyond the traditional areas and organize and budget for recruiting and staff development as a normal operational function (Task Force, 1989).

Institutions

Institutions, through their graduate colleges, colleges of education, divisions of student affairs, academic departments, and specific programs need to be more thoughtful, intentional, and focused in their efforts to recruit prospective students in student affairs preparation programs. Program materials stressing meaningful educational experiences and professional involvement must be developed and distributed appropriately. Adequate funding, through meaningful assistantship opportunities, fellowships, scholarships, and other forms of financial aid must be made available to students, and advertised early. The creation of financial incentives (fee/tuition remission, time off) for student affairs professionals to pursue part-time and full-time graduate studies on or off campus must be developed (Task Force, 1989). Consideration of the needs of diverse graduate students must be attended to. These considerations should include available support services, career development services, descriptions of minority communities both on and off campus, accessibility, cost of living, diversity of cultural life and cocurricular programming (Cowell, 1985).

Professional Associations

The ACPA-NASPA Task Force (Task Force, 1989) made several recommendations directed to professional associations. Some of those recommendations include the development of a highly sophisticated multimedia recruitment campaign to target different audiences and inform them about student affairs as an attractive and viable career choice, appropriate undergraduate and graduate studies, and experiences which are appropriate to satisfying careers and successful practice. Professional associations must provide accessible and relevant career materials for all levels of education, including K-12, high school, and college (Komives, 1993). In addition, professional associations are encouraged to continue to collaborate with other associations, graduate programs, and student affairs practitioners in the development of resources and programs designed to recruit promising and competent new professionals into the field. Professional associations, particularly ACPA and NASPA, must advance and further refine the activities of the National Week for Careers in Student Affairs to recruit individuals into the profession, and encourage practitioners to view recruitment as a basic responsibility of the student affairs division and graduate preparation faculty on college campuses. Professional associations should consider following the ACUHO-I model, which offers paid summer internships away from the home campus to undergraduates who have been identified as being particularly promising for careers in student affairs. Professional associations are encouraged to launch a sustained, national campaign among current members of the profession to increase sensitivity to and an acceptance of their professional obligation for identifying and recruiting promising people into graduate preparation programs. Professional associations should adopt specific marketing strategies to inform the most relevant publics of the profession of the field's benefits to students and faculty in higher education and to reverse the current lack of image and visibility. In addition, career sessions should continue to be offered during regular conferences designed both for potential and current professionals. Professional associations should also utilize campus student leadership courses for identifying promising students and for exposing them to opportunities in the field and to graduate study (Task Force, 1989).

Professional associations are urged to include in these efforts a framework designed to assist potential graduate students with decisions about entry into the field (essential values of the profession, skills and competencies required, educational experiences, career opportunities, qualifications sought in candidates, etc.). Professional associations should be continually developing scholarship opportunities, and sponsoring research efforts that will assist in the improvement of recruitment practices and interventions.

CONCLUSION

Even though the numbers of students and programs has increased, there is still much work to do with regard to recruitment, selection, and retention of qualified graduate students in student affairs preparation programs. Three current challenges face the profession. First, faculty, practitioners, institutions, and professional associations must all assume responsibility for the recruitment of highly qualified graduate students who are underrepresented in our preparation programs and in the field. Second, they must improve the recruitment and training process to better ensure that those who graduate from preparation programs will be retained in the field. Finally, they must demand that those who are being considered for entry-level positions in student affairs have the appropriate educational training and background to assume such positions.

REFERENCES

Andreas, R. E., Komives, S., Kuh, G. D., Lyons, J. W., McEwen, M., Roper, L., Schuh, J. H., Snyder, M. B., & Whitt, E. J. (1993). *A faculty-practitioner dialogue on student affairs preparation.* Paper presented at the pre-conference workshop of the National Association of Student Personnel Administrators, Boston, MA.

Appleton, J. R., Briggs, C. M., & Rhatigan, J. J. (1978). *Pieces of eight.* Portland, OR: National Association of Student Personnel Administrators.

Arns, R. G. (1983, October). *Strategic planning: Can the promise be fulfilled?* Paper presented at the meeting of the International Society for Educational Planning.

Baron, P. B. (1987, September/October). Graduate student recruitment. *Communicator,* pp. 8-12.

Beeler, K. D. (1991). Graduate student adjustment to academic life: A four-stage framework. *NASPA Journal, 28,* 163-171.

Blackburn, R. T., Chapman, D. W., & Cameron, S. M. (1981). Cloning in academe: Membership and academic careers. *Research in Higher Education, 15,* 315-327.

Canon, H. (1989). Student services and secular sin: Beyond ethical codes. In R. Young & L. Moore (Eds.), *The state of the art of professional education and practice* (pp. 48-55). Alexandria, VA: ACPA.

Carpenter, D. S. (1983). The student affairs profession: A developmental perspective. In T. K. Miller, R. B. Winston Jr., & W. R. Mendenhall (Eds.), *Administration and leadership in student affairs* (pp. 147-166). Muncie, IN: Accelerated Development.

Cheatham, H. E., & Phelps, C. E. (1995). Promoting the professional development of graduate students of color. In A. S. Pruitt-Logan & P. D. Isaac (Eds.), *Student services for the changing graduate student population* (New Directions for Student Services, no. 72, pp. 91-99). San Francisco: Jossey-Bass.

Cohen, P. A. (1983, April). *College grades and adult achievement: A meta-analysis of empirical research.* Paper presented to the meeting of the American Educational Research Association, Montreal.

Coomes, M. D., Belch, H. A., & Saddlemire, G. L. (1991). Doctoral programs for student affairs professionals: A status report. *Journal of College Student Development, 32,* 62-68.

Cowell, P. (1985, Fall). Recruitment and retention for graduate student diversity. *The Journal of College Admissions,* 27-31.

Daloz, L. A. (1986). *Effective teaching and mentoring: Realizing the transformational power of adult learning experiences.* San Francisco: Jossey-Bass.

DeFour, D., & Hirsch, B. (1990). The adaptation of Black graduate students: A social network approach. *American Journal of Community Psychology, 18,* 487-503.

Erwin, M. C. (1992). [Job opportunities during selected weeks in the Chronicle of Higher Education]. Unpublished raw data.

Erwin, M. C. (1993). [Job opportunities during selected weeks in the Chronicle of Higher Education]. Unpublished raw data.

Holmes, D., Verrier, D., & Chisholm, P. (1983). Persistence in student affairs work: Attitudes and job shifts among master's program graduates. *Journal of College Student Personnel, 24,* 438-443.

Hoyt, D. P. (1966). College grades and adult accomplishments: A review of research. *Educational Record, 47,* 70-75.

Hunter, D. E. (1992). How student affairs professionals choose their careers. *NASPA Journal, 29,* 181-188.

Keim, M. C. (1985, March). *Student affairs preparation programs: Progressive, paralyzed, or perishing?* Paper presented at the meeting of the American College Personnel Association, Boston, MA.

Keim, M. C. (1991). Student personnel preparation programs: A longitudinal study. *NASPA Journal, 28,* 231-242.

Keim, M. C., & Graham, J. W. (1994). *Directory of graduate preparation programs in college student personnel 1994.* Washington, DC: ACPA.

Kirby, A. F., & Woodard, D. (Eds.). (1983). *Career perspectives in student affairs.* NASPA Monograph Services, Vol. 1. Washington, DC: National Association of Student Personnel Administrators.

Komives, S. R. (1990). Student affairs careers in postsecondary settings. In N. Garfield & B. Collison, (Eds.). *Careers in counseling and human development* (pp. 31-48). Alexandria, VA: American Association for Counseling and Development.

Komives, S. R. (1993). Graduate education: A focus on possibilities, problems and the promise of the doctorate. In M. J. Barr (Ed.). *Handbook for Student Affairs Administration* (pp. 390-411). San Francisco: Jossey-Bass.

Komives, S. R., & Kuh, G. (1988). The right stuff: Some thoughts on attracting good people to student affairs work. In R. B. Young & L. V. Moore (Eds.), *The state of the art of professional education and practice* (pp. 1-20). Alexandria, VA: American College Personnel Association.

Malaney, G. D. (1984). An analysis of financial aid in the recruitment of graduate students at the Ohio State University. *Journal of Student Financial Aid, 14,* 11-19.

Malaney, G. D. (1985). An organizational perspective of graduate student recruitment: A resource dependence approach. *The Review of Higher Education, 8,* 375-386.

NASPA. (1990). *Consider a career in college student affairs.* Washington, DC: Author.

Pruitt, A. S., & Isaac, P. D. (1985). Discrimination in recruitment, admission, and retention of minority graduate students. *Journal of Negro Education, 54,* 525-536.

Rentz, A. L, & Knock, G. H. (1990). *Student affairs careers: Enhancing the collegiate experience.* Alexandria, VA: American College Personnel Association.

Rentz, A. L, & Saddlemire, G. L. (1987). *Careers in the college student personnel profession.* Alexandria, VA: American College Personnel Association.

Richmond, J., & Sherman, K. J. (1991). Student-development preparation and placement: A longitudinal study of graduate students' and new professionals' experiences. *Journal of College Student Development, 32,* 8-16.

Saddlemire, G. (Ed.). (1974). *The practitioner considers the preparation program: Report of a conference on the preparation of college student personnel - student development workers.* Bowling Green, OH: College Student Personnel Department.

Sagaria, M. A., & Johnsrud, L. K. (1991). Recruiting, advancing, and retaining minorities in student affairs: Moving from rhetoric to results. *NASPA Journal, 28,* 105-120.

Samson, G. E., Graue, M. E., Weinstein, T., & Walberg, H. J. (1984). Academic and occupational performance: A quantitative synthesis. *American Educational Research Journal, 21,* 311-321.

Sedlacek, W. E., & Brooks, G. C. (1976). *Racism in American education.* Chicago, IL: Nelson-Hall.

Stamatakos, L. C. (1981). Student affairs progress toward professionalization: Recommendations for action - Part I. *Journal of College Student Personnel, 22,* 105-113.

Task Force on Professional Preparation and Practice. (1989). *The recruitment, preparation and nurturing of the student affairs professional.* A report of the American College Personnel Association and the National Association of Student Personnel Administrators. Washington, DC: NASPA.

Tracey, T. J., & Sedlacek. W. E. (1985). The relationship of noncognitive variables to academic success: A longitudinal comparison by race. *Journal of College Student Personnel, 26,* 405-410.

Trimble, R. W., Allen, D. R., & Vidoni, D. O. (1991). Student personnel administration: Is it for you? *NASPA Journal, 28*(2), 156-162.

Young, R. B. (1985). Impressions of the development of professional identity: From program to practice. *NASPA Journal, 23*(2), 50-60.

Young, R. B. (1986). An exploratory study of admissions information and success in a preparation program for student personnel workers. *Journal of College Student Personnel, 27,* 131-136.

Young, R. B., & Moore, L. V. (Eds.). (1988). *The state of the art of professional education and practice.* Alexandria, VA: American College Personnel Association.

Chapter Six

Student Affairs Faculty: Characteristics, Qualifications, and Recommendations for Future Preparation

Nancy J. Evans and Terry E. Williams

Student affairs faculty are different in many ways from members of the professoriate who teach in the liberal arts and sciences. Not only must they fulfill the demands facing all university faculty, they must also meet the expectations of the profession for which they are preparing students. Often they are the one faculty member with expertise in student affairs who teaches in a program. As the only student affairs faculty member they teach most of the core curriculum, are responsible for program promotion, recruitment, advisement, and placement of students, and conduct research expected of them by their institutions. Exacerbating these stresses, faculty enter the student affairs professoriate with a wide variety of educational experiences and often with little formal preparation to assume a faculty role.

In this chapter we review the existing literature, drawing on results obtained from a national survey conducted to determine the characteristics and qualifications of full-time faculty in student affairs preparation programs, as well as the environment in which they work. Based on this data, we make recommendations concerning the necessary qualifications of faculty with regard to knowledge, values, skills, and behaviors. Finally, we provide suggestions for the preparation of future student affairs faculty. While it is important to note that many adjunct faculty teach in student affairs programs, this chapter focuses mainly on full-time faculty who have their primary affiliation in student affairs.

CHARACTERISTICS AND QUALIFICATIONS OF CURRENT FACULTY

Who are the faculty in student affairs who are preparing individuals to enter the profession? How have they themselves been trained for their role as educators? Little information about student affairs faculty is available in the literature. We obtained information first by examining data provided in the *1994 Directory of Graduate Preparation Programs in College Student Personnel* (Keim & Graham, 1994). Then, to find out more about the characteristics of student affairs faculty, during the summer of 1995 we surveyed the 95 full-time faculty listed in the *1994 Directory* (Williams & Evans, 1995). We received responses from 63 individuals, a 66% return rate.

Demographic Characteristics

A profile of the characteristics of student affairs faculty drawn from Keim and Graham (1994) and Williams and Evans (1995) is provided in Table 6-1. Fully one-third of the faculty are assistant professors and less than half are full professors. Almost a quarter of all student affairs faculty have received their degrees since 1990. All but one person responding to our survey (Williams & Evans, 1995) was in a tenure-track position; 41 (65%) currently hold tenure. Having a relatively low number of senior level faculty may be problematic to the discipline in terms of securing the academic status that comes with holding the rank of full professor.

Men continue to outnumber women at the full and associate levels but there are more women than men at the assistant professor level, suggesting that the make-up of the faculty is starting to resemble the student affairs field where the lower ranks are dominated by women (McEwen, Engstrom, & Williams, 1990). On the average, women faculty have received their degrees more recently than men indicating that more women have been entering the teaching ranks in recent years.

Reflecting these demographics, faculty in student affairs are relatively young, ranging in age from 33 to 69; with a mean age of 49 and a median age of 48 (Williams & Evans, 1995). One-fourth of the faculty were age 55 or older, however, suggesting that a number of them may be close to retirement. If they do retire in the near future, they are likely to be replaced by younger, less experienced faculty since senior level positions are hard to retain because of budget constraints facing higher education.

As is true of student affairs practitioners (see Chapter 5), faculty are predominantly Caucasian (87%). Six faculty (10%) are African-American and one person is Asian-American. Seven individuals (11%) indicated that they have some type of disability. The lack of diversity among student affairs faculty undoubtedly contributes to the field's lack of ability to attract diverse students into preparation programs (see Chapter 5).

Academic Preparation

Faculty who teach in student affairs preparation programs come from different academic backgrounds. The data in Table 6-1 (from Williams & Evans, 1995) demonstrate the wide variety of academic disciplines in which student affairs faculty have studied. Since there is no undergraduate major for student affairs, it is not surprising that faculty have bachelors degrees in many different disciplines. Perhaps more surprising, and distressing, is that more than one-third of the faculty have masters degrees in fields other than college student personnel or counseling and that 14% have doctorates in fields other than college student personnel, counseling, or higher education, majors one would expect student affairs faculty to have pursued. The diversity of preparation faculty themselves have received may contribute to the lack of agreement concerning the components of quality student affairs preparation at both the masters and the doctoral levels (see Chapter 7).

Faculty listed in the *1994 Directory* (Keim & Graham, 1994) received their doctorates from a wide variety of institutions. The 37 faculty who completed degrees in 1980 or later are alumni of 21 different institutions. In the last 15 years, only eight institutions have granted doctoral degrees to more than one current student affairs faculty member. These schools are Indiana (5), Iowa (4), Maryland (3), UCLA (2), Texas A & M (2), Purdue (2), Ohio State (2), and Northern Illinois (2).

Professional Experience

The average faculty member has held full-time teaching positions for a total of about 12 years at two different institutions (Williams &

Table 6-1
Characteristics of Full-Time Student Affairs Faculty

Rank

Gender	Assistant		Assoc.		Full		Not Reptd		Total	
	N	%	N	%	N	%	N	%	N	%
Male	12	(39)	13	(59)	33	(80)	-	-	60	(64)
Female	18	(58)	9	(41)	8	(20)	-	-	34	(36)
Not Reptd	1	(03)								
Total	31	(33)	22	(23)	41	(43)	1	(01)	95	(100)

Field of Academic Study

Bachelors	%	Masters	%	Doctorate	%
teachers educ	21	counseling	35	counseling	35
social science	16	CSP	30	higher ed	32
business	13	other	35	CSP	19
literature	13			other	14
other	37				

Decade of Doctoral Degree Completion

Decade	Men		Women		Not Reported	Total	
	N	%	N	%	N	N	%
Before 1960	2	(04)	-	-	-	2	(02)
1960-1969	13	(24)	2	(06)	-	15	(16)
1970-1979	26	(48)	10	(29)	-	36	(38)
1980-1989	5	(09)	12	(34)	-	17	(18)
1990 or later	8	(15)	11	(31)	1	20	(21)
Not Reported					5	5	(05)
Total	54	(57)	35	(37)	6 (06)	95	(100)

Source: Williams & Evans, 1995.

Evans, 1995). About half of the faculty (51%) have held part-time/adjunct faculty positions at some time during their careers and about one-quarter (24%) have served as full-time visiting faculty. The latter data may indicate that moving into a full-time faculty position immediately after completing a doctorate is not necessarily the norm in student affairs.

Most faculty also have significant work experience both within and outside of student affairs. Many (84%) have held full-time student affairs staff positions, averaging a total of 10 years in such positions. A few faculty (16%) have held full-time university staff positions not in student affairs, for an average of 12 years, and over half (57%) have worked full-time outside of higher education for an average of 3 years. As a result of their professional work experience, faculty are likely to be knowledgeable of the issues facing student affairs practitioners and to understand the skills they need to work effectively in the field.

THE CURRENT ENVIRONMENT FOR STUDENT AFFAIRS FACULTY

The environment in which faculty work creates many demands upon their time and talents. Preparation for a faculty position in student affairs must be informed by the type of activities in which the faculty member will be engaged. The work environment of student affairs faculty is primarily shaped by three constituencies: student affairs practitioners, students enrolled in their programs, and the institutions of higher education in which they are employed.

Expectations of Faculty Held by the Student Affairs Field

Unlike many other graduate fields, student affairs preparation is closely linked to the profession it prepares students to enter. For example, two professional student affairs organizations recently issued a joint report on the status of preparation and practice in student affairs (Task Force, 1989). In this document, the ACPA-NASPA task force laid out a number of expectations for faculty. They called on student affairs educators to "provide superior preparation that links theory with practice, research knowledge with conventional wisdom, and materialistic career ambitions with altruistic purpose for all students in graduate preparation programs" (p. 18). They advocated increased collaboration between faculty and student affairs practitioners with regard to recruitment, curricular development, research, and field experience for students. They also listed skills, competencies, and attributes needed by new professionals, stressed the importance of faculty involvement in practitioner-oriented professional associations, and advocated faculty outreach to student affairs practitioners locally.

A number of professional association statements and studies have listed expected competencies for new student affairs professionals (Task Force, 1989; *Continuing the Dialogue*, 1995; Council for the Advancement of Standards, 1992; Garland & Grace, 1993; Hyman, 1988). These statements propose to faculty that new student affairs professionals must be prepared to engage in an ever increasing range of activities such as facilitating student and staff development, collaborating with faculty and other institutional agents, providing expert advice on all aspects of student life, enhancing learning environments for students and contributing to the academic mission, creating a multiculturally sensitive environment, being change agents, and carrying out sound management and administrative practices.

In addition to preparing new professionals, student affairs faculty are often expected to attend to the continuing professional development needs of those staff already in the field (Penn & Trow, 1987; Young, 1988), provide direct assistance and consultation to practitioners, and collaborate with practitioners in conducting research and evaluation of programs (Upcraft, 1994). (See Chapters 8 and 9 for further discussion of these expectations.)

Perhaps in response to these expectations, student affairs faculty are very active in professional student affairs associations. Sixty-eight per cent of the 63 respondents to our survey (William & Evans, 1995) indicated that, since becoming full-time faculty members, they have served in an elected leadership role for a professional organization. Respondents are active in the following professional organizations: ACPA (51), NASPA (39), ACES/ACA (13), and ASHE (15). Faculty indicated that 7% of their time is taken up by professional association service and another 8% by activities such as consultation and accreditation work.

Student Expectations of Faculty

A recent study by Hunter (1992) suggests that most individuals enter student affairs preparation programs with very little previous knowledge about the field. As a result of the varied backgrounds students bring and their lack of knowledge of the field, student affairs faculty spend a significant amount of time advising, socializing students into the profession, and providing basic information about various aspects of student affairs and its philosophical and theoretical underpinnings.

Students in student affairs graduate programs expect personalized attention and significant involvement with their faculty. In a study of women doctoral students in education, Heinrich (1995) found that students expect their faculty to be mentors and are deeply disappointed when they do not fulfill this role. Rogers (1992) also noted that students saw faculty role modeling as a powerful way of developing their own leadership skills. However, current reward structures for faculty do not credit informal involvement with students (Love, Kuh, MacKay, & Hardy, 1993).

Institutional and Programmatic Demands on Faculty

Colleges of Education, like other units in higher education, have been faced with decreased enrollments and budget cuts, often necessitating downsizing. The ACPA-NASPA Task Force on Professional Preparation and Practice (Task Force, 1989) noted:

> Often teacher education is seen as the core function of (Colleges of Education), and allied graduate programs are seen as peripheral to this basic mission. When budget cutting and reorganization are necessary, as has been the case for the past decade or so. . . , efforts to save the core faculty and programs may result in a reduction of support of graduate programs. (p. 6)

This trend has resulted in the merger of small graduate programs, such as student personnel or higher education, with other programs, such as educational administration or counseling (Cooper, 1986). As a result, student affairs graduate programs are threatened with a loss of identity.

Along with a loss of identity, programs have also lost faculty. Based on her longitudinal study of student affairs preparation programs, Keim (1991) noted that the number of full-time faculty has decreased. In 47 programs that furnished data from 1973 until 1987, the number of full-time faculty dropped from 75 to 61 with the average number of full-time faculty per program dropping from 1.7 in 1973 to 1.3 in 1987.

Recent data also indicate that the number of full-time faculty in student affairs programs is continuing to decrease. An analysis of information reported by 83 programs in the *1994 Directory of Graduate Preparation Programs in College Student Personnel* (Keim & Graham, 1994) revealed a total of 95 full-time faculty (an average of only 1.1 full-time faculty per program). On a positive note, fewer programs reported in 1994 (N= 26, 31%) than in 1987 (N=61, 54%) that they have no full-time student affairs faculty.

Additionally, Keim (1991) reported an increase in the number of courses required to complete masters degrees and slightly more student affairs doctoral courses being offered. Program coordinators further stated that their programs were undergoing curriculum revision that would result in the addition of even more courses to conform to CAS or CACREP standards.

Decreases in the number of full-time faculty per program, coupled with increased curricular demands, create serious concerns for student affairs faculty. For example, faculty in student affairs programs often do not have the luxury of becoming specialists. They must teach a wide range of classes and work with large numbers of students with varied needs and interests (Penn & Trow, 1987). Faculty we surveyed (Williams & Evans, 1995) taught an average of seven graduate classes and one undergraduate class during the year (including summers). They averaged five different course preparations during a typical calendar year. Instruction took up an average of 38% of their time.

Faculty responding to our survey reported that their advising loads averaged 25 students per year, ranging from 2 to 70 students. Faculty were currently directing an average of 5 dissertations (range = 0-18) and 7 masters theses or final papers (range = 0-25). Faculty devote 11% of their time to advising graduate students.

Student affairs faculty are faced with heavy teaching and advising loads at the same time that universities are expecting greater research productivity for promotion and tenure (Task Force, 1989). Half of the faculty in our survey indicated that over the last 3-5 years they had experienced greater pressure from their institution to increase the amount of scholarship they publish and 40 (63%) noted that they had experienced increased pressure to acquire more grant funding. They reported that 22% of their time is spent in research and scholarly activity.

For the last three years, our survey respondents reported that they had published an average of 5 refereed journal articles, 3 non-refereed articles, 3 book chapters, 1 edited book, and 1 authored book. Since becoming faculty members, they had also authored an average of 5 grant proposals (range = 0-35) of which, remarkably, an average of 4.8 had been funded (range = 1-32).

Current reward structures in higher education do not take into account the significant amount of administrative work required of faculty in small graduate programs. Faculty in our study indicated that they spend an average of 17% of their time administering their graduate programs and another 8% of their time in service to their institutions.

Student affairs preparation programs have always relied on administrators to serve as adjunct faculty. To maintain programs in the face of additional demands and budget cuts, use of part-time faculty has become even more the norm. Faculty we surveyed indicated that, in their programs, an average of 3 graduate courses each year (range = 0-8) are taught by full-time student affairs practitioners who serve as adjunct faculty.

Young (1989) found that part-time faculty served in various roles, including supervising fieldwork, teaching required and elective courses, and serving on program committees. As Love et al. (1993) noted, however, when the number of adjunct faculty is high, community and shared educational goals can decrease.

RECOMMENDED QUALIFICATIONS FOR FACULTY

Living up to the expectations of the profession, enrolled students, and one's university requires that faculty possess a comprehensive knowledge base as well as values congruent with the student affairs profession and skills to carry out the wide variety of tasks required of them. Since consensus has not been achieved with regard to the preparation necessary to enter the student affairs professoriate (Beatty & Stamatakos, 1990), prospective faculty members are often left to guess about the coursework and experiences that will enhance their chances of entering their chosen field. In this section we outline the knowledge base, values, and skills we believe are necessary to successfully fulfill the role of a faculty member in a student affairs preparation program, supporting our ideas wherever possible with survey data and literature.

Knowledge Base

In the following chapter, McEwen and Talbot discuss doctoral level curricula in student affairs. As they note, no doctoral level standards have been proposed to prepare either student affairs administrators or faculty. The faculty we surveyed identified, in order of importance, the following content areas as important in the preparation of student affairs faculty: (1) the student affairs profession (including developmental and environmental theory, students, history, philosophy, current issues), (2) counseling and multicultural issues, (3) higher education, (4) research design and analysis, and (5) teaching and learning.

Since many faculty will be entering programs as the sole or primary student affairs educator, they must be prepared to cover the entire student affairs curriculum outlined in the CAS Standards (1992) (see Chapter 7). To teach this curriculum, potential faculty must be well versed in several content areas.

Multicultural awareness. McEwen and Roper (1994) convincingly argue that a multicultural perspective must be infused throughout the entire student affairs curriculum. To create this type of curriculum, future faculty must be provided with in-depth education about various student populations, diverse higher education environments, multicultural models of organizational development, developmental and counseling theories applicable to non-dominant student populations, and student affairs' role in serving multicultural students.

American higher education. Potential faculty must have a good understanding of the historical development of American higher education as well as the issues currently facing higher education institutions. They must be knowledgeable of the diversity of institutional types, missions, and goals, as well as changing student demographics in higher education.

The student affairs profession. Knock, Rentz, and Penn (1989) stress the importance of student affairs faculty having a strong background related to the philosophical underpinnings of the profession. In addition, they must be familiar with the origins and development of student affairs practice, its various traditions, and its values (Young & Elfrink, 1991b). They must be aware of the broad spectrum of student affairs functional areas and the unique challenges faced by each area.

The theoretical foundations of student affairs continue to expand. Faculty must be grounded in theories of student development, organizational behavior and management, person-environment interaction, leadership, involvement, social construction, and the helping relationship. They must also be very familiar with theory-to-practice models and their uses in student affairs.

Finally, faculty must be aware of current issues in the field and professional and ethical standards to which student affairs professionals and units must adhere.

Theories of teaching and learning. To teach effectively, faculty must be knowledgeable of theories related to teaching and learning. This knowledge base includes cognitive/learning styles, creation of teaching/learning environments, and theories and methods related to the instructional process, including principles of critical pedagogy.

Research design and analysis. Programs must make an increasing commitment to teach both qualitative and quantitative methodologies (Love, et al., 1993) and faculty must be familiar with both methods of research. They must also understand the processes involved in evaluation research and assessment of needs, environments, and outcomes.

Values, Skills, and Behaviors

While the knowledge possessed by faculty is important to their success in academe, the values, behaviors, and skills they bring to their positions may be even more crucial. Students and colleagues often remember personal qualities and ways in which a faculty member interacted with them and carried out their role, more so than the depth of the knowledge they shared.

If faculty are to instill values in the students with whom they work, for instance, they must profess those same values and consistently base their actions on them. Young and Elfrink (1991a) have identified aesthetics, altruism, community, equality, freedom, human dignity, justice, and truth as core student affairs values. Faculty must exhibit these values in their interactions with others, the decisions they make, the goals they strive for, and the stands they take on issues.

Faculty must also demonstrate a genuine commitment to a multicultural perspective including being open to learning more at both an affective and cognitive level about working with diverse individuals. Young (1985) stressed the importance of faculty establishing relationships of mutual respect with all students and demonstrating through their actions a true appreciation of differences. Brown (1985) also underscored the importance of acknowledging and attending to students' differing needs. Students and colleagues are quick to see through statements that are words only, without actions to back them up.

Creamer and Shelton (1988) noted that both the personal and professional development of student affairs graduate students must be attended to if they are to become effective professionals. Faculty must be willing to relate to students on a personal, affective level as well as on a cognitive level in the classroom (Evans, 1988). The most powerful moments in students' graduate careers are often the times when they are able to share something very personal and significant with a faculty member. To allow such moments to happen, faculty must be approachable, sincere, and available to students.

Brown (1985) suggested that mentoring relationships between students and their faculty are an important component of student affairs preparation. Mentoring is especially important to assist students in learning aspects of a field about which most know very little and finding their niche among the varied professional options. Rogers (1991) found that faculty in preparation programs develop leadership in students through mentoring, encouraging professional involvement, and modeling leadership behavior as well as through coursework. As part of the mentoring process, faculty also have a responsibility to assist students in career planning and job search efforts (Richmond & Benton, 1988).

Faculty must demonstrate through their actions a commitment to scholarship and learning. Modeling what it means to be a professional and a scholar through one's activities, conversations, and active involvement in research and other projects with students helps students to develop a desire for lifelong learning and scholarly pursuit. Penn and Trow (1987) suggested that this type of role modeling is the most important aspect of the faculty member's job.

Teaching is, of course, a major aspect of a faculty member's role. Varied experiential learning techniques, such as case studies, simulations, site visits, and field experiences are particularly important in working with the concrete learners who often enroll in student affairs programs (Penn & Trow, 1987). Conceptual study must be integrated with practical experience (Forney, 1994; Young, 1985). Projects that connect students with practicing professionals (see Hunter & DeLuca, 1986) and encouragement to become involved in professional associations and activities are particularly important for socializing students into the student affairs profession.

Accomplishing all these tasks requires a broad range of skills. To interact well with students outside of, as well as inside the classroom, and to relate with student affairs professionals effectively, faculty must possess strong interpersonal skills. They must be "people persons" in addition to good scholars.

RECOMMENDED PREPARATION FOR STUDENT AFFAIRS FACULTY

Entering the student affairs professoriate today is not easy. Coomes, Belch, and Saddlemire (1991) found that of 775 students enrolled in student affairs doctoral programs, 20% (105) aspired to faculty positions. However, informal review of job listings in the last decade suggests that faculty positions available in student affairs programs (as well as counselor education and higher education programs looking for student affairs specialists) have generally numbered less than 10 per year and sometimes fewer.

With the elimination of a mandatory retirement age for faculty, it is hard to predict future employment trends. While many faculty may decide to continue working as long as their health is good, early retirement incentives may induce others to leave their positions at a younger age. With only 16 faculty in our survey age 55 or older, prospects for large numbers of positions becoming available to new faculty seem dim. In addition, downsizing in Colleges of Education may result in elimination of positions that do become open, especially in small graduate programs.

How, then, are potential faculty to be prepared for success in this competitive job market? In addition to appropriate coursework in the areas outlined previously, relevant experiences, mentoring, and socialization are necessary.

Student affairs faculty believe that professional experience as a student affairs practitioner is important for establishing credibility, both with students and with student affairs professionals. It is difficult to effectively "sell" a position or action or discuss the implications of a real life case study if one has never had to implement what one is advocating. Being able to talk about one's own work in the field and to understand the intricacies of various issues strengthens one's teaching and helps in establishing positive connections with practitioners. Faculty in our survey rated professional experience in student affairs as a very important (5.0 on a 6-point scale) qualification for faculty.

Few programs offer a doctorate in student affairs. More typically, the doctorate is in higher education, counselor education, or educational leadership with a specialty in student affairs. Faculty in our study were most likely to recommend obtaining a doctorate in higher education (34), followed by student affairs (28), and counseling (14). The major field seems less important than the specific coursework potential faculty members have taken and the scholarly credentials they present. Students should be aware, however, that their major field selection may dictate the types of programs to which they will be attractive candidates. For example, a counselor education-based student affairs program may be wary of a candidate with a higher education degree who does not understand the "culture" of a counseling program and may not be prepared to teach counseling courses or supervise a counseling practicum.

Helping students learn what it means to be a faculty member is an important responsibility for faculty mentors. Potential faculty must be provided with opportunities to "do the things that faculty do" (for example, work on research projects, give papers at professional conferences, teach classes, assist in administrative aspects of running a preparation program). First, such activities will be an important "reality check" for aspiring faculty. Second, they will help to build resumes that will assist students in securing positions. And finally, they will assist individuals in making the transition from a student role to that of a faculty member.

Newell and Kuh (1989) reported that 71% of the higher education faculty they surveyed indicated that their departments had a "practitioner" orientation. Since an important aspect of preparation for students interested in becoming faculty is learning the "culture" of academe (Love, et al., 1993), such administratively-oriented programs might not be as appropriate as a more research-oriented program. Prospective doctoral students interested in faculty careers may want to note the programs listed earlier that have prepared faculty in recent years. While there are no guarantees that they will produce new faculty in the future, they at least have some track record for doing so.

In recent years, at least some programs have been encouraging students to consider teaching careers. Assistant professors in our study were much more likely than associate or full professors to report that they had been encouraged to consider a faculty career and had been mentored to assume such a role.

An increasingly important skill for any potential faculty member is facility with research methodology and writing for publication. Delworth and Hanson (1989) recommended early and ongoing involvement in research projects as part of doctoral preparation. From a survey designed to solicit suggestions for improving research training in counseling, programs were encouraged to involve students in research teams, to see that first year students gained hands-on research experience, and to emphasize research design rather than statistics (Galassi, Stoltz, Brooks, & Trexler, 1987). These suggestions seem appropriate for would-be student affairs faculty as well. Assistant professors we surveyed were more likely than associate or full professors to have co-presented research with faculty and to have co-authored with faculty while they were graduate students.

Given the realities of a very tight job market, students aspiring to faculty roles would be well advised to develop back-up plans, either in administration or in positions such as institutional research and planning. With the increasing reliance on part-time faculty, aspiring faculty might look for such positions on campuses with student affairs programs where they might be able to secure adjunct faculty roles. Continuing involvement in faculty-oriented associations, such as Commission XII of ACPA and the Association for the Study of Higher Education, as well as continuing scholarly activity and persistence in the job market may lead to full-time academic positions at a later point in one's career.

CONCLUSION

Full-time student affairs faculty number only 95 individuals teaching in 83 programs. These numbers have been decreasing over the last decade and are likely to continue to decrease given the economic conditions facing higher education and the vulnerability of small graduate programs.

While men still predominate at the senior ranks, the majority of assistant professors are women. Less than 10% of all student affairs faculty are people of color. Faculty are relatively young; the median age is 48 and over half of the faculty received their doctorates after 1980. Thirty-five percent have yet to receive tenure. The relatively large number of young, female, untenured faculty in student affairs suggests that they may be especially vulnerable if decisions must be made about allocation of resources or distribution of workload, particularly if there are no senior student affairs faculty in their program to offer support and to fight for equity.

Doctoral preparation of student affairs faculty is most likely to be in counseling or higher education, with less than 20% receiving degrees specifically in student affairs. The lack of in-depth preparation specifically in student affairs at the doctoral level is problematic, especially when faculty are required to cover the gamut of the student affairs curriculum. Limited faculty and resources in student affairs programs, however, often precludes offering specialized doctoral level coursework.

Most faculty have previously held staff positions in student affairs. Extensive professional experience in the student affairs field certainly adds to faculty credibility in the classroom and with student affairs practitioners. Many faculty have also held part-time or visiting faculty positions prior to obtaining full-time positions. Given the difficulty of obtaining a full-time student affairs teaching position, such positions may become even more common in the career paths of our faculty.

The work environment for student affairs faculty is demanding. Faculty report teaching heavy loads, advising large numbers of students, and providing significant service to professional associations in addition to spending almost one-quarter of their time on research and scholarship. Despite heavy workloads, they are very productive, regularly submitting and securing grants and publishing in professional journals. What price do faculty pay for their level of productivity? Open-ended comments on our survey suggest that the biggest issue facing student affairs faculty is lack of time to get everything done that must be done. Informally, faculty report working nights, weekends, and vacations and never feeling caught up. Are the rewards of seeing an article in print or obtaining excellent class evaluations worth the constant stress and exhaustion that many faculty feel? Is there any solution to this problem?

Carrying out the responsibilities associated with being a student affairs faculty member requires comprehensive preparation. To be successful both in the very limited and competitive job market facing potential student affairs faculty candidates and in the demanding field itself, students must carefully prepare for their roles. Current faculty have a responsibility to mentor students who desire to be faculty members by working with them on research projects, presentations, and publications as well as providing teaching opportunities. They must also help them to truly understand the demands of a faculty career in student affairs and prepare themselves mentally for these demands. If we are to effectively prepare student affairs practitioners to function in an increasingly complex and diverse higher education environment, we must first more carefully and intentionally attend to the preparation of student affairs faculty who will teach them.

REFERENCES

Beatty, D. L., & Stamatakos, L. C. (1990). Faculty and administrator perceptions of knowledge, skills, and competencies as standards for doctoral preparation programs in student affairs administration. *Journal of College Student Development, 31,* 221-229.

Brown, R. D. (1985). Graduate education for the student development educator: A content and process model. *NASPA Journal, 22*(3), 38-43.

Continuing the dialogue: Creating an agenda for student affairs educa-

tion, preparation, and professional development. (1995, February). Breakfast dialogue at the NASPA IV-East Regional Conference, Dearborn, MI.

Coomes, M. D., Belch, H. A., & Saddlemire, G. L. (1991). Doctoral programs for student affairs professionals: A status report. *Journal of College Student Development, 32,* 62-68.

Cooper, J. H. (1986, February). *Higher education as a field of study: Some future prospects.* Paper presented at the meeting of the Association for the Study of Higher Education, San Antonio, TX. (ERIC Document Reproduction Service No. ED 268 905)

Council for the Advancement of Standards in Higher Education. (1992). *Preparation standards and guidelines at the master's degree level for student affairs professionals in higher education.* College Park, MD: Author.

Creamer, D., & Shelton, M. (1988). Staff development: A literature review of graduate preparation and in-service education of students. *Journal of College Student Development, 29,* 407-414.

Delworth, U., & Hanson, G. R. (1989). Future directions: A vision of student services in the 1990s. In U. Delworth & G. R. Hanson (Eds.), *Student services: A handbook for the profession* (pp. 604-618). San Francisco: Jossey-Bass.

Evans, N. J. (1988). Practicing what we teach: Implications of the new scholarship on women for student affairs preparation. *Journal of College Student Development, 29,* 499-501.

Forney, D. S. (1994). A profile of student affairs master's students: Characteristics, attitudes, and learning styles. *Journal of College Student Development, 35,* 337-345.

Galassi, J. P., Stoltz, R. F., Brooks, L., & Trexler, K. A. (1987). Improving research training in doctoral counseling programs. *Journal of Counseling and Development, 66,* 40-44.

Garland, P. H., & Grace, T. W. (1993). *New perspectives for student affairs professionals: Evolving realities, responsibilities and roles.* ASHE-ERIC Higher Education Report No. 7. Washington, DC: The George Washington University, School of Education and Human Development.

Heinrich, K. T. (1995). Doctoral advisement relationships between women. *Journal of Higher Education, 66,* 447-469.

Hunter, D. E. (1992). How student affairs professionals choose their careers. *NASPA Journal, 29,* 181-188.

Hunter, D. E., & DeLuca, L. (1986). Enhancing the socialization of new student affairs professionals. *The Vermont Connection, 7,* 10-16.

Hyman, R. E. (1988). Graduate preparation for professional practice: A difference of perceptions. *NASPA Journal, 26,* 143-150.

Keim, M. C. (1991). Student personnel preparation programs: A longitudinal study. *NASPA Journal, 28,* 231-242.

Keim, M. C., & Graham, J. W. (1994). *Directory of graduate preparation programs in college student personnel 1994.* Washington, DC: ACPA.

Knock, G. H., Rentz, A. L., & Penn, J. R. (1989). Our philosophical heritage: Significant influences on professional practice and preparation. *NASPA Journal, 27,* 116-122.

Love, P. G., Kuh, G. D., MacKay, K. A., & Hardy, C. M. (1993). Side by side: Faculty and student affairs cultures. In G. D. Kuh (Ed.), *Cultural perspectives in student affairs work* (pp. 37-58). Lanham, MD: ACPA.

McEwen, M. K., Engstrom, C., & Williams, T. E. (1990). Gender diversity within the student affairs profession. *Journal of College Student Development, 31,* 47-53.

McEwen, M. K., & Roper, L. D. (1994). Incorporating multiculturalism into student affairs preparation programs: Suggestions from the literature. *Journal of College Student Development, 35,* 46-53.

Newell, L. J., & Kuh, G. D. (1989). Taking stock: The higher education professorate. *Review of Higher Education, 13,* 63-90.

Penn, J. R., & Trow, J. J. (1987). Expanding graduate education. In L. V. Moore & R. B. Young (Eds.), *Expanding opportunities for professional education* (New Directions for Student Services, no. 37, pp. 39-51). San Francisco: Jossey-Bass.

Richmond, J., & Benton, S. (1988). Student affairs graduates' anticipated and actual placement plans. *Journal of college Student Development, 29,* 119-124.

Rogers, J. L. (1991). Leadership education in college student personnel preparation programs: An analysis of faculty perspectives. *NASPA Journal, 29,* 37-48.

Rogers, J. L. (1992). Graduate student views of leadership education in college student personnel preparation programs. *NASPA Journal, 29,* 169-179.

Task Force on Professional Preparation and Practice. (1989). *The recruitment, preparation and nurturing of the student affairs professional.* A report of the American College Personnel Association and the National Association of Student Personnel Administrators. Washington, DC: NASPA.

Upcraft, M. L. (1994). The dilemmas of translating theory to practice. *Journal of College Student Development, 35,* 438-443.

Williams, T. E., & Evans, N. J. (1995). [Characteristics, qualifications, and work environments of student affairs faculty]. Unpublished raw data.

Young, R. B. (1985). Impressions of the development of professional identity: From program to practice. *NASPA Journal, 23*(2), 50-60.

Young, R. B. (1988). The profession(alization) of student affairs. *NASPA Journal, 25,* 262-266.

Young, R. B. (1989). The perceptions and roles of adjunct faculty. *Journal of College Student Development, 30,* 168-170.

Young, R. B., & Elfrink, V. L. (1991a). Essential values of student affairs work. *Journal of College Student Development, 32,* 47-55.

Young, R. B., & Elfrink, V. L. (1991b). Values education in student affairs graduate programs. *Journal of College Student Development, 32,* 109-115.

Chapter Seven

Designing the Student Affairs Curriculum

Marylu K. McEwen and Donna M. Talbot

Graduate curricula in student affairs have evolved significantly within the past century. The first graduate program in student affairs was established in 1913, although there is evidence of persons providing student affairs functions at least as far back as 1880, and perhaps as early as the mid-1800s (Lloyd-Jones, 1949).

The focus of this chapter is on the formal curriculum in student affairs, its history, professional standards, and specific components of the curriculum. The majority of attention has been given to the masters degree curriculum, accepted as the minimal level of education for student affairs practice. Greater variation and less consensus exist for doctoral-level education.

HISTORICAL CONTEXTS

Histories of student affairs portray the evolution of both professional practice and preparation. The value of attention to the history of the design of student affairs curricula lies in three areas: (a) understanding the disciplinary and historical context for student affairs curricula; (b) identifying key curricular components that have been an ongoing part of the curriculum; and (c) describing curricular trends.

Knowing and understanding the foundations of student affairs curricula is important to the continuing development and evolution of professional training.

Early Preparation of Student Affairs Professionals

For the first 40-50 years of the student affairs profession's existence, the professional preparation of most student affairs practitioners consisted primarily of on-the-job training. With the establishment of student affairs professional associations betwee 1916 and 1924, continuing training and education of student affairs professionals occurred through these national associations, both at their professional conventions and eventually through their professional journals (see Chapter 4).

Formal graduate programs in student affairs can be traced to 1913 at Teachers College, Columbia University, which "set up a program of special training, exclusively on a graduate level, designed to train 'deans and advisers of women'" (Lloyd-Jones, 1949, p. 262). Prior to this first graduate program in student affairs, student affairs professionals with graduate degrees would have studied in a great variety of disciplines, from more closely related disciplines such as education, psychology, and sociology, to somewhat less directly related areas of study such as English, history, and mathematics. Even the program established at Teachers College in 1913 brought together specialists from a variety of fields.

According to Lloyd-Jones (1949), "the first Masters of Arts degree and the Diploma of Dean of Women were granted at Teachers College in 1914" (p. 262). The curriculum leading to the Diploma of Dean of Women in 1914 at Teachers College included specific courses such as the hygiene of childhood and adolescence, biology as related to education including sex education, a full year of educational psychology, history of the family, educational sociology, the philosophy of education, management of the corporate life of the school, problems of administrative work, the psychology of religion, and "a practicum in which concrete problems confronted by the dean of women were discussed" (Lloyd-Jones, 1949, pp. 262-263).

LaBarre (1948), in a study undertaken in 1946, found that approximately 50 institutions provided training for college level personnel work; 37 of these programs offered both masters and doctoral degrees. Based on the comprehensive training programs which existed at many institutions, Lloyd-Jones (1949) concluded that there was firm evidence, by the late 1940s, that "intellectual training *is* offered in this field" (p. 263).

Training and preparation for professional practice, historically and continuing to this day, are rooted both in experience and practice (an apprenticeship model) and in formal graduate work. According to Wrenn (1949), almost all of the 110 institutions responding in 1946 to LaBarre's (1948) survey reported inclusion of an internship in their formal training programs.

Wrenn (1949) also discussed his perceptions of graduate programs in student personnel. He believed that some minimal standardization among graduate programs existed at that time, but that much more needed to be done and that programs needed to push further and to push "upward from . . . [their] present status" (p. 272). Wrenn, quoting from his article in the May 1948 *Journal of Higher Education*, stated eloquently that a comprehensive study of the person was central, but clearly not enough. He spoke of the importance of studying an individual's immediate environment, but also of the necessity of examining the greater environment "of society itself" (Wrenn, 1949, p. 273). Wrenn further stated that there should be three components of knowledge in all training of personnel workers: (a) skills for working with individuals, including counseling, appraisal, and adjustment among others; (b) knowledge of organizations, particularly student affairs' place in organizational structures and organizational dynamics; and (c) "an awareness of values" (p. 273), by which he meant an overriding philosophy about and of personnel work, clear assumptions and intentionality about the values held and acted upon, and "a sense of the contribution to be made to society" (p. 273). The early development of professional education in student affairs is clearly reflected in contemporary standards and practice.

Formal Statements Concerning Professional Preparation

According to Miller (1991), the first formal statements related to professional preparation for student affairs professionals were put forth in the 1960s. The second and more comprehensive statement, a revision of a 1964 statement by the Council of Student Personnel Associations in Higher Education (COSPA), was published by COSPA in 1967 as "Guidelines for Graduate Programs in the Preparation of Student Personnel Workers in Higher Education" (COSPA as cited in Miller, 1991).

Evolution, revision, and subsequent reiterations of these 1967 guidelines resulted in 1986 in a formal set of standards and guidelines for "Preparation . . . at the Master's Degree Level for Student Affairs Professionals" (Council for the Advancement of Standards in Higher Education [CAS], 1986). What set the 1986 standards apart from others were their development and adoption by the Council for the Advancement of Standards in Higher Education (CAS), a consortium of more than 20 professional associations concerned with promoting quality of programs and services for students in higher education. These 1986 CAS standards were subsequently revised in 1992, and it is that current statement of standards for professional preparation which is discussed in this chapter.

MASTERS DEGREE PROGRAMS

The overall goal of a masters degree curriculum in student affairs is to prepare competently trained individuals to perform the broad range of practice in student affairs. Specifically, the curriculum should embrace a two-pronged objective: (a) to provide thorough theoretical background and knowledge related to understanding students, higher education, and the practice of student affairs; and (b) to develop effective student affairs practitioners through guided and supervised experiences in student affairs. The 1992 CAS Standards address these dual purposes of student affairs graduate programs.

The interweaving of theory and practice in graduate preparation should be central to student affairs graduate programs. Too much theory with too little practice may yield an intellectual understanding of the profession and its knowledge bases without the concurrent facility, supervision, and experience in effective practice. On the other hand, professional practice and experiential education, without an adequate base in theory and literature, produces a trained apprentice, rather than someone with the intellectual and scholarly training and understanding of the persons and organizations with which one works and practices. A fine blending of both theory and practice is essential for the effective education *and* practice of student affairs professionals.

Key Issues in the Curriculum

Issues central to the design of a student affairs curriculum include (a) the content of the formal curriculum; (b) the nature and quantity of applied experiences; (c) the place of research within the curriculum; (d) the length of the graduate program; (e) the nature of the graduate students in the curriculum, including criteria for admissions and retention; (f) the nature and composition of the faculty, including their qualifications and expertise, their number and representativeness, and whether they are full-time or part-time; and (g) the nature and quality of the scholarly and interpersonal community related to the graduate program. Overarching and essential components of the curriculum are professional ethics and the creation of an ethical and caring community. Another important issue which should be integral to graduate programs in student affairs relates to the program's responsiveness to contemporary and emerging issues.

Central to the CAS standards is that the masters degree represents the *minimal* requirement for professional practice. It is readily acknowledged that there are student affairs practitioners whose highest educational degrees are bachelors degrees or whose graduate degrees are in areas not directly related to student affairs. Further, many of these individuals are competent practitioners and active professionals. Such persons may or may not have the body of knowledge related to student affairs. Nevertheless, the core belief about the professional practice of student affairs is that persons will hold a masters degree in student affairs or a closely related area. This belief is also reflected in the CAS standards for programs and services for students in functional areas.

The CAS Preparation Standards and Guidelines at the Master's Degree Level for Student Affairs Professionals in Higher Education (1992) prescribe a comprehensive set of professional knowledge and supervised practice *essential* for minimum competency in student affairs. The standards describe "education leading to established minimum competencies, knowledge, skills, attitudes, and values appropriate to professional practice" (CAS, 1992, p. 1) in student affairs. The guidelines illuminate, describe further, and enhance the essential elements represented in the standards. The foundation of these standards is that "student affairs is a professional field in higher education that promotes student learning and development" (p. 1).

In the CAS preparation standards, it is fully acknowledged that the implementation of these standards must occur within the "contexts of institutional mission," "graduate school policies," "faculty expertise," and faculty "perspectives on ideal practice in the profession" (p. 1). Further, "creative approaches to professional education are encouraged" (p. 1).

Mission of the Masters Degree Program

Central to the design of student affairs curricula is the development of a clear statement of mission and objectives regarding the program. The responsibility of developing a mission statement and program objectives rests with the program faculty (CAS, 1992). It is suggested that, in developing the mission and objectives, program faculty should involve "collaborating student affairs professionals and relevant advisory committees" (CAS, 1992, p. 2). It is expected that the statement be written to provide appropriate markers and assessment of student attainment and program effectiveness. Such a mission statement should be "readily available to current and prospective students and to cooperating faculty and agencies" (p. 2). Further, a mission statement should be reviewed periodically and revised as appropriate.

The CAS guidelines encourage program faculty in the development of the mission statement and program objectives to consider and draw upon a wide net of recommendations from relevant professional and governmental groups; program constituents including current students, alumni/alumnae, and associated professionals; and national, regional, state, and local legislative bodies. Relevant societal issues, trends, and needs should also be considered in program development.

Not only do the mission statement and program objectives represent a broad and general portrait of the program and its goals, but the CAS guidelines suggest that "mission and objectives . . . specify mandatory and optional areas of study and . . . include a plan for assessing student progress throughout the program of study" (pp. 2-3). Further, it is suggested that "the mission and objectives may address recruitment, selection, retention, employment recommendations, curriculum, instructional methods, research activities, administrative policies, governance, and program evaluation" (p. 3). In essence, the program's mission and objectives must represent clearly and concretely the broad intent of the program.

Recruitment and Admission

Although a comprehensive discussion of recruitment and retention of qualified graduate students is provided in Chapter 5 of this book, it should be noted here that a section of the CAS standards on recruitment and admission addresses admissions processes and the obligations to prospective as well as current students. Programs *must* have readily available accurate descriptions of the program, qualifications of program faculty, and data regarding student persistence, graduation, and post-graduation plans (either further study or employment).

Written admissions criteria must exist and should be provided to prospective students and program faculty; these criteria must include the institution's criteria for admission to graduate study. Admissions decisions must be based on these criteria.

Criteria for students admitted to a program should include not only strong interpersonal skills, intellectual abilities, and a student affairs career goal, but also "the potential to serve a wide range of students with varying developmental levels and backgrounds, and the capacity to be open to self-assessment and growth" (p. 3). Further, faculty are strongly encouraged to use criteria known to predict success in the program for students with varying backgrounds and characteristics. For example, non-cognitive variables (Sedlacek, 1987, 1991; Tracey & Sedlacek, 1984, 1985), listed in Chapter 5, may be useful criteria in considering students who have been underrepresented in higher education.

Essential Components of the Curriculum

Three components are essential to masters degree curricula in student affairs. These include Foundational Studies, Professional Studies, and Supervised Practice. Foundational Studies include the history and evolution of higher education and student affairs as well as knowledge from other disciplines which underlie the practice of student affairs. Professional Studies embrace five related areas, including (a) student development theory, (b) student characteristics and effects of college on students, (c) individual, group, and organizational interventions, (d) organization and administration of student affairs, and (e) assessment, evaluation, and research. Supervised Practice involves formal practica and internships consisting of supervised work in at least two distinct areas of professional practice. Competence in each of these three components represents minimum knowledge for all master's degree graduates in student affairs.

Foundational Studies. Study in disciplines and literatures that provide the basis and foundation for student affairs knowledge and practice constitute this component. Such foundations include history of higher education, educational philosophy, psychology, and sociology. Also included are the research foundations and sociocultural foundations of higher education. Study of the history and philosophy of student affairs is an essential part of this component. Other disciplines and literatures which can inform student affairs practice are also appropriate for inclusion. Examples of such disciplines and literatures include international education, management, human development, and ethics.

Professional Studies. Professional studies represent the core knowledge bases for work in student affairs. The five areas of study include student development theory; student characteristics and effects of college on students; individual, group, and organizational interventions; organization and administration of student affairs; and assessment, evaluation, and research. Knowledge in these five areas, taken together, provide bases for student affairs professionals in knowing students, student populations, and demographics of who goes to college; identifying and assessing outcomes and value-added benefits for persons who attend college; understanding the psychological and sociocultural bases of who students are and how they learn and develop in college; developing and providing interventions with individuals, groups, and organizations; understanding the organization and administration of student affairs units and divisions and how they fit within institutional structures and organizations; and understanding and conducting assessment of students and environments, program evaluation, and related research.

Student development theory. This area should address theories and research about how students learn and develop. A comprehensive examination of students' development should take place. Specific facets of development include intellectual and cognitive development; moral development; and spiritual development—the structures and processes one uses to think and to reason. Psychosocial development includes the kinds of issues students are preoccupied with, such as career, self, self in relation to others, competence, and values. Identity dimensions are a third area of student development. These dimensions include racial, ethnic, and cultural identity; sexual identity; and gender identity, among others. It is not the biological descriptors of one's self which are important, but what those biological descriptors mean to an individual, psychologically and socioculturally. A fourth kind of developmental theory concerns learning styles, the consistent and persistent differences among individuals in terms of how they relate to the world. Person-environment and campus ecology theories represent the fifth kind of theory focus; theories and perspectives in this area concern the interactions between individuals and environments and how those environments affect or mediate students' learning and development.

Not only is the area of student development theory identified by the CAS standards as essential to a student affairs curriculum, but the concept of student development and the related student development theories represent one of the hallmarks of the student affairs profession. Brown (1972), Miller and Prince (1976), and Knefelkamp (1982) have articulated how student development represents one of the most important premises of student affairs.

Student characteristics and effects of college on students. There are two primary aspects of this area of study. Student characteristics concerns an in-depth examination of who attends college and what happens with them, in terms of demographic characteristics, such as gender, race/ethnicity, age, socioeconomic status, and academic ability and preparation. Student characteristics also includes attention to specific groups of students, not only in regard to characteristics cited above, but also pertaining to resident status (commuters and residents), full-time and part-time students, adult students, international students, first-generation college students, and student athletes. Particular subsets of students who have unique experiences in the academic community are important for study.

The second aspect of this area of study concerns the effects of college on students. Issues such as retention and attrition, value-added outcomes of college, and student satisfaction with the college experience should be considered.

Individual, group, and organizational interventions. This area includes "studies of techniques and methods of assessing, design, and implementation of interventions with individuals, groups, and organizations" (CAS, 1992, p. 6). A premise of this standard is that the curriculum should provide opportunities for graduate students in student affairs to develop knowledge and competence in "advising, counseling, instructing, mediating, leading, and managing" in order to "assist individuals, groups, and organizations" (p. 7). Counseling, group dynamics, and organizational development are at the heart of this standard, and the CAS standards indicate that "students' programs of study should include substantial instruction" (p. 7) in these three knowledge areas. The CAS standards further acknowledge that "intervention skills [in these three areas] are complex and require periods of time to practice under supervised conditions" (p. 7).

Organization and administration of student affairs. This area includes studies of theory underlying organization and administration of student affairs, namely, organizational, management, and leadership theory. It also includes study of the many functional areas of student affairs, the varying manners in which they are organized within the institution, and organizational and administrative issues related to these functional areas. Central and essential to this area is the study of professional issues in student affairs and higher education; ethics of the profession, including formal ethical statements; and standards for practice (see, in particular, the CAS standards for more than 20 functional areas).

Assessment, evaluation, and research. This area is a comprehensive examination of "studies of student and environmental assessment" (CAS, 1992, p. 7), program evaluation studies, and studies of research methodologies. In essence, student affairs professionals should be competent in assessing student needs, students' learning and development, and student outcomes of the educational experience. They should also know how to assess educational environments. Student affairs professionals should also know how to conduct evaluations of programs. Further, they should be able to critique research studies and have had experience in "designing, implementing, and reporting a research study" (CAS, 1992, p. 8). Hunter and Beeler (1991) offer excellent questions concerning inclusion of the study of research in graduate programs.

Supervised Practice. Critical to the learning of competencies as a student affairs professional is supervised experience and practice in student affairs. The CAS standards prescribe a minimum total of 300 hours of supervised practice consisting of at least two distinct experiences. This requirement may be accomplished by completing two practica or internships in different settings consisting of substantively different learnings and experiences, or by completing one practicum/internship and one graduate assistantship which involves "substantive experience and professional supervision" (CAS, 1992, p. 8). Practical experiences should include work representing the full range of student affairs practice, including work with individual students and groups of students; "program planning, implementation, and evaluation; staff training and supervision; and administrative functions and processes" (p. 8). The CAS standards acknowledge that "appropriate consideration and provisions should be made for students with extensive experience in student affairs" (p. 8).

Preparation of students for practica and internships is required. Such preparation involves prior learnings, knowledge of ethical practice, advanced site placement, collaboration with on-site supervisors, and articulation of responsibilities for the practicum or internship. It also includes appropriate assessment, feedback, and remediation, where necessary, of students' skills and competencies.

"Supervision must be provided by competent on-site professionals working in cooperation with qualified program faculty" (CAS, 1992, p. 8). Both on-site supervisors and students, as well as program faculty, must comply with ethical principles and standards of the American College Personnel Association (ACPA, 1990), the National Association of Student Personnel Administrators (NASPA, 1995), and other relevant professional associations.

Principles of the Graduate Program

Affirmative Action, Equal Opportunity, and Access. The CAS standards for masters degree programs specify that the "academic preparation unit must adhere to the spirit and intent of equal opportunity laws in all activities" (CAS, 1992, p. 9). The two components specifically targeted in this standard are equal access and hiring and promotion policies. Further, faculty and administrators are expected to "take affirmative action that strives to remedy significant staffing imbalance, particularly when resulting from past discriminatory practices" (p. 9). Such affirmative hiring should occur when faculty teaching in a graduate program are not representative of the graduate student body or of the demographics of students in postsecondary institutions in the United States. For example, faculties which are comprised of one racial/ethnic group, often White, or primarily of one sex should work appropriately and diligently to hire, when positions are available, persons who would add to the diversity of the faculty. When positions are not available, creative means (such as guest speakers, visiting scholars, and professional mentors) should be considered to enhance the diversity of experiences and opportunities available to graduate students and faculty in the program.

Faculty. Although Evans and Williams provide a comprehensive discussion of student affairs faculty in Chapter 6, it is important to note specifications in the CAS standards for student affairs faculty. According to the CAS Standards (1992), essential to a graduate program in student affairs are the "equivalent of two full-time faculty members with primary teaching responsibilities in the student affairs preparation program" (p. 10). The Standards further specify that at least one of those persons "must be devoted full time to the program" (p. 10) and that there must be a "program director who is qualified by preparation and experience to manage the academic program and to supervise research, curriculum development, and field placements" (p. 10).

In essence, this standard specifies that, minimally, a graduate program in student affairs should have at least one full-time faculty member and the equivalent of one additional faculty member. This "second" faculty position may be another full-time faculty member or a collection of part-time faculty or full-time student affairs professionals who devote part of their work to the graduate preparation program. Simply stated, there should be adequate faculty for the maintenance, care, and nurturing of graduate students and a quality graduate program.

Also included in the CAS standards are the requirements for continuing professional development of program faculty and adequate support through staff, resources, and facilities for operation of the program and for faculty to devote sufficient time to their faculty responsibilities. Guidelines (suggestions but not requirements) regarding faculty and staff address a "reasonable faculty-student ratio" (CAS, 1992, p. 10), appropriate teaching loads, a system for involving professional practitioners in the academic program, and the importance of collaboration with student affairs professionals in multiple components of the academic program.

Institutional Responsibilities. Responsibilities of the institution to the graduate program, although implied above, are underscored. These responsibilities, in order to have and maintain an adequate graduate program, include providing an appropriate number of qualified faculty and support staff; supporting the continuing professional development of faculty; and providing sufficient resources, library resources, facilities, and research support for the program.

Responsibilities to Students. The CAS Standards (1992) also specify responsibilities to and for students enrolled in the graduate program. These include "high quality academic advising" (p. 11) by faculty, "professional career assistance" (p. 11), and availability of financial support. Specific forms of financial support include "graduate assistantships, fellowships, work-study, research funding, travel support, and other financial aid" (p. 12).

Ethics. Ethics are an essential component of professional practice specifically addressed by the CAS Standards. Components of the Ethics Standard include (a) ethical compliance and behavior of faculty; (b) faculty competence; (c) instruction of students regarding ethics;

(d) communication to students of ethical expectations and information regarding graduate student liability; (e) regular review of students; and (f) faculty responsibility regarding employment-related recommendations.

First, faculty are expected to "comply with all ethical principles and standards of the American College Personnel Association [ACPA] and the National Association of Student Personnel Administrators [NASPA]" (CAS, 1992, p. 13) as well as with ethical principles and standards of other relevant professional associations as appropriate. It is the responsibility of all program faculty to model ethical behavior and practice, including academic integrity to students and to colleagues. Faculty must "demonstrate the highest standards of ethical behavior and academic integrity in all forms of teaching, research, publications, and professional service" (p. 13). Faculty must be "skilled as teachers and knowledgeable about current theory, research, and practice in areas appropriate to their teaching or supervision assignments" (p. 13).

Second, faculty are expected to "instruct students in ethical practice and in the principles and standards of conduct of the profession" (p. 13). Although not specified directly, it is appropriate and probably essential that faculty instruct students about complex issues of academic integrity, such as intellectual property and scholarly documentation. Ethical statements of ACPA (1990), NASPA (1995), and related professional associations and institutional academic honesty and academic integrity codes are useful sources upon which to draw.

The Standards also specify that "ethical expectations of graduate students must be disseminated in writing on a regular basis to all students" (CAS, 1992, p. 13). In addition, "faculty must inform all students of . . . institutional and program policies regarding student liability when working with others under supervision" (p. 14). The Standards suggest that "programs may wish to establish policies requiring students to hold membership in particular professional associations and to purchase liability insurance prior to entering into practica or internships" (p. 14). Program faculty will want to know their institutional policies and practices regarding liability and may want to consult with institutional legal counsel regarding such issues.

Third, faculty of an academic program are required to engage in an *annual* evaluation of "students' progress and suitability for entry into the student affairs profession. Evaluation of students' ethical behaviors must be included" (CAS, 1992, p. 14). An essential component of regular evaluation of students is that expectations of students must be identified by faculty and communicated to students annually in writing, and that a process for an annual review of students must be established and in place. Further, faculty are expected "in case of significant problematic behaviors to communicate to the student the problems identified and the remediation required" (p. 14). The Standards suggest that where issues and concerns are identified, faculty have a responsibility to work with students for appropriate remediation.

Fourth, the Standards address faculty members' responsibility to "respond to requests for employment-related recommendations by students" (CAS, 1992, p. 14). It is also stated that "when endorsement cannot be provided [by a faculty member] for a particular position, the student must be informed of the reason for non-endorsement" (p. 14). In essence, faculty must be ethical in endorsements, and such endorsements should be based on knowledge of the student and the student's "competencies, skills, and personal characteristics" (p. 14).

Program Evaluation. The CAS Standards (1992) require that "planned procedures for continuing evaluation of the program must be established and implemented" (pp. 14-15). The guidelines for this standard on program evaluation indicate the value and importance of reviewing "policies and procedures relating to recruitment, selection, retention, and career services" as part of this process. The guidelines suggest that evaluations should occur at least once every five years.

Incorporated in the guidelines is the recommendation that there should be multiple criteria for evaluating program effectiveness, including student knowledge and competencies, professional accomplishments of graduates, and "quality of faculty teaching, advising, and research" (CAS, 1992, p. 15). Further, evidence regarding the evaluation of program effectiveness should come from multiple sources, including former students, employers of program graduates, clientele served by graduates, and formal program reviews.

BENEFITS AND CHALLENGES OF ACCREDITATION AND STANDARDS

A common approach to ensuring quality in educational programs has been the establishment of professional standards and the practice of accreditation. Both are forms of self-regulation. Although the CAS Standards are embraced in this chapter, we believe it is useful to examine critically the role of standards in designing student affairs graduate programs. Clear benefits are derived, but certain cautions and even perhaps disadvantages are also incurred.

Some benefits of the CAS Standards are that they provide common minimal requirements and additional guidelines for designing student affairs curricula. Further, the CAS Standards through a comprehensive process have been developed with revisions and input from numerous professional associations and ultimately have been agreed upon by CAS directors who are representatives of more than 25 professional associations. In addition, voluntary standards such as the CAS standards permit flexibility and creativity in program design, development, and revision often not possible through formal accreditation standards.

Professional standards also provide guidance for program design and development (Mable, 1991), help to enhance program quality (Ebbers & Kruempel, 1991; Kuh, Whitt, & Shedd, 1987. Mable, 1991), offer guides for program improvement and enhancement (Mable, 1991), and promote program and professional accountability (Jacoby & Thomas, 1991). The existence of professional preparation standards also potentially enhances credibility (Kuh et al., 1987). Professional standards also provide a means of program assessment and redesign.

Disadvantages of the CAS Standards are that there is no requirement or external monitoring for programs to either attain or to maintain these standards; adherence to these standards is voluntary and self-regulatory. Further, especially with no external review process, there are likely to be widely varied interpretations of the written standards which may not be congruent with the intent of the standards. Third, in practice the standards may not necessarily be commonly accepted.

Kuh et al. (1987) offer cautions about the CAS Standards. First, they are concerned that the CAS Standards "will do what standards for other fields have done, that is, reinforce the status quo" (p. 95). They also express concern that the standards do not reflect adequately emergent paradigm principles (p. 98). Kuh et al. encourage persons to be flexible in interpreting the CAS Standards to embrace emergent paradigm perspectives and philosophy.

Accreditation for student affairs master's degree programs exists only through the Council for Accreditation of Counseling and Related Educational Programs (CACREP, 1994). Although CACREP's standards for student affairs programs once closely reflected the CAS standards, they have become increasingly discrepant over time, despite recommendations from practitioners and faculty in student affairs professional associations. CACREP seems to best serve those programs with a comprehensive counseling focus; this is only a small percentage of the student affairs programs. Miller (1991) cited concerns of faculty about the appropriateness of the CACREP standards and CACREP accreditation for programs in student affairs. The greater the focus of the program on student development and student affairs administration, the less likely it is that faculty view CACREP standards and accreditation as relevant to their programs. In 1995, these perspectives, coupled with CACREP's unwillingness to act upon the concerns and recommendations of student affairs faculty regarding the 1994 CACREP Standards, resulted in ACPA's withdrawal from membership on the CACREP Board. With this separation, ACPA requested (B. N. Anderson, personal communication, February 3, 1995) that CACREP "discontinue the use of the term 'student affairs' and related terms such as 'student development' and "college student personnel' in describing the nature of the programs which the body [CACREP] accredits" (D. Forney, personal communication, September 26, 1994). In 1997, there is no "formal link" or collaboration between CACREP and any primarily student affairs identified professional associations. Despite this fact, CACREP continues its practice of evaluating and accrediting student affairs graduate programs, and a number of student affairs faculty continue to seek CACREP accreditation for their programs.

This divergence within the counseling and student affairs professions about standards and accreditation raises several important issues, however. Subsequent to ACPA's withdrawal from the CACREP Board, some faculty involved in student affairs graduate programs within departments and units which value and seek CACREP accreditation have expressed concern about the tension which is created for faculty and their students between embracing CACREP accreditation versus the CAS Standards. Some faculty in CACREP-accredited student affairs graduate programs also view the 1992 CAS Standards and ACPA's withdrawal from CACREP as moving away from a time-honored tradition of counseling as a foundation of student affairs graduate programs and preparation. Further, some faculty support CACREP because accreditation aids them in securing resources for their graduate programs. Thus, it appears that the student affairs profession needs to continue to struggle with and to promote further discussion of whether or not it embraces a goal of program accreditation and, specifically, how the profession will include, not exclude, those graduate programs that have achieved accreditation by CACREP.

As a means of quality assurance and yet an alternative to accreditation, a committee of CAS, evolving from a joint NASPA-ACPA committee on quality assurance, is discussing a voluntary program registry. A registry would involve self-study by programs and submission of self-study data to a review body. Program review by on-site external reviewers could be a component of a program's being placed on the registry. A form of program registry and an effort at quality assurance of graduate programs in student affairs already exists in designation in the *Directory of Graduate Preparation Programs in College Student Personnel 1994* (Keim & Graham, 1994) of programs that meet the American College Personnel Association's Commission XII (Graduate Professional Preparation) minimal criteria of

> at least one full-time faculty member in the program, at least four content courses about student services/affairs/development and the college student/environment, a program of at least two academic years in duration, and at least one student personnel practicum opportunity for students in the program. (p. v)

Issues of quality assurance and self-regulation will likely be important topics of discussion over the next five to ten years and hold important implications for student affairs graduate programs.

DOCTORAL EDUCATION IN STUDENT AFFAIRS

Doctoral education in student affairs, according to LaBarre's 1948 study (as cited in Wrenn, 1949), has been provided for at least half a century. Consensus and clarity about the nature of doctoral education, however, has not been achieved in the same manner as that for masters degree programs in student affairs. In fact, according to Komives (1993), "until recently . . . far less attention has been paid to doctoral preparation" (p. 393). Additionally, there are no established standards, and few, if any, guidelines about the mission or curriculum of doctoral programs in student affairs (Beatty & Stamatakos, 1990; Coomes, Belch, & Saddlemire, 1991). Within the limited literature about doctoral study in student affairs, however, are some important suggestions and considerations for the design of doctoral curricula.

Guidelines for Doctoral Curricula

Two key issues in developing a doctoral program are the mission and goals of the doctoral program and the particular emphasis or focus of the program. A third key issue concerns the kind of background, both academic and experience-based, the doctoral program builds upon. Delworth and Hanson (1989) underscore that a doctoral program should be based upon an entry-level professional curriculum in student affairs. This implies that all doctoral students should complete, either prior to or early in their doctoral program, the equivalent of a master's curriculum in student affairs.

Delworth and Hanson (1989) suggest that the core of doctoral education in student affairs should be "demonstrated competence in research" (p. 613) and "demonstrated mastery of core and specialized competencies . . . in at least one of the role orientations or models of practice" (p. 614). These role orientations or models include the "administrator role/administrative model," the "counselor role/counseling model," the "student development role/student development educator model," and "the campus ecology manager role/ecological model." They further state that it is desirable at the doctoral level to have mastery of more than one of these models and that leadership in the profession should be the focus of education at the doctoral level.

Two dimensions that should distinguish doctoral programs, and ultimately doctoral graduates, from master's degree study or from a series of courses beyond the master's degree are research and leadership. Further, the doctoral degree, especially the Ph.D., is considered a research degree. As such, it includes formal research training and the demonstration, usually through a dissertation, of competence in research. Delworth and Hanson (1989), in identifying research competence as part of the core of doctoral training, believe that "real comfort with and appreciation of research is acquired only through systematic involvement in relevant research projects over a period of time" (p. 614) and recommend "the early and continued involvement of doctoral students in research projects" (p. 614).

We believe that the goal of doctoral programs in student affairs should be to develop expert practitioners or scholar-practitioners and also, for some doctoral programs, to develop persons to assume faculty positions. Delworth and Hanson's (1989) emphasis on doctoral education as training for leadership is congruent with this goal. Some of the important questions concern how this goal is best accomplished. What are the value-added contributions of doctoral study in student affairs? How are programs distinguished from masters programs, from a series of additional courses, and from doctoral study in related disciplines? How is professional leadership developed and fostered in a doctoral program? How is true research competence not only developed, but research and scholarly contributions sustained?

Beatty and Stamatakos (1990), based on the responses from student affairs administrators and student affairs faculty, identified six general competency areas for doctoral-educated student affairs professionals. These include (a) theoretical competence—"an in-depth understanding of the historical, philosophical, and theoretical foundations" (p. 227) of student affairs; (b) scholarly competence—"the development and perpetuation of scholarship through inquiry, critical interpretation, investigation, research, and writing" (p. 227); (c) functional competence—"the development, maintenance, or enhancement of those skills needed to perform both simple and complex functions in an effective manner" (p. 227); (d) transferal competence—"the ability to transform theoretical and philosophical foundations of student affairs administration into practical applications" (p. 227); (e) environmental competence—"an understanding of and the ability to work within and to help shape the environment" (p. 227) of student affairs; and (f) human relations competence—"the ability to understand, direct, communicate with, and interact with primary constituents, colleagues, and peers" (p. 227) in higher education. What is not articulated by Beatty and Stamatakos is how these competencies are different from or more complex than those expected of graduates of masters degree programs in student affairs.

Kuh et al. (1987) advise doctoral students to "take courses in history and philosophy of science that introduce concepts and vocabularies that enable them to conduct and critique research and administrative practice in both conventional and emergent paradigm language" (p. 97). In discussing implications of the emergent paradigm for graduate preparation in student affairs, Kuh et al. state that "knowledge producers and scholar-practitioners will need varying amounts of time to process, internalize, and discover applications of emergent paradigm qualities. A time constraint cannot be placed on a process that will demand a considerable amount of creative energy" (pp. 101-102).

Komives (1993) identified ten areas of basic questions for prospective doctoral students to use in assessing potential doctoral programs. These same areas are useful in thinking about important components of a doctoral program. They include (a) who the faculty are, and what their professional interests and expertise are; (b) the nature of faculty-student interaction, including both full-time and adjunct faculty; (c) the culture of the program, including the student culture, student interests, and program supports; (d) areas of specialty available in the program and in related programs and departments; (e) core requirements of the program, including course work and other requirements such as comprehensive exams; (f) teaching modes within the program, including the nature and variety of learning experiences, and the currency of course content; (g) program policies and requirements such as residency, internships, and time limits for the degree; (h) financial support, in the forms of assistantships, fellowships, research funds, and travel support; (i) ethics of the program, such as the core program values, the nature of the program community and environment, and the nature of relationships within the program; and, (j) the connections with professional practice, both at the host institution as well as at nearby institutions and professional agencies (Komives, 1993, pp. 404-405). We add to Komives' areas that of dissertations, both the topics and kind of research pursued, the quality and completion rate, and the nature and degree of support for dissertation completion.

The Nature of Doctoral Study in Student Affairs

Both the identification and the description of doctoral programs related to student affairs are difficult. In the *Directory of Graduate Preparation Programs in College Student Personnel 1994* (Keim & Graham, 1994), 43 doctoral programs with an emphasis in student affairs were identified. Eighteen of the programs were housed in counseling departments, and 22 programs were located in departments of higher education and educational leadership; three programs existed in departments which embraced both counseling and administration. Yet, according to Komives (1993), citing Crosson and Nelson's 1984 study, 47 higher education administration doctoral programs indicated the availability of a specialization in student affairs. This discrepancy (47 vs. 22) is puzzling, and underscores some of the confusion about the location and nature of doctoral programs in student affairs.

Coomes et al. (1991), in their survey of doctoral programs listed in the 1987 *Directory of Graduate Preparation Programs in College Student Personnel* (Keim & Graham, 1987), found that doctoral programs were located in colleges and schools of education, but in a variety of academic departments, including counselor education, educational leadership and policy studies, and higher and adult education. They also found that 63% of the programs included an emphasis in student affairs.

For the doctoral programs listed in the 1994 *Directory* (Keim & Graham, 1994) that were housed in counseling departments, counseling and counselor education were at the core of the curriculum. For those programs located in departments of higher education and educational leadership, courses in higher education and educational administration formed the core of the doctoral curriculum. Included in the data provided by program directors was the "number of student services/affairs/development courses available *exclusively* for *doctoral* students." The range of responses to this question was 0 to 30; three responses were not usable. Eighteen programs indicated that they offered no courses in student affairs exclusively for doctoral students. The modal response of programs that did offer courses exclusively for doctoral students was 3 courses ($n = 9$ programs); 7 programs offered 5-9 courses exclusively for doctoral students, and 1 program indicated an offering of 30 courses. Based on reviewing the specific doctoral courses identified for each program in the 1994 *Directory*, however, fewer than five programs appeared to offer substantial specialized, post-masters courses in student affairs. Related to these findings from the 1994 *Directory* is Townsend and Wiese's (1992) question of "whether preparation in student development, rather than in the more general field of higher education, would be considered more critical preparation for student affairs administrators" (p. 57).

The data that most doctoral programs offer student affairs as a specialization within either counselor education or higher education rather than as a separate and distinct program suggest questions about what constitutes doctoral study in student affairs. Does there, and should there, exist doctoral-level study in student affairs with definition and focus unique from that of disciplines such as higher education and counselor education? Do doctoral programs or emphases in student affairs embrace specialized and advanced-level knowledge in student affairs? Or is the connection between the particular discipline (e.g., higher education or counselor education) only loosely or not at all tied into student affairs? Do doctoral programs in higher education emphasize only the administrative dimensions of student affairs rather than core theoretical knowledge about student affairs? Similarly, do those programs in counselor education focus only on the interpersonal realm of student affairs rather than specialized and advanced-level knowledge in student affairs? Do doctoral programs build on a masters level curriculum in student affairs, as Delworth and Hanson (1989) suggest? Or, do most doctoral programs with a student affairs emphasis or specialization only offer equivalents to masters-level study in student affairs? In regard to specialized knowledge about college students, an area of study at the heart of student affairs, Beatty and Stamatakos (1990) found that, for doctoral preparation in student affairs, knowledge of the college student was ranked 8th (out of 15) by student affairs faculty and did not appear at all in the top 15 rankings of student affairs administrators.

Based on the data about where student affairs doctoral programs are located and in consideration of the questions raised above, three possible conclusions about the current nature of doctoral study in student affairs might be reached. One possibility is that the existence of student affairs doctoral programs primarily within higher education and counselor education doctoral programs may suggest that there is insufficient advanced (beyond masters) content which is specialized and unique to the student affairs field to create separate-standing student affairs doctoral programs. A second possibility is that doctoral study should consist of study in another discipline, such as higher education, counselor education, or related fields, rather than in student affairs. A third hypothesis is that perhaps the development of doctoral curricula in student affairs parallels the early development of masters programs and that consensus has yet to be reached on what constitutes a specialized doctoral curriculum in student affairs. Other pertinent questions concern what "training for leadership in the profession" (Delworth & Hanson, 1989, p. 614) means and whether that equates with the study of administration, what is unique to advanced study of student affairs and what is the core knowledge base, and, finally, whether indeed consensus about doctoral curricula is even a desired outcome.

Next Steps Toward Clarity about Doctoral Curricula

Based on the above discussion, it is apparent that doctoral study in student affairs appears to be institution-specific with little to no professional consensus. One attempt to address the confusion and lack of clarity about doctoral study is an initiative within CAS, begun in 1994, to consider the feasibility of developing standards and guidelines for doctoral programs in student affairs. Because of the variability within doctoral programs, where they are housed, and with what professional associations program faculty identity, gaining input and generating discussion about such standards is an even greater challenge than developing standards for masters degree programs in student affairs. Preliminary discussions revolve around the value of developing a working document describing the various approaches to doctoral study in student affairs, perhaps accompanied by some overarching philosophy, principles, and questions about what should constitute doctoral study in student affairs. The need for a comprehensive description of doctoral programs in student affairs has also been identified (Miller, Creamer, Gehring, & McEwen, 1996).

CURRENT, EMERGING, AND FUTURE ISSUES

One of the greatest challenges facing higher education in general, and student affairs more specifically, is the rate at which knowledge is growing and the "half-life" of current information—the speed at which current information is disseminated and discarded as no longer relevant (Moore, 1995; Toffler, 1990). Additionally, while institutions of higher education have existed relatively separate from the "real world," as is captured by the term "the ivory tower," changing attitudes toward accountability, consumerism, and self-regulation are beginning to erode the walls that once insulated academic freedom from public whim and government intrusion. Relating these concerns to professional preparation in student affairs, it is easy to understand the importance of and challenges to an evolving curriculum.

Influences of Change

The overriding and pervasive issues discussed in the first section of this book will impact student affairs education. First, one undeniable change which is current and on-going is the shift in the college student population from being homogeneous (White, male, affluent and presumably heterosexual) to being incredibly heterogeneous and diverse in more ways than can be defined (Commission on Minority Participation in Education and American Life, 1988; Evans & Wall, 1991; Parker, 1988). There have been increasing demands from students, parents, faculty, and professional associations for knowledgeable and skilled professionals who can work effectively with a diverse student body (Iasenza, 1989; Jones, 1990; McEwen & Roper, 1994; Sue, Arredondo, & McDavis, 1992; Talbot, 1996). Second, increasing knowledge about learning styles and teaching have led to the integration into higher education of less traditional styles of pedagogy (liberation theology, feminist pedagogy, critical pedagogy, computer-centered pedagogy) (Evans, 1988), new models/ways of thinking (constructivism, chaos theory) (Freire, 1970, 1989; Manning, 1994; Nemiroff, 1992, Rhoads & Black, 1995), and curricular transformation (Schuster & Van Dyne, 1985). Given these different pedagogies and ways of thinking, combined with the acknowledgment of a diverse student population and different learning styles, faculty, in order to be effective, will need to provide more educational opportunities that involve more than cognitive processes. The curriculum will need to be designed and structured so that material and information are delivered on both affective and behavioral levels, as well as a cognitive one; the classroom environment will need to be a safe place to explore and share sensitive and challenging information and experiences (Lewis, 1990; Sue, Arredondo, & McDavis, 1992; Tatum, 1992).

Foundational studies. While it may seem that the Foundational Studies (history of higher education, educational philosophy, psychology, sociology, history and philosophy of student affairs, and research and sociocultural foundations of higher education) in the curriculum should remain the same regardless of emerging and future issues, the emergence of revisionist history and growth of support for constructivist thinking (Beattie, 1995; Carnella & Reiff, 1994; Martin, 1994; Toffler, 1981) may help to reframe the contexts in which higher education has been defined. For example, it has only been in recent years that there has been a greater emphasis on the role and impact of women's colleges, historically Black colleges and universities, and tribal colleges in higher education. As emerging technologies and less positivistic methods of thinking grow, how information has been shared, interpreted, and recorded regarding the foundations and history of higher education may be reshaped and take on new meaning. As history, including the history of higher education, is reported by individuals who were not acknowledged or valued earlier, perceptions about the "ivory tower" are reconstructed. These examples are just a few of the ways that new information and the embracing of diverse populations and perspectives will redefine the history of higher education.

Professional Studies and Supervised Practice. Probably the areas of the student affairs curriculum that have and will continue to require the greatest changes to incorporate emerging and future issues in higher education are Professional Studies and Supervised Practice. With the recognition that most of the student development theories were developed by studying White, middle to upper class, heterosexual (or assumed to be so) men and generalized to all students, faculty and practitioners are questioning the applicability of these theories for the populations who now fill institutions of higher education. Currently, there is a push to include theories which focus on "special populations" such as women, ethnic minorities, international students, students with disabilities, non-traditional students, and students who are gay, lesbian, or bisexual (McEwen & Roper, 1994; Rifenbary, 1995). This push is driven by another related area which is emphasized and undergoing great changes in the student affairs curriculum: student characteristics and effects on college students. Professional associations have already taken the initiative to include ethical standards which require professionals to value individual differences, as well as have knowledge and skill to work with diverse constituents (American College Personnel Association, 1990; American Counseling Association, 1995).

Teaching becomes even more complicated as institutions work on ways of incorporating distance learning and "educational communities" that never reside or take classes on campus. To address these issues, professional preparation will need to incorporate newly developing theories and theoretical foundations from other disciplines. The business world and corresponding educational programs are already struggling with change in the knowledge-intensive and technological age. They are doing this by addressing the roles of "intangible assets," developing frameworks for the storage and "protection of knowledge" as a resource, embracing a drive towards chaos and strategic management in an era of chaos, and developing and understanding the "dynamics of cognitive technological maps" (Lorange, Chakravarthy, Roos, & Van de Ven, 1993). In essence, the business world has accepted technology and many of the implications as it relates to competition and the "bottom line;" their new goal is to find a way to capitalize on growing technologies by developing systems and strategies for managing the unknown future. Student affairs programs will also need to embrace and understand growing technologies that appear on our campuses so that students will be able to skillfully negotiate cyberspace and responsibly handle the ethical implications of doing so. In addressing this issue at a recent NASPA IV-E conference, Pavela (1996) shared the story of a traditional people in this country—the Amish. While most people believe that the Amish reject technology, this is not true. When a new technology is introduced to the Amish, they evaluate it as a community to determine if the new development is consistent with and enhances their mission. Perhaps we need to teach the future student affairs professionals to examine the new technologies in light of their institutions' missions and goals, instead of wholeheartedly entering the "bigger, better, faster race" of the information age.

Emerging issues that seem to threaten the shift to a more representative, global student body are conservative societal trends, political backlashing, and economic struggles in the U.S. We see these issues emerge in the attacks on affirmative action and minority scholarships, in the cutting of government-backed financial aid for students' education, and in the growth of outspoken conservative groups on campuses. However, patterns still indicate that institutions of higher education will continue to admit a very diverse student body. Some of these changes are being facilitated by increased legislation such as the Americans with Disabilities Act of 1990 (ADA), Civil Rights legislation, and sexual harassment/assault policies which are tied to federal aid. In response, preparation programs are compelled to reevaluate the curriculum related to individual and group interventions, as well as legal knowledge and skills.

It will be the responsibility of future student affairs professionals to develop policy and provide services/programs for students who represent diverse groups and who have special needs; the curriculum will need to adapt to provide the necessary information and resources for these new professionals. While it may seem that these challenges are the same ones that are faced today, an added dimension which makes these issues seem so imminent is the growing willingness of the courts to infringe on and take part in shaping the regulation of higher education. The development of several law related publications for faculty, staff, and administrators in colleges and universities (e.g., Pavela's *Synthesis* and *Synfax*; Gehring's Legal Issues column in the *NASPA Newsletter*; Kaplin and Lee's (1995) *The Law of Higher Education*) gives evidence of the impact of legal issues in higher education. More emphasis in the curriculum may need to be given to developing administrators who are savvy about the law and legal issues that impact the learning environment.

Another transformation of the curriculum is driven by both internal and external pressures and issues. Assessment, evaluation and research are becoming increasingly important in practice and will need to have greater emphasis in graduate preparation as the government and the public demand more accountability from higher education. There is also a growing emphasis on qualitative research as a more holistic method for understanding student populations (Stage & Associates, 1992). In an era of shrinking budgets and increasing accountability, student affairs professionals will need the skills to be able to "prove" that services and programs benefit students in some way of importance to the institution.

Finally, the Supervised Practice promises to be the laboratory in which all the current, emerging and future issues come to life. Because of restructuring and down-sizing in response to economic concerns, what were once student affairs functional areas (admissions, advising, international student affairs, financial aid, career counseling, etc.) are now reporting to other divisions in the institution, such as academic affairs and auxiliary enterprises. In some institutions, student affairs divisions are being eliminated all together. This change provides another layer of complication as supervised practice is designed. In many colleges and universities, it will be necessary for students to utilize student affairs philosophy and practices in areas that are not governed by these same professional beliefs. Graduate programs will need to do a better job of bridging the gap between student affairs and other divisions in the institution. Students will need to develop the skills and language to be able to serve their constituents regardless of who supervises them. As always, there is the constant challenge of providing a sound theoretical and philosophical professional orientation without ignoring the practical applications that are necessary to function in student affairs. Professionals who supervise the practical experiences in the field (and who hire graduates) consistently request certain "skill areas" in students. Those areas include budgetary and financial expertise, varying degrees of computer proficiency, supervisory abilities, assessment and research skills, and communication skills (K. Atwater, B. Merkle, B. Kocher, T. Powell, D. Swartz, & M. LaPlante, personal communication, May 10, 1996; Sandeen, 1992).

An additional consideration is the place of community service in a student affairs curriculum, both given the needs for responsiveness to our communities and the emerging emphasis within the academy upon service-learning (Jacoby, 1996; Jones, Lenski, & Sagaria, 1997; O'Meara & Burton, 1996). Perhaps student affairs curricula should be modeling and reflecting what educational institutions, both high schools and postsecondary institutions, seem to be increasingly expecting of their students.

CONCLUSION

While it is impossible to see the future, especially in an era when the half-life of information is estimated to be approximately 3-4 years (Moore, 1995), it is imperative that student affairs educators watch the patterns and anticipate the needs of educational institutions. In the broadest sense, perhaps we should return to Wrenn's (1949) suggestion that one of the three main components of a student affairs curriculum should be "a sense of the contribution to be made to society" (p. 273). We should also heed Johnson and Sandeen's (as cited in Miller, 1991) recommendation that program curricula should be considered and developed through the "'filter of the future' to better ensure that entry-level professionals will be prepared to meet the challenge of change" (p. 58). This is the only way that professional preparation will be viable and that graduates of student affairs programs will be prepared to effectively and ethically serve institutions and their constituents.

REFERENCES

American College Personnel Association. (1990). Statement of ethical principles and standards. *Journal of College Student Development, 31,* 197-202.

American Counseling Association. (1995). *Code of ethics and standards of practice.* Alexandria, VA: Author.

Beattie, M. (1995). *Constructing professional knowledge in teaching.* New York: Teachers College Press.

Beatty, D. L., & Stamatakos, L. C. (1990). Faculty and administrator perceptions of knowledge, skills, and competencies as standards for doctoral preparation programs in student affairs administration. *Journal of College Student Development, 31,* 221-229.

Brown, R. D. (1972). *Student development in tomorrow's higher education —A return to the academy.* Alexandria, VA: American Personnel and Guidance Association.

Carnella, G. S., & Reiff, J. C. (1994). Individual constructivist teacher education: Teachers as empowered learners. *Teacher Education Quarterly, 21,* 27-38.

Coomes, M. D., Belch, H. A., & Saddlemire, G. L. (1991). Doctoral programs for student affairs professionals: A status report. *Journal of College Student Development, 32,* 62-68.

Council for Accreditation of Counseling and Related Educational Programs. (1994). *CACREP accreditation standards and procedures manual.* Alexandria, VA: Author.

Council for the Advancement of Standards in Higher Education. (1992). *Preparation standards and guidelines at the master's degree level for student affairs professionals in higher education.* College Park, MD: Author.

Commission on Minority Participation in Education and American Life. (1988). *One-third of a nation.* Washington, DC: American Council on Education.

Delworth, U., & Hanson, G. R. (1989). Future directions: A vision of student services in the 1990s. In U. Delworth, G. R. Hanson & Associates (Eds.), *Student services: A handbook for the profession* (2nd ed., pp. 604-618). San Francisco: Jossey-Bass.

Ebbers, L. H., & Kruempel, B. J. (1992). Student affairs programs: Should they be accredited? *NASPA Journal, 30,* 59-65.

Evans, N. J. (1988). Practicing what we teach: Implications of the new scholarship on women for student affairs preparation. *Journal of College Student Development, 29,* 499-501.

Evans, N. J., & Wall, V. A. (1991). *Beyond tolerance: Gays, lesbians, and bisexuals on campus.* Washington, DC: American College Personnel Association.

Freire, P. (1970). *Pedagogy of the oppressed.* New York: Continuum.

Freire, P. (1989). *Education for critical consciousness.* New York: Continuum.

Hunter, D. E., & Beeler, K. J. (1991). Peering through the "looking glass" at preparation needed for student affairs research. In K. J. Beeler & D. E. Hunter (Eds.), *Puzzles and pieces in wonderland: The promise and practice of student affairs research* (pp. 106-123). Washington, DC: National Association of Student Personnel Administrators.

Iasenza, S. (1989). Some challenges of integrating sexual orientations into counselor training and research. *Journal of Counseling and Development, 68,* 73-76.

Jacoby, B. (Ed.). (1996). *The practice of service-learning in higher education.* San Francisco: Jossey-Bass.

Jacoby, B., & Thomas, W. L., Jr. (1991). Professional standards and the accreditation process. In W. A. Bryan, R. B. Winston, Jr., & T. K. Miller (Eds.), *Using professional standards in student affairs* (New Directions for Student Services, no. 53, pp. 19-28). San Francisco: Jossey-Bass.

Jones, S. R., Lenski, T. J., & Sagaria, M. A. D. (1997, March). *Innovative approaches for integrating service-learning into the curriculum.* Paper presented at the joint conference of the American College Personnel Association and the National Association of Student Personnel Administrators, Chicago, IL.

Jones, W. T. (1990). Perspectives on ethnicity. In L. V. Moore (Ed.), *Evolving theoretical perspectives on students* (New Directions for Student Services, no. 51, pp. 59-72). San Francisco: Jossey-Bass.

Kaplin, W. A., & Lee, B. A. (1995). *The law of higher education: A comprehensive guide to legal implications of administrative decision making* (3rd ed.). San Francisco: Jossey-Bass.

Keim, M. C., & Graham, J. W. (Eds.). (1987). *Directory of graduate preparation programs in college student personnel.* Washington, DC: American College Personnel Association.

Keim, M. C. R., & Graham, J. W. (Eds.). (1994). *Directory of graduate preparation programs in college student personnel 1994.* Washington, DC: American College Personnel Association.

Knefelkamp, L. L. (1982). Faculty and student development in the 80's: Renewing the community of scholars. In H. F. Owens, C. H. Witten, & W.

R. Bailey (Eds.), *College student personnel administration: An anthology* (pp. 373-391). Springfield, IL: Charles C. Thomas.

Komives, S.R. (1993). Advancing professionally through graduate education. In M. J. Barr & Associates, *The handbook of student affairs administration* (pp. 390-411). San Francisco: Jossey-Bass.

Kuh, G. D., Whitt, E. J., & Shedd, J. D. (1987). *Student affairs work, 2001: A paradigmatic odyssey.* Washington, DC: American College Personnel Association.

LaBarre, C. (1948). *Graduate training for educational personnel work.* Washington, DC: American Council on Education.

Lewis, M. (1990). Interrupting patriarchy: Politics, resistance, and transformation in the feminist classroom. *Harvard Education Review, 60,* 467-488.

Lorange, P., Chakravarthy, B., Roos, J., & Van de Ven, A. (Eds.). (1993). *Implementing strategic processes: Change, learning, and co-operation.* Cambridge, MA: Blackwell Publishers.

Lloyd-Jones, E. (1949). The beginnings of our profession. In E. G. Williamson (Ed.), *Trends in student personnel work* (pp. 260-264). Minneapolis: University of Minnesota Press.

Mable, P. (1991). Professional standards: An introduction and historical perspective. In W. A. Bryan, R. B. Winston, Jr., & T. K. Miller (Eds.), *Using professional standards in student affairs* (New Directions for Student Services, no. 53, pp. 5-18). San Francisco: Jossey-Bass.

Manning, K. (1994). Liberation theology and student affairs. *Journal of College Student Development, 35,* 94-97.

Martin, R. J. (1994). Multicultural social reconstructionist education: Design for diversity in teacher education. *Teacher Education Quarterly, 21,* 77-89.

McEwen, M. K., & Roper, L. (1994). Interracial experiences, knowledge and skills of master's degree students in graduate programs in student affairs. *Journal of College Student Development, 35,* 81-87.

Miller, T. K. (1991). Using standards in professional preparation. In W. A. Bryan, R. B. Winston, Jr., & T. K. Miller (Eds.), *Using professional standards in student affairs* (New Directions for Student Services no. 53, pp. 45-62). San Francisco: Jossey-Bass.

Miller, T. K., Creamer, D. G., Gehring, D. D., & McEwen, M. K. (1996, March). *Doctoral program standards: Is you is or is you ain't?* Paper presented at the annual conference of the American College Personnel Association, Baltimore.

Miller, T. K., & Prince, J. S. (1976). *The future of student affairs: A guide to student development for tomorrow's higher education.* San Francisco: Jossey-Bass.

Moore, K. (1995, February). *Women in leadership: Preparing for the 21st century.* Paper presented at the annual meeting of NASPA IV-East, Dearborn, MI.

National Association of Student Personnel Administrators. (1995). Standards of professional practice. In *NASPA Member Handbook 1995-1996* (pp. 15-16). Washington, DC: Author.

Nemiroff, G. H. (1992). *Reconstructing education: Toward a pedagogy of critical humanism.* New York: Bergin & Garvey.

Nuss, E. (1993). The role of professional associations. In M. J. Barr & Associates, *The handbook of student affairs administration* (pp. 364-377). San Francisco: Jossey-Bass.

O'Meara, K., & Burton, S. (1996, March). *Teaching student development theory through service-learning.* Paper presented at the annual conference of the American College Personnel Association, Baltimore.

Parker, W. M. (1988). *Consciousness-raising: A primer for multicultural counseling.* Springfield, IL: Charles C. Thomas Publisher.

Pavela, G. (1996, February). *Critical law and policy issues in 1996.* Preconference workshop presented at the National Association of Student Personnel Administrators - Region IV East conference, Indianapolis, IN.

Rhoads, R. A., & Black, M. A. (1995). Student affairs practitioners as transformative educators: Advancing a critical cultural perspective. *Journal of College Student Development, 36,* 413-421.

Rifenbary, D. (1995). Reentering the academy: The voices of returning women students. *Initiatives, 56*(4), 1-10.

Schuster, M. R., & Van Dyne, S. R. (1985). Stages of curriculum transformation. In M. R. Schuster & S. R. Van Dyne (Eds.), *Women's place in the academy: Transforming the liberal arts curriculum* (pp. 13-29). Totowa, NJ: Rowman & Allanheld.

Sedlacek, W. E. (1987). Black students on White campuses: 20 years of research. *Journal of College Student Personnel, 28,* 484-495.

Sedlacek, W. E. (1991). Using noncognitive variables in advising nontraditional students. *NACADA Journal, 11*(1), 75-82.

Stage, F. K., & Associates. (1992). *Diverse methods for research and assessment of college students.* Lanham, MD: University Press of America.

Sue, D. W., Arredondo, P., & McDavis, R. J. (1992). Multicultural counseling competencies and standards: A call to the profession. *Journal of Multicultural Counseling and Development, 20,* 64-88.

Talbot, D. M. (1996). Master's students perspectives on their graduate education regarding issues of diversity. *NASPA Journal, 33,* 163-178.

Tatum, B. D. (1992). Thinking about race, learning about racism: The application of racial identity development theory in the classroom. *Harvard Education Review, 62,* 1-24.

Toffler, A. (1981). Education and the future: An interview with Alvin Toffler. *Social Education, 45,* 422-426.

Toffler, A. (1990). *Powershift.* New York: Bantam Books.

Townsend, B. K., & Wiese, M. (1992). The value of a doctorate in higher education for student affairs administrators. *NASPA Journal, 30,* 51-58.

Tracey, T.J., & Sedlacek, W.E. (1984). Noncognitive variables in predicting academic success by race. *Measurement and Evaluation in Guidance, 16,* 172-178.

Tracey, T.J., & Sedlacek, W.E. (1985). The relationship of noncognitive variables to academic success: A longitudinal comparison by race. *Journal of College Student Personnel, 26,* 405-410.

Wrenn, C. G. (1949). An appraisal of the professional status of personnel work, part I. In E. G. Williamson (Ed.), *Trends in student personnel work* (pp. 264-280). Minneapolis: University of Minnesota Press.

Part Three

Linkages Between Student Affairs Practice and Preparation

Because it is an applied field, student affairs preparation must be closely aligned with practice. If they are to prepare new practitioners to effectively function in the changing world of higher education, it is contingent on student affairs faculty to maintain contact with practitioners and to stay current with issues facing the field. Student affairs faculty also have an obligation to assist practitioners in understanding new theory and research that may have implications for how practitioners do their work. In turn, practitioners have an obligation to feed back to preparation programs information about issues they are facing and to provide assistance in recruiting and training individuals who will be effective in addressing those issues.

As the authors of the previous chapters have demonstrated, the forces impacting student affairs as a field and student affairs practitioners as individuals are many and challenging. Faculty, too, face many changes and crises as they attempt to educate new members of the profession. By working together, practitioners and faculty can proactively address the issues the student affairs field faces. The two chapters in this section examine ways in which such linkages can occur. The first chapter describes continuing education needs and strategies for student affairs practitioners while the second chapter looks at ways in which student affairs practice and preparation currently interface and offers ideas for increased interaction.

In a field that is changing as rapidly as student affairs, the preparation an individual receives in a graduate preparation program is soon outdated. In addition, many individuals enter student affairs without formal training in the field, many preparation programs do not meet minimal standards for educating student affairs professionals, and disagreement exists over what constitutes appropriate preparation. As Stan Carpenter notes in Chapter 8, as a result of these issues, quality assurance is a major concern facing the profession. Continuing education plays an important role in addressing this concern.

Carpenter outlines the principles and practices related to continuing education and considers them within the context of student affairs. He goes on to address the role of student affairs faculty in continuing professional education, stating his belief that faculty have an obligation to provide leadership in these efforts. Faculty need to be involved in setting the agenda for what is to be learned, for seeing that continuing professional education is delivered, for instilling in students the desire for ongoing learning, and for assessing the outcomes of continuing education efforts. Carpenter concludes his chapter by proposing a number of action steps to insure that continuing professional education receives the attention it deserves in the student affairs profession. As Carpenter stresses, "only through life-long learning can we hope to keep up" with the changes outlined in earlier chapters of this book.

Continuing education is only one arena in which student affairs practitioners and faculty interface. In Chapter 9, Susan Komives provides many other examples of linkages at the local campus and regional/national level. She examines ways in which practitioners can support student affairs preparation programs as well as opportunities for graduate programs to support student affairs practice, noting that students provide the natural bridge between the two areas. An important area in which preparation and practice intersect is in the placement of program graduates. Komives discusses issues related to recruitment of new professionals and advocates for ethical practice with regard to hiring processes. The role of professional associations in encouraging practitioner-faculty interchange is also stressed in Chapter 9. Finally, Komives examines ways in which linkages occur in other professions, such as medicine and law. She encourages student affairs professionals to consider ways of applying strategies borrowed from these professions.

If student affairs is to continue to be a viable and vital profession, practitioners and faculty must work together to provide ongoing education for current and future professionals. This section provides challenging, yet practical, steps for carrying out this goal.

Chapter Eight

Continuing Professional Education in Student Affairs

D. Stanley Carpenter

Just as some campuses and some practitioners in student affairs have to cope with the various cutting edge issues noted in this book and some do not, not everyone in the field takes seriously the need to continually sharpen skills and learn new practices. Continuing professional education (CPE), long a fixture in such fields as medicine, psychology, and counseling has always been treated in haphazard fashion by the student affairs profession. Many, if not most, professionals go to conferences, attend seminars, and read professionally, but there is little systematic, corporate access and accountability for these activities and no way to formally record them. But a consensus is building in the field that this state of affairs cannot long continue if we are to remain viable and relevant.

This chapter focuses on continuing professional education in the student affairs profession. The purpose is to examine the nature and status of CPE in student affairs and other fields, to offer some theoretical perspectives, and to raise some provocative points. Some will find the chapter troubling, others infuriating, and still others may find it helpful and hopeful. In any case, the recommendations and observations are those of the author and are intended to advance the dialogue.

The debate in the literature about the status of student affairs work as a field of endeavor seems to have resulted in a consensus in at least one area. Whether student affairs is an ". . . emerging profession" (Carpenter, Miller, & Winston, 1980, p. 21), does not meet the classical criteria for professional status (Bloland, 1987; Komives, 1988; Stamatakos, 1981), or is continuing in its ". . . professionalization" (Young, 1988, p. 262), it seems to be clear that ". . . every author has linked its [student affairs'] status to the professional education of its practitioners" (Young, 1994, p. 243). Further, the notion that student affairs practitioners form a viable professional community, present in almost all current writing and speaking in this area, leads inescapably to the same conclusion. To many, professional education is synonymous with the preparation necessary to enter a given field or occupation. However, Smutz, Crowe, and Lindsay (1986) asserted that ". . . continuing learning always has been an obligatory part of the professional's role" (p. 385). The position taken in this chapter is that student affairs work is a profession and that its practitioners must engage in career-long professional education.

Any professional community must attend to three principal sets of commonalities (Carpenter, 1991). First, a profession must share knowledge, goals, and objectives in sufficient detail, clarity, and coherence so that they can be identified and discussed. Second, the profession must create and enforce formal and informal sanctions with regard to professional practices and behaviors. The third set of processes has to do with socialization and regeneration of members. All of these professional "knowings" have to be taught and otherwise communicated to new individuals as they enter the field. The most accepted and convenient model for accomplishing this goal in professions is some kind of common academic and practical experience such as medical or law school, culminating in a licensure examination process certifying the individual as having at least entry level competence. In such established professions, there is also a concomitant obligation to continue to keep up with newly developed knowledge, procedures, and mores, enforced by varying mechanisms including state and federal statutes, restrictions on practice areas, requirements for membership in professional organizations, third party payers, and the like (Smutz, et al., 1986). This obligation of continuous learning was once fulfilled by informal activities like reading journals, consultations with colleagues, and attending conferences. An informal approach is no longer sufficient to meet the learning needs of professionals because of the explosion of knowledge, technology, and public attitudes toward professional competency. The traditional and established professions, then, attend to, value, and provide for the ongoing, career-long preparation of the their practitioners through more or less formal continuing professional education activities that are regulated and sanctioned in a variety of ways.

For student affairs professionals, the picture is not so clear. The efforts of the Council for the Advancement of Standards for Higher Education (CAS), most recently embodied by the 1992 revision, to establish standards for practice and professional preparation have been widely honored more in the breach than in the observance. The Council for the Accreditation of Counseling Related Educational Programs (CACREP) 1992 Standards seem to have left out any student affairs preparation program which is not heavily—much more heavily than most are—counseling oriented (Forney, 1994). Only in the 1994 version of the *Directory of Graduate Preparation Programs in Student Personnel* (Keim & Graham, 1994) did Commission XII (Professional Preparation) of ACPA finally allow a notation that certain programs meet *minimal* standards, while other programs, listed side by side, did not. Revealingly, out of 83 programs requesting a listing in the directory, only 47 met these standards (which are considerably short of the CAS standards). If, as has been posited, professional preparation ". . . refers to formal education in theory and research about student development and effects of college attendance, student affairs application skills, values, and professional practices and to formal education in other related disciplines" (Creamer et al., 1992, p. 5), and if student affairs work is a complex, professional activity, requiring specific knowledge, skills, and values (Carpenter, 1994), this state of disarray of the fundamental base of professional preparation is deplorable.

But that's not the weird part, as John Belushi said on "Saturday Night Live." Worse than the spectre of poor preparation is the fact that many (and possibly most) people enter the field (that is, obtain their first professional position) with no student affairs training or education at all. Incredibly, that first professional position is sometimes that of Senior Student Affairs Officer of an institution (Paterson, 1987)! Given these facts, it would seem that continuing professional education would be a critical need. However, ". . . reliable and widely acknowledged systems of . . . continuing professional education and recognition and reporting systems for student affairs do not exist" (Creamer et al., 1992, p. 3). At issue, then, are two of the most important concerns of any profession: ". . . professions have an altruistic motive to maintain the competence of their practitioners based on their service orientation; however, they also have a need to limit external regulation in order to ensure the most favorable conditions for their members to practice" (Smutz, et al., 1986, p. 389). In other words, student affairs must pay attention to quality assurance or someone else most certainly will—ignoring, or at best interpreting, professional values and standards.

Efforts to address quality assurance in student affairs practice have been hampered by a lack of consensus about what constitutes appropriate professional preparation, who best should control or prescribe practices on individual campuses, the proper role of professional associations, including jurisdictional disputes among the generalist organizations and the specialized ones, and concerns about diversity in the profession. The diversity argument is most appealing, since student affairs has been an inclusive field virtually from its outset. There are so many different kinds of institutions, students, and practitioners that the profession is best served by a sort of laissez faire approach to entry and practice, many contend. However, the traditional professions also deal with diverse clienteles, but still have stringent standards. Given that such standards may perpetuate privilege among certain classes and groups, the problem becomes one of re-inventing the term "profession" to embrace diversity. Since student affairs is in the process of determining its own professional structure intentionally, this redefinition is not only possible, but likely. There is no good reason why sincere, tough-minded efforts cannot be made to raise the quality of initial preparation and CPE without leaving anyone behind. Especially if we make diversity a cornerstone of professional learning and practice, student affairs as a field should be able to improve services to all clienteles and exclude only those who refuse to commit to competence.

In any case, efforts have begun. Building upon reports from the Task Force on Professional Preparation and Practice (1989) and Creamer and Woodard (1992), a small study group was commissioned in 1992 and created a "proposal for action by professional associations" (Creamer et al., 1992). Pointing to the CAS standards (1992) and the ACPA (1993) and NASPA (1992-93) codes of ethics, the group contended that ". . . assessment of professional competencies and needs, continuing professional education, and recognition and reporting systems are . . . crucial aspects of quality assurance" (p. 3). The group went on to proclaim the ethical obligation of professional associations to ensure the quality of professional preparation and practice, to emphasize diversity of programs and practitioners, to decry current models of certification and accreditation, to recognize that student affairs practitioners enter the field with varying training and that there is a need to provide continuing professional education in student affairs to allied professionals who practice with college students, and to argue that practitioners should be recognized for improving their knowledge and practice through continuing professional education. Further, ". . . (a) quality professional practice requires life-long continuing professional education, (b) principles of adult education should form the basis for continuing professional education, and (c) continuing professional education can take place in many forms and arenas" (Creamer et al., 1992, p. 11). To date, in response to this clear call for action and other pressures, Commission XII is considering some sort of mechanism for quality assurance for professional preparation programs and the ACPA Council for Professional Development has endorsed the Creamer report and is pursuing many of the recommendations as a part of its agenda. A Committee on Continuing Professional Education was also formed by ACPA to further the CPE agenda. The scope of this chapter is too limited to deal with all the aspects of quality assurance. The remainder of this chapter will discuss continuing professional education.

PRACTICES AND PRINCIPLES OF CONTINUING PROFESSIONAL EDUCATION (CPE)

Appropriate and competent professional practice requires formal and informal learning experiences to be ongoing. Responsibility for this learning accrues to the individual professional, but should be facilitated by the profession in some structural way. This is the fundamental basis for the notion of continuing professional education (CPE). There are four principal stakeholder groups in CPE: the public, the professions, CPE providers, and CPE participants (Smutz, et al., 1986).

The public interest is frequently (but not exclusively) represented by various kinds of licensing bodies and procedures. CPE is often required for renewal of licenses in response to consumer issues and regulatory concerns regarding professional competence. Requirements are usually expressed in hours and specific activities are chosen by the participants. "All states require continuing professional education in at least one licensed occupation" (Smutz, et al., 1986, p. 389). Mandatory CPE is thought to protect the public from practitioners who would not otherwise keep up to date, remove inadequate professionals, increase professional interaction, improve public confidence, and result in better informed and current practice (Lowenthal, 1981). There are voices to the contrary, however, who claim that mandatory CPE violates adult education precepts and does not guarantee professional competence (Brockett, 1992), perhaps because CPE is ". . . only one component of continuing competence" (Smutz, et al., 1986, p. 389).

The professions themselves clearly have a large stake in CPE deriving from conceptual issues—evolution of the profession; performance issues—knowledge, practice, and practitioner enhancement; and collective identity issues—credentialing, professional subculture creation, and relations with other vocations and service users (Smutz, et al., 1986). Consequently, professional associations often ". . . regulate CPE . . . through monitoring the quality of CPE offered to their members through program approval mechanisms, and through imposing their own CPE requirements, making certification, specialization, or membership dependent on CPE" (p. 389).

Continuing Professional Education providers form a stakeholder group, as well. Principal providers are ". . . universities and professional schools, professional associations, employing agencies, and independent providers" (Cervero & Young, 1987, p. 405). The relative importance of each of these groups varies from profession to profession, and they interact with each other in unpredictable ways to serve the needs of practitioners and employing organizations. For example, many student affairs divisions have strong staff development programs that often involve faculty members from preparation programs. And, of course, in student affairs, the employing organization is a college or university. Some independent providers work with employers and with professional associations. There is much interaction, but perhaps not enough interdependence (Cervero & Young, 1987), an issue that will be discussed further below. A principal goal of CPE should be to encourage and enable professionals to learn independently, which is not frequently done in initial preparation programs (Suter, Green, Lawrence, & Wathall, 1981). Paradoxically, providers should be attempting to reduce participant reliance upon their own services.

Participants in CPE have a variety of needs and motivations. This diversity makes it hard to match programs with individuals (Gonnella & Zeleznik, 1983). Participant motivations to engage in CPE go far past enhanced competence and include affiliation and interaction with colleagues (Cervero, 1981), renewal (Caplan, 1983), and increased professional self-awareness (Baskett & Marsick, 1992). Houle (1980) pointed out the difference between continuing education and continuing learning, noting that CPE implies formal activities, but professional learning can occur in a variety of contexts, even unplanned ones. In fact, ". . . individuals are faced with choosing that combination of formal and informal activities best suited to their own needs" (Smutz, et al., 1986, p. 392). According to Klevans et al. (1992), this choice process ". . . does not refer to self-perceived learning needs but rather to a self-administered testing process that provides confidential, personal information to participants based on external, profession-defined criteria" (p. 17). Combined with Schön's (1987) call for education of practitioners who can deal with factual, procedural, and reflective knowledge, this self-assessment model can form the basis of a comprehensive system of initial professional preparation and CPE for student affairs.

Apart from stakeholder issues, the modern theory and practice of CPE is beset with other controversies. The very notion of professions has been under attack for some time as elitist and unnecessarily individualistic (Baskett & Marsick, 1992). Research on learning is challenging time-honored ideas of what kinds of knowledge exist and which are important to professional practice, how learning occurs, where knowledge comes from, appropriate learning cycles and resources, and the impact of CPE. It would appear that the time is ripe for a re-examination of CPE and, indeed, all professional education structures, by most professions (Baskett & Marsick, 1992). It is in this context that student affairs begins truly to define its own career-spanning educational processes.

CPE IN STUDENT AFFAIRS WORK

Several assertions seem pertinent and warranted based upon the above review.

1. The student affairs profession needs to come to some agreement as to the structure of the profession in order to address preparation and education needs. For the moment, it is not clear who is a member of the profession or should be. Universities and colleges include varying functional areas under the rubric of student affairs and other titles. There are numerous national and regional associations exercising leadership and purveying educational programming. The most promising attempt at common cause is the CAS Standards (1992), but even these are not universally known or used.

2. Relatedly (and perhaps belatedly), the nature and form of initial preparation for the profession need to be addressed.

The CAS Standards (1992) call for a two-year full-time curriculum that is carefully laid out, encourages flexibility and diversity, and includes supervised practice. As mentioned above, barely half of the programs calling themselves professional preparation meet Commission criteria, let alone the CAS Standards. People are routinely hired at every level in the profession with no professional education, training, or experience (Creamer et al, 1992). In this author's opinion, the profession must quickly begin to address some kind of quality control process for masters degree preparation programs or abandon all pretense of coherence.

3. Acknowledging that people enter the field in many different ways and with different levels of preparation, and that many allied professionals such as counselors, psychologists, nurses, doctors, and attorneys also practice in student affairs venues (Creamer et al., 1992), CPE must take several different forms and be conducted on multiple levels. If quality assurance is truly a goal of the profession, then all who practice, however limited their role or background in the area, must be given the opportunity to enhance their skills and knowledge.
4. Student affairs work is a sufficiently diverse, inclusive, and amorphous label to suggest that statutory licensure is not a fruitful approach. Further, the process of so clearly defining the field and its practice as to make licensure viable would risk destroying much of the vitality and vibrance of campus life, to say nothing of shutting off innovation. Approaches to systematizing professional preparation and CPE must be voluntary in nature and depend upon the altruistic motivations of members of the profession, at least initially and probably long term.
5. Professional associations have a large role to play in organizing and delivering CPE. Until recently, they have not taken that role seriously in any systematic way. Sessions are offered, speakers are hired, themes are played out, workshops are sponsored, all apparently willy-nilly, with little continuity and less coherence from year to year. Professional associations are the national umbrella groups such as ACPA and NASPA, regional groups affiliated (or not) with the larger ones, and specialty associations such as ACUHO-I, ACU-I, and many others. Ideally, all interested and concerned parties will come together in some fashion to address CPE and other

professional education and practice problems. Again, the best model so far is CAS (1992).

Not unexpectedly, given its status as an emerging profession, student affairs professional preparation, both initial and continuing, is in an unsettled state. This is good news. Intentional change and innovation are actually easier in an environment where stakeholder interests are not solidified and concretized. It should be possible for agreements to be reached and structures created to solve problems. Random activity means that inertia is not a problem.

Cervero and Young (1987) proposed a model of interdependence for the provision of CPE. In a very few fields, there is a monopoly on CPE, implying no interdependence. More often, parallelism and competition occur. In the former, providers ignore each other and in the latter, they know each other exist, but assume that there is a large enough market for everyone. More interdependent strategies are cooperation and coordination. Cooperation usually means ad hoc arrangements, while coordination may mean formal agreements or informal parceling out of market niches. Collaboration is the most interdependent strategy of all, in which interested parties work together toward mutual goals.

In student affairs, providers of CPE are usually faculty members in preparation programs, faculty members from ancillary or related areas, or practitioners who have become familiar with one or more specific areas of theory or practice. Many of the practitioner providers also perform a formal faculty role on an adjunct or part-time basis for a preparation program. Continuing professional education activities are either sponsored by one or more professional associations, one or more preparation programs, one or more employing universities or colleges, or some combination of the above, in all possible permutations. There are very few independent providers of CPE in student affairs, and even they almost always work under the sanction of an association or an employer. In terms of the interdependence model, then, CPE in student affairs already enjoys a fair amount of cooperation and coordination, although parallelism and competition are present. Clearly, no one group has a monopoly and there is not sufficient agreement on process or outcomes to foster true collaboration. Assuming that collaboration is not a foreign concept to student affairs practitioners, professional associations, and preparation program faculty, progress should be possible. What appears necessary is leadership, which gets at the main point of this chapter.

THE ROLE OF FACULTY IN CPE

Preparation faculty and programs have an obligation to provide leadership to CPE efforts in order to enhance and maintain the competence of professionals they originally educated because growth of knowledge and technology make it inefficient and difficult for individual practitioners to stay current, even though it is their responsibility to do so; because demographics dictate re-training as opposed to continually producing fresh entrants for the field; and because the failure to do so means that other organizations with conflicting interests may not focus on the competence of professional practitioners appropriately (Smutz, et al., 1986). Further, faculty create and disseminate new information as a part of their roles and have access to the best thinking from many disciplines.

Arguments against faculty leadership in CPE are that there exist value differences between practitioners and preparers and that program faculty in most professions typically have little contact with clients or proper practice resources. These arguments are less compelling in student affairs, since preparation programs are co-located with practice sites, practitioners routinely advise on curricular matters, and supervised practice is a vigorous and normal part of preparation. Faculty should have major roles to play in restructuring student affairs CPE in the areas of content, delivery, process, and outcomes.

Content

In student affairs, as in perhaps few other professions, faculty and practitioners are closely joined. Professional association leadership can be characterized as a mix of senior professors and practitioners. Teachers have traditionally helped to set the agenda for the profession. If anything, these relationships should intensify and become more formalized. In determining the proper nature of the field, and hence the proper training and education, both theory and application are critical. It is significant that many such efforts are already ongoing and all involve both faculty and practitioners. For example, CAS (1992), the NASPA Reasonable Expectations Project (Kuh, Lyons, Miller, & Trow, 1995), the ACPA Student Learning Imperative statement (ACPA, 1994), the Committee on Continuing Professional Education (Creamer & Claar, 1995), and this book, among other efforts, all involve study of the nature of the profession and what should be taught to enhance practice and competence. Faculty already use these and other sources as grist for their curricular mills for initial preparation. The logical next step is to synthesize and approach a dynamic consensus on the most important skills and knowledge for each level of student affairs practice. What needs to be known at entry into the profession and what should be taught at succeeding stages of professional development? What do persons who have no previous student affairs background or education minimally need to know to function as professionals? What do allied professionals need to learn and when? If these questions were answered, basic subject matter for CPE would be apparent. From this base, faculty should take the lead in identifying new knowledge as it becomes available and seems likely to impact practice, in collaboration with practitioners, probably under the rubric of the professional associations. Effectively, faculty should take the lead in a team approach to setting an ongoing, change-oriented CPE agenda for the profession. Such a compilation would ideally be interdisciplinary, incorporate past, present, and future research findings, be flexible and open to innovation, and clearly reflect practical knowledge and application difficulties.

Delivery

Faculty have equally large responsibility for appropriate and timely delivery of CPE. Not only should they directly deliver CPE in local, regional, and national venues, but also they should act as consultants to practitioners who wish to do so. Faculty are the curricular experts of the profession. As such they should act as peer reviewers for CPE approaches and materials and have a strong impact on what is to be offered to practitioners. To be sure, practitioners know better how to supervise practical experiences, but even here, faculty can aid in the reflection characteristic of true and complete learning.

Faculty can contribute greatly in bringing to the field cutting edge instructional methods, distance learning techniques and strategies, adult education models and methods, and curriculum development knowledge. If students are initially prepared using these methods, they will expect high quality CPE. Practitioners with good ideas could collaborate with faculty for optimum delivery. Faculty modeling could make obsolete the "three points and an overhead" method of conference presentation, which, of course, faculty "popularized" in the first place. The creation of modules or "road shows" for use by trained practitioners to provide CPE for others is but one example of how faculty impact could be multiplied far past their numbers. Finally, faculty should monitor the quality of CPE offerings.

Process

The most important obligation facing faculty under any model or rubric is that of instilling in entry level professionals the notion that their education and learning have just begun. This should be done by ensuring that the masters curriculum is current and provides a base for CPE; by teaching and modeling professionalism; by keeping up with and helping to create new knowledge and approaches; and by understanding and participating in the credentialing of CPE processes as they evolve and change. Faculty should field test new material and promising instructional approaches for CPE. They should develop an active, two-way advisory relationship with practitioners in proximity to them. Faculty should obviously pay attention to their own professional development, including CPE. They should actively teach and embody the processes of peer review.

One immediate step that faculty should take is to agree upon and implement some sort of preparation program registry that provides an incentive for programs to follow the CAS Standards (1992). Traditional accreditation is not advocated here, but rather a voluntary process involving a serious self-study, the report of which would be evaluated by peers (without expensive and unnecessary site visits) and suggestions made. Programs which agreed to do this and met the CAS Standards would be listed in a directory which would provide a resource for students seeking preparation. Faculty should feel ethically bound to make sure that prospective students would know the difference between a "registered" (or some other designation) program and one which ignores the industry standard. Over time a reverse Gresham's Law process would occur in which the good programs would drive out the weak. There is sufficient room for diversity and inclusiveness in the CAS Standards that good programs need have no fear of evaluation. In some sense, if student affairs work is unwilling to codify its basic preparation, there is little point in discussing CPE. After all, if you do not care where you are, it does not matter where you are going.

Outcomes

Faculty should take the lead in assessing the results of initial preparation and CPE. There is a fair amount of information available about how colleges impact students (Pascarella & Terenzini, 1991). How student affairs practitioners facilitate those outcomes is not as well researched. Faculty should collaborate with practitioners to evaluate professional practice with an eye toward improving CPE content and processes. Faculty should also help in creating instruments for the self-assessment of individual practitioners at all levels as they strive to enhance their own practice through further training and education. This approach, favored by CAS and suggested by the Interassociation Committee on Continuing Professional Education (ICCPE, Creamer & Claar, 1995), would keep the responsibility for CPE where it belongs—in the hands of the practitioner, but with guidance from the profession (Klevans et al., 1992). The point of CPE (indeed, the principal point of a profession) is assurance of quality practice. Faculty bring research and conceptual skills and objectivity to the measurement of practice outcomes that are unlikely to be duplicated by most practitioners.

To summarize these points, preparation program faculty should be the research and development arm of the profession as it conceives and implements an organized program of CPE. Practitioners have a huge role in both content and process, associations provide the framework for discussion and delivery, employers provide incentives and resources, but faculty are needed to make the whole thing work.

PROPOSED NEXT STEPS

The first step in formulating an intentional plan for student affairs CPE is the obvious one—to find out what is already being done and examine it in its entirety. The ICCPE (Creamer & Claar, 1995) was working with NASPA and the Professional Development Council (PDC) of ACPA to do just that and disseminate a calendar for the use of the members of the profession. Unfortunately, the ICCPE stopped short of its goal, but many of its activities have been assumed by the PDC. Assuming that any CPE process in the future will be partly, and probably largely, market driven, what exists now will provide valuable clues about what should exist.

But there will be gaps, especially if the conception of CPE grows to include, as it should, the education of persons with no previous professional training and allied professionals. Content and skills necessary for every level of student affairs practice and for persons of every conceivable background should be addressed. When this CPE "curriculum" is compiled, it should be broadly disseminated among all members of the professional community for review and comment. Of particular interest will be the input of preparation program faculty, CAS, ACPA's Senior Scholars, specialty and regional associations, and the various sub-groups of ACPA and NASPA, such as Commissions, Standing Committees, and Networks. Each of these groups include faculty members who should play active roles in the debates. What should emerge is a "snapshot" of the CPE needs of the profession on or about a certain date. Periodic review by appropriate groups should be undertaken in order to keep this CPE agenda fresh, vital, and current. The best group for this activity may be CAS or some interassociation group, heavily involving preparation faculty.

Given that the content is known, the next step in implementing a CPE plan in student affairs would be attention to delivery. Providers of all types should be required to submit proposals to some appropriate sanctioning body, either the review body mentioned above, some arm of CAS, or bodies within the various associations that agree to standards and the peer review process. Again, faculty should be heavily involved, given their expertise in teaching and learning and their experience in peer review. Just as clearly, practitioners need to be involved, since they will bring a sense of the practical and provide market and field feedback. Accepted proposals would receive recognition and successful participants in the programs would be awarded Student Affairs Continuing Professional Education Credits (SACPEC's) as appropriate for the effort and time expended. Programs without sanction or not accepted after peer review would not be eligible for use by professionals in any contemplated certification or registry processes (see below).

Professional preparation masters programs should take the lead in the credentialing movement in student affairs by moving toward a program registry involving professional associations. Those that meet current and future CAS standards should be recognized. Those that do not should be helped to develop or cease calling themselves student affairs preparation programs.

Creamer et al. (1992) state that ". . . practitioners who engage in improving their professional practice should receive recognition for those achievements" (p. 12). Clearly, if student affairs is not to move toward licensure, and it should not, CPE is always going to be voluntary. Currently, participation in a professional preparation program that adheres to the CAS Standards is voluntary, but most would agree that such training gives an advantage in placement and practice to those who do so. Similarly, if a professional registry were created and made contingent upon proper initial preparation or its equivalent in CPE, appropriate early career supervision, and ongoing levels of CPE, then many would choose to participate in order to excel at their practice. According to this model, a person would be graduated from a registered preparation program, be supervised for some period by a more senior registered professional (who had participated in CPE appropriate for such supervision), and then attain full registry. Continuing registry would be granted if the person fulfilled an annual CPE obligation. There could also be different levels of CPE for entry level, mid-level, and senior student affairs workers and certification or further registry for specialties in student affairs such as residence life, student activities, or student financial aid. A person thus educated and learning continually should be an attractive applicant for any student affairs division concerned about quality of professional practice. Clearly, many years of transition would be needed before such a model was fully in place.

CONCLUSION

The preceding section was originally titled "Brave New World or Modest Proposal" but both of those phrases imply a negative view. Rather, this entire chapter is meant as positive food for thought and to advance the dialogue in CPE. It is perhaps trite to say that higher education and student affairs are at a crossroads—in many ways, they always have been. However, it is certain that technology, the new accountability, and the "new" college goers demand innovative thinking and ever-changing practice. Only through life-long learning can we hope to keep up.

REFERENCES

American College Personnel Association. (1993). Statement of ethical principles and standards. *Journal of College Student Development, 34,* 89-92.

American College Personnel Association. (1994). *The student learning imperative.* Washington, DC: Author.

Baskett, H. K. M., & Marsick, V. J. (1992). Confronting new understandings about professional learning and change. *Professionals' ways of knowing: New findings on how to improve professional education* (New Directions for Continuing Education, no. 55, pp. 7-15). San Francisco: Jossey-Bass.

Bloland, P. A. (1987, March). *Are we a profession?* Paper presented at the joint national conference of the American College Personnel Association and the National Association of Student Personnel Administrators, Chicago, IL.

Caplan, R. M. (1983). Continuing education and professional accountability. In C. McGuire, R. P. Foley, A. Gorr., R. W. Richards et al. (Eds.),

Handbook of health professions education (pp. 319-350). San Francisco: Jossey-Bass.

Carpenter, D. S. (1991). The student affairs profession: A developmental perspective. In T. K. Miller, R. B. Winston, & W. Mendenhall (Eds.), *Administration and leadership in student affairs* (2nd ed., pp. 212-231). Muncie, IN: Accelerated Development.

Carpenter, D. S. (1994). Student affairs and the paradigm wars: Some thoughts on professional practice in the 1990's. *NASPA Journal, 32*(1), 31-36.

Carpenter, D. S., Miller, T. K., & Winston, R. B. (1980). Toward the professionalization of student affairs. *NASPA Journal, 18*(2), 16-22.

Cervero, R. M., & Young, W. H. (1987). The organization and provision of continuing professional education: A critical review and synthesis. In J. Smart (Ed.), *Higher education: Handbook of theory and research, Vol. III* (pp. 402-431). New York: Agathon Press.

Cervero, R. M. (1981). A factor analytic study of physicians' reasons for participating in continuing education. *Journal of Medical Education, 56,* 29-34.

Council for the Accreditation of Counseling and Related Educational Programs (CACREP). (1992). *Accreditation procedures manual and application.* Alexandria, VA: Author.

Council for the Advancement of Standards for Higher Education. (1992). *Preparation standards and guidelines at the master's degree level for student affairs professionals in higher education.* College Park, MD: Author.

Creamer, D., & Claar, J. (1995). *Report of the Interassociation Committee on Continuing Professional Education to the NASPA and ACPA Boards.* Unpublished paper available from the authors.

Creamer, D. G., & Woodard, D. B. (1992). *Accrediting and credentialing in college student affairs: The role of ACPA and NASPA.* Unpublished paper commissioned by ACPA and NASPA. Washington, DC: ACPA.

Creamer, D. G., Winston, R. B., Schuh, J., Gehring, D., McEwen, M. L., Forney, D., Carpenter, D. S., & Woodard, D. B. (1992). *Quality assurance in college student affairs: A proposal for action by professional associations.* Report published by the American College Personnel Association and the National Association of Student Personnel Administrators.

Forney, D. (1994). *Chair's report to Commission XII.* American College Personnel Association Annual Conference, Indianapolis, IN.

Gonnella, J. S., & Zeleznik, C. (1983). Strengthening the relationship between professional education and performance. *Strengthening connections between education and performance* (New Directions for Continuing Education, no. 18, pp. 59-72). San Francisco: Jossey-Bass.

Houle, C. O. (1980). *Continuing learning in the professions.* San Francisco: Jossey-Bass.

Keim, M., & Graham, J. (1994). *Directory of graduate preparation programs in student personnel.* Washington, DC: ACPA.

Klevans, D. R., Smutz, W. D., Shuman, S. B., & Bershad, C. (1992). Self-assessment: Helping professionals discover what they do not know. *Professionals' ways of knowing: New findings on how to improve professional education* (New Directions for Continuing Education, no. 55, pp. 17-27). San Francisco: Jossey-Bass.

Komives, S. R. (1988, March). *The art of becoming professional.* Paper presented at the annual conference of the American College Personnel Association, Miami, FL.

Kuh, G., Lyons, J., Miller, T., & Trow, J. A. (1995). *Reasonable expectations: Renewing the educational compact between institutions and students.* Washington, DC: NASPA.

Lowenthal, W. (1981). Continuing education for professionals: Voluntary or madatory? *Journal of Higher Education, 52,* 519-538.

National Association of Student Personnel Administrators. (1992-93). Standards of professional practice. In *Member handbook* (pp. 17-18). Washington, DC.: Author.

Pascarella, E. T., & Terenzini, P. T. (1991). *How college affects students.* San Francisco: Jossey-Bass.

Paterson, B. G. (1987). An examination of the professional status of chief student affairs officers. *College Student Affairs Journal, 8*(1), 13-20.

Schön, D. A. (1987). *Educating the reflective practitioner: Toward a new design for teaching and learning in the professions.* San Francisco: Jossey-Bass.

Smutz, W. D., Crowe, M. B. , & Lindsay, C. A. (1986). Emerging perspectives on continuing professional education. In J. Smart (Ed.), *Higher education: Handbook of theory and research, Vol. II* (pp. 385-423). New York: Agathon Press.

Stamatakos, L. C. (1981). Student affairs progress toward professionalism: Recommendations for action. *Journal of College Student Personnel, 22*(2 & 3), 105-113, 197-205.

Suter, E., Green, J. S., Lawrence, K., & Wathall, D. B. (1981). Continuing education of health professionals: Proposal for a definition of quality. *Journal of Medical Education, 56 (Suppl.),* 687-707.

Task Force on Professional Preparation and Practice. (1989). *The recruitment, preparation, and nurturing of the student affairs professional.* Washington, DC: NASPA.

Young, R. B. (1988). The profession(alization) of student affairs. *NASPA Journal, 25,* 262-266.

Young, R. B. (1994). Student affairs professionals' perceptions of barriers to participation in development activities. *NASPA Journal, 31,* 243-251.

Chapter Nine

Linking Student Affairs Preparation with Practice

Susan R. Komives

Preparation programs in higher education and student affairs are unique among all campus graduate programs. No other graduate fields prepare professionals whose sole objective is to work in the very environment in which their graduate education occurs—on a college campus. The whole environment truly becomes a learning laboratory for these graduate students. This uniqueness provides an opportunity and an obligation for a dynamic reciprocity between preparation programs and practice. Indeed, successful preparation and effective practice depend on it.

This connection of preparation occurring in the environs of practice helps mitigate the discrepancy found in many other fields between the "proverbial 'ivory tower' and . . . the 'real world'" where communication is rare (Murphy, 1991, p. 22). Faculty are involved in practice at local, regional, and national levels and practitioners support graduate programs in many ways. The state of the art of linking preparation and practice is generally healthy—a unique strength of this field.

The state of the art of linking preparation and practice may be good, but it is not consistent. The promise and potential of this interface always exceeds reality and leaves room for improvement. The rapid pace of changing knowledge in the future will require us to move away from a prevailing traditional preparation model of faculty-conducting-the-courses and practitioners-supervising-the-internships as two essentially non-interacting sets. Murphy (1991) suggested that "preparation programs should be designed by both professors and practitioners and combine theoretical understandings, skills training, and clinical experiences into coherent and integrated programs of learning" (p. 25). Indeed, effective organizations (and perhaps professional fields) in the future will likely be those "based on a model of organizational learning in which learning is seen as a process of continuing conversation among organization stakeholders" (Boyatzis, Cowen, Kolb, & Associates, 1994, p. 240).

This chapter will explore the current state of the linkage between preparation and practice at the local campus and regional/national level (Task Force, 1989). A range of practices will be identified that illustrate existing linkages along with recommendations for where linkages should be built or enriched. Illustrations of actual practices were obtained primarily through open e-mail solicitation of information through such lists as CSPTALK (a list of graduate CSP faculty coordinated at the University of Louisville) and STUDEV (a list of practitioners and faculty coordinated at the University of Toledo). These examples are not the only or best applications but serve as useful illustrations. Among the linkage practices to be explored is the employment of professionally educated new professionals. The chapter will also include models of practice from other professions that have implications for student affairs preparation and practice.

BEING SCHOLAR-PRACTITIONERS

To use the terms "practitioner" or "faculty" may overly simplify these complex roles. For example, practitioners actually have many professional orientations and come through many diverse preparation routes. In addition to those in traditional student affairs roles with graduate degrees in student affairs or higher education, other professionals may be from related professional fields (e.g., counseling psychology, health education, social work) or may be using their expertise from unrelated fields in specialty roles with students (e.g., reading specialists, medical staff). Faculty also may have come from related fields (e.g., counselor education, educational psychology) and have little experience in student affairs or higher education jobs or come from student affairs practice and have little experience being researchers or scholars.

One's professional orientation is central to how effective a linkage can be developed in any particular setting. Whether in practice or in preparation, in the broadest view, one needs to be, to some extent, both a scholar (one interested in advancing knowledge, promoting inquiry, understanding findings, learning and sharing new strategies and approaches) and a practitioner (implementing interventions effectively, being oriented to quality service and education, effectively applying theory and research in practice). In a simplistic way, there may be a continuum (i.e., practitioner-practitioner; practitioner-scholar; scholar-practitioner; scholar-scholar) where either extreme end results in limited effectiveness.

I expect that most people in this field intentionally try to incorporate some aspect of both scholar and practitioner, yet there are hundreds of people in the student affairs field who have not read a recent journal, do not attend convention programs, have no campus-based continuing professional education program (see Chapter 8), have never conducted an outcomes or evaluation study, and conduct no research. While there is much theory-based practice and research occurring, some critics see little of either in the field (Bloland, Stamatakos, & Rogers, 1994). Bob Brown puts that criticism in context by noting we still hear too much questioning of "the value of research and theory as they relate to practice. This question comes up for all services fields (e.g., nursing, education, counseling, etc.) so student affairs should not feel unique or particularly low on that totem pole" (R. Brown, personal communication, May 12, 1995). Likewise, there are faculty who have not attended a student activities program, advised an undergraduate student, or attended a student affairs administrative staff meeting in years. They may be operating from outmoded ideas of reality.

It is the premise of this chapter that we should be committed to establishing, promoting, nurturing, and advancing linkages between preparation programs and practice. Collaborative approaches are essential to enhance practice and to model and educate generations of new professionals. This collaboration is so essential that the field has included it as ethical practice. The American College Personnel Association's ethics statement (1993) specifies that student affairs professionals will:

> Contribute to the development of the profession (e.g., recruiting students to the profession, serving professional organizations, educating new professionals, improving professional practices, and conducting and reporting research). (p. 90)

The ACPA/NASPA Task Force on Preparation and Practice (Task Force, 1989) observed that this field has done a good job taking advantage of the many opportunities to link preparation and practice, perhaps better than other fields of study, but that we can do better. The Task Force noted that "national efforts are sporadic, regional activities are uneven, and individual campus interface ranges from interdependent and supportive to neglectful or hostile. We will likely never be totally satisfied that we are doing all that is possible with the rich opportunities to interface" (p. 25). However, there is no research evidence to substantiate that observation; the field needs an intentional study to identify the nature of linkages.

LOCAL LINKAGES

Many campuses with graduate programs have campus policies or practices that define and perhaps limit the nature of the desirable structured relationship between administrators and faculty. For example, some campuses do not allow administrators to teach courses on-load or do not permit graduate programs to sponsor undergraduate credits, but many can. Campuses without graduate programs may not be permitted to be internship sites (citing limitations on staff time) and may not be funded to offer assistantship equivalents, but many are. Individual campus policies, then, may drive the nature of the formal relationship, even if many options exist in the informal arena.

In a campus culture that expects scholar/practitioner models and symbiotic links, the ideal model may be the most permissive. In such a model, graduate programs can formally appoint qualified administrators as affiliate or adjunct faculty, including opportunities for practitioners to teach courses, to advise graduate students and supervise their research, and to serve as core faculty for the graduate program. Concurrently in this model, the program might support practice with activities such as sponsoring academic credit to support student development education (for example, offering resident assistant or orientation courses, sponsoring leadership courses to be coordinated by student activities staff, and offering credits for such undergraduate experiential education as community service and service learning). Possible linkages between student affairs practice and preparation programs on college campuses are noted in Figure 9-1 and discussed below.

Practitioners Supporting Graduate Programs

Individual practitioners often support their own graduate alma mater through student referrals, guest presentations, and annual gifts

Figure 9-1
Examples of Local Practice/Preparation Linkages

Faculty, Students, and Preparation Programs' Contributions to Practitioners and to Practice	
STRUCTURED	♦ serve on office advisory boards ♦ serve on student affairs committees ♦ provide/attend staff development (offer CEUs if possible ♦ award alums for excellence in practice ♦ maintain contact with program alums ♦ stay active in local/regional/national professional associations ♦ offer credit-bearing courses for student affairs offerings
INFORMAL	♦ conduct joint research/writing ♦ consult ♦ network with/among program alums ♦ link graduate student resources to campus/local needs ♦ collaborate in service learning activities
Practitioners' Contributions to Faculty, Students, and Preparation Programs	
STRUCTURED	♦ supervise internships ♦ offer assistantships ♦ teach graduate courses ♦ serve on program advisory boards ♦ financially sponsor programs ♦ offer various experiential learning opportunities ♦ serve as faculty advisor to graduate students ♦ serve as affiliate/adjunct faculty
INFORMAL	♦ recruit students to the field ♦ support one's own alum graduate program ♦ participate in student/faculty research ♦ offer data bases/research options ♦ hire professionally-educated graduates ♦ read professional literature ♦ mentor graduate students

to support program activities such as student research. Many practitioners also actively recruit to the field by identifying promising student leaders and sponsoring them into the profession, guiding them in the graduate application process, and in understanding the career field. Careers in Student Affairs Week activities are held on many individual campuses to support recruitment to the field with focused efforts to recruit students from diverse ethnic and racial backgrounds (see Chapter 5).

Various student affairs offices have been supportive of graduate preparation through such activities as supporting student research, involving program faculty and students in professional development programs, and sharing networks for job openings. Practitioners on nearby campuses without graduate programs can serve on program advisory boards, create internship programs, and contract with program faculty for research and other consultation.

Individual practitioners offer hot topic or current issues seminars, teach special topic short courses, or regular graduate courses. On some campuses many practitioners with doctoral degrees hold formal adjunct or affiliate appointments. Accepting an affiliate faculty appointment usually means accepting a formal role in managing the program, such as serving on graduate program committees (e.g., admissions). It is undeniable that practitioners teaching in student affairs graduate programs benefit the program; however, there is mixed opinion on whether such affiliations aid administrators in being viewed as scholars or bridge builders with other campus faculty (Clement & Rickard, 1992).

Graduate student affairs and higher education programs probably have more practitioners teaching as adjuncts or affiliates than do most other graduate fields. While some campuses do not allow or encourage administrators to teach, most practitioners enjoy that experience if it is available to them. Crosson and Nelson (1984) estimate that 58% of the part-time faculty teaching in higher education programs concurrently hold appointments as administrators on those campuses. Keim (1991) reports nearly 700 faculty members in student affairs programs, of whom only 105 are full-time and the remaining 595 are part-time administrators or counselors. This very strong link between preparation and practice is illustrative of good relationships but, sadly, may also signal that Colleges of Education do not hold student affairs programs in high regard since these numbers average out to fewer than one full-time faculty member per program.

Some programs are comprised solely of practitioners. For example, at Oregon State University almost all of the Student Affairs department heads (e. g., housing, financial aid) teach at least one course and all advise graduate students. A number of the "junior" staff also teach or lead seminars in their areas of expertise. Roger Penn estimates this involvement of 15 staff equates to about 4 F.T.E. faculty. While creating a different kind of program than CAS standards and ACPA Commission XII criteria suggest; he observes, "This set up then gives us no choice but to align theory closely to practice" and "gives us greater diversity in instruction and helps the students to stay focused on the realities of practicing in the field" (R. Penn, personal communication, July 27, 1995). In many places, practitioners are officially attached to a graduate program. Many would agree with the University of Hawaii-Manoa's Jan Javinar who observed that "by using adjuncts like me, the emphasis/bias(?) is on making theory practical and promoting a theory-based practice" (personal communication, May 12, 1995).

Graduate Programs Supporting Practice

Full time graduate faculty must be supportive of the student affairs divisions at their campus and create and nurture intentional links with nearby programs. Ideally, graduate faculty should support the campus' agenda for undergraduate students, support the student affairs division's goals, and be another friendly bridge for student affairs administrators to the faculty arena. These connections can include serving on special functional area advisory boards (e.g., Career Center Advisory Board or Living-Learning Center Assessment Committee), being a sympathetic faculty member appointee to student-oriented committees (e.g., Campus Retention Committee), or serving as a consultant (either in a process role or expertise role) regarding various campus needs and issues.

Graduate faculty have a special responsibility to ensure a quality experience for the graduate students in the program. Graduate faculty must "assure that field supervisors are qualified to provide supervision to graduate students and are informed of their ethical responsibilities in this role" (ACPA Ethics, 1993, p. 91). Sadly, in too many programs, students seek and manage their own field work experiences with little to no involvement from busy faculty. Some programs (e.g., Bowling Green State University) have extensive field work manuals with excellent supervision guidelines, yet professional associations have no suggested standards of practice or other teaching guidelines for field work supervisors.

Many faculty have demonstrated commitments to be highly engaged with practitioners, but if these supportive patterns are infrequent or nonexistent, intentional action is needed to establish a more effective symbiosis. This symbiotic relationship requires great understanding of both the faculty and administrative cultures. Many faculty were previously practitioners and likely understand the stress and challenge of working in a student affairs role. Practitioners who have never been full time faculty need to understand the different world of the faculty/academic culture. Graduate faculty have little or no support staff, few technological resources, meager budgets, and must manage all recruitment, admissions, and aspects of program community, while researching and publishing to meet professional goals and expectations of the faculty reward system. In Chapter 6, Evans and Williams identify other aspects of the faculty role that require understanding.

Students Bridge Preparation and Practice

Graduate students are often the main bridges and boundary spanners between preparation programs and practitioners. They become instrumental to campus offices as student workers through their assistantships or continuing in their full time jobs. Students bring the latest of their learning to their assistantship and work sites and in turn bring those living case studies to the classroom. Ted Miller illustrates this interaction with a University of Georgia practice of students using the CAS Functional Area Standards and Guidelines to assess their internship and practicum sites, helping both the student and the site (T. Miller, personal communication, May 12, 1995).

Assistantship systems range from placement of graduate students primarily by the graduate program (such as the Ohio State Student Personnel Assistant-SPA-program), facilitated assistantship placements where employers make hiring decisions but link with the graduate program for campus visitations (such as University of Maryland College Park, Indiana University, Bowling Green State University, Iowa State), to campuses without many assistantships but who help students with part-time work (e.g., Pennsylvania State University, Teacher's College). Some campuses like California State University-Long Beach have additional creative programs like their Protege program offering ten half time paid positions in the second year (Keim & Graham, 1994). Most practitioners and faculty alike would agree that CSP programs bring a talented pool of new professionals into campus offices and establish a good "feeder" of quality candidates for the campus (M. Cuyjet, personal communication, May 12, 1995). Most campus offices prefer student affairs graduate students to those from other academic programs (M. Dannells in Keim & Graham, 1994, p. 103).

Most campuses with a graduate preparation program depend on the program as a source of graduate student staff who fill assistantships or become part time staff in student affairs offices. Likewise, the program depends on campus offices to provide these professionally related jobs for experience and as a source of funding for graduate student education. Most assistantships or part time jobs are excellent experience, but students often identify the need for more developmental supervision and more integration of their formal classroom learning with their job expectations.

The tremendous benefits of close practice-program relationships can bring unique and sensitive problems. Serious ethical issues can emerge if work relationships are not carefully designed. Often work supervisors are concurrently faculty in student affairs courses; they need to exert great care to not mix work performance evaluation with classroom outcomes. Students also find themselves in multiple roles with each other—students in the same class may be on the same staff, some even as supervisors of others. The ACPA ethics statement (1993) specifies that preparation program faculty will:

> Assure that required experiences involving self-disclosure are communicated to prospective graduate students. When the program offers experiences that emphasize self-disclosure or other relatively intimate or personal involvement (e.g., group or individual counseling or growth groups), professionals must not have current or anticipated administrative, supervisory, or evaluative authority over participants. (p. 91)

It is virtually impossible not to have some multiple relationships in the small campus student affairs world. Where these dual relationships exist, staff of both graduate preparation and work settings should explicitly discuss the ethical implications of these potentially conflicting interactions. "Considering that the relationships and reputation gained from assistantship employment will persist after graduate study, students should carefully assess the true work load, expectations, and office culture as students cannot afford not to do well in this related work experience" (Komives, 1993, p. 400). Inexperienced workers (i.e., new masters students) will likely need careful mentoring to avoid potentially conflicting relationships.

Faculty and practitioners share a precious responsibility. Applied fields must develop the whole student and not merely expose them to the knowledge bases of a discipline (Boyatzis et al., 1994, p. 132). The best wisdom of the Student Personnel Point of View (American Council on Education, 1937) taught us to value holistic development and we must insist on that perspective for our graduate students.

Curricular Linkages

Internships and counseling practica supported by reflective seminars exist in almost all programs and have long served as the best example of preparation-practice collaboration. On some campuses, internship site placements are facilitated through consortia or other structural relationships like the seven campus "Metroversity" that includes the University of Louisville (M. Cuyjet, personal communication, May 12, 1995). Some campuses also offer courses in which a major component is to link the students as consulting teams in practice (e.g., Environmental Assessment courses that review and make recommendations to actual institutional "clients"). The nine different consulting teams in a Technology in Student Affairs class at Western Kentucky University evaluated the technological applications of 27 different student affairs offices using this approach (A. Hughey, personal communication, May 16, 1995). Many courses would benefit from a redesign to include this type of experiential component. The University of Vermont has instituted such a class recently on Institutional Research emphasizing practical research in applied settings as a collaboration between the student affairs division and the program (K. Manning, personal communication, August 12, 1995).

Advisory Boards

Wise campus leadership practices support the involvement of appropriate share holders and stake holders in the assessment and revision of practice. Various campus offices and graduate programs need to develop more formal mechanisms (i.e., advisory boards) to keep a dynamic flow of information and advice coming into programs.

An advisory board is "a group of volunteers that meets regularly on a long-term basis to provide advice and/or support to an institution or one of its subunits" (Teitel, 1994, p. 3). Too often advisory boards are formed solely for public relations functions with little or no meaningful role or involvement of participants in influencing the unit for which the board is established. Some functional areas (e.g., resident life academic programs) or cross functional areas (e.g., interdisciplinary developmental studies, wellness programming) would benefit by involving the external shareholders and stakeholders in those functions and preparation program faculty would be useful additions to such functions as advisors to those in practice.

Graduate programs, likewise, would benefit by the advice and linkage created by an advisory board of both host campus staff and those from diverse nearby institutions who supervise internships and hire program graduates. Some campuses (e.g., California State University-Long Beach) established advisory boards of area college student affairs professionals to build a support base for the students and the program when the program was founded. Others have established advisory boards to address specific issues such as recruiting African American graduate students. Teitel (1994) clarifies that an advisory board is most likely to be effective when (a) the representatives of the unit involved (e.g., faculty) truly want the input of the members of the board; (b) the members of the board are genuinely interested, have useful information, and receive effective recognition; (c) processes and structures exist to insure the board's usefulness like regular meetings, appropriate information, and a "sense of engagement and ownership" (p. v); and (d) "expectations about the roles of the committee in providing advice and support are clear, consistent, and well communicated" (p. v). Sadly, advisory boards mandated by accreditation or certification requirements often slip into becoming ineffective or "rubber stamps" (Teitel, 1994, p. 29) for the unit that created them.

Few advisory boards actually exist. Faculty report such problems as scheduling, lack of clerical support to facilitate meetings, and faculty workload issues as problems working against adding new interventions even as useful as advisory boards. Advisory boards might best be established around specific functions and tasks that could fit the pace of the programs and participants instead of slipping into meaninglessness. Advisory meetings might even serve a good purpose to bring share holders and stake holders together for a type of focus-group activity to advise program faculty or a Total Quality Management (TQM) or Continuous Quality Improvement (CQI) team to address a specific process or issue. Such advisory meetings could be scheduled at regional or national conventions to bring alumni and those from nearby institutions into the process.

Sometimes all we need to do is ask for feedback. Tom Jackson Jr. at the University of Texas-El Paso shared that he hired an alumni of the program at Emporia State University and subsequently met the program director who asked him to comment on what the program needed to do from the perspective of an employer of a recent grad. Tom said "Of course I did just that. My point was . . . *he asked me to respond* about the program from a practitioner's viewpoint" (personal communication, May 12, 1995).

SUGGESTIONS FOR PROMOTING LINKAGES

Practitioners and faculty who want to develop more intentional linkages might consider some of the following suggestions:

Recommendations for Graduate Programs.

1. Establish an advisory board, conduct limited focus group meetings, or establish a TQM or CQI team with host campus and regional campus personnel. See Teitel's (1994) *The Advisory Committee Advantage* for useful guidance on this kind of support.
2. Interact with assistantship and internship supervisors. While most campuses do interact with internship supervisors at least to evaluate the student's learning, some also have well developed supervision criteria and large networks of assistantship supervisors well aware of the curricular requirements of the program. Informed supervisors can become true partners to help the student have a good experience.
3. Establish clinical professorships or appoint adjunct faculty for internship supervision to emphasize the importance of intentionally designed field work experiences for students. Someone keenly in touch with issues of practice should direct these seminars, process this learning with students, and inform site supervisors about the role of this kind of learning in the students' program.
4. Specify previous employment in student affairs as a job requirement for faculty appointment. The "easiest, quickest, and surest way to bridge the gap between the delivery and practices" of student development and student affairs administration is "to appoint more professors who have" student affairs experience (Murphy, 1991, p. 23).
5. Encourage "clinically-based sabbaticals" (Murphy, 1991, p. 23) to return teaching faculty to some aspect of practice and active involvement with undergraduates or undergraduate programs and services.
6. Consider affiliating administrators who may get sabbaticals

or professional leave time as a practitioner-in-residence to bring that reflective person into graduate students' lives and provide a base for that practitioner to develop new ideas for practice (H. Belch, personal communication, May 12, 1995).

Recommendations for Practitioners.

1. Stay in touch with your own graduate program. Holly Belch observed "I think those practitioners who did keep in touch with what was happening in prep programs [did it through] staying in touch with their own prep program faculty" (personal communication, May 12, 1995). Nothing will replace the umbilical cord relationship connecting alumni to their program. Programs value the feedback from alumni in their diverse settings because they can uniquely integrate the changing needs of the field with what the program needs to offer. Many alumni would agree with an Indiana University alum who wrote that in the first couple of years when financial support of the program wasn't possible, he was geographically close enough at least to donate his time through guest presentations and team teaching, sustaining his commitment to the program and bringing advice from practice into the classroom (J. Vander Putten, personal communication, July 26, 1995).
2. Identify and recruit prospective students for your alma mater and to the profession in general. Faculty would agree with Kathy Manning from the University of Vermont when she comments on the alumni referrals, "I'm amazed at how that shapes our program—sets expectations before the students arrive . . ." (personal communication, August 12, 1995).
3. Seek student and faculty consultation from nearby programs. Practitioners can identify short term and long term projects for consultation and involvement of graduate students (perhaps even through formal class assignments). Students engaged in these projects can form learning teams with the practitioners on-site for collaborative relationships and co-teaching.
4. Encourage practice-focused research. The field needs this research to advance and new professionals need to learn how research, assessment, and evaluation can influence policy and practice.

5. Develop expectations for supervisors of graduate assistants (GAs) to provide teaching-supervision. It is reasonable to expect supervisors to use the syllabi of courses to guide the GA and intentionally reinforce their learning. Supervisors need to "take the time to try to make those 'connections' with [GAs] between what they are doing on site and what is going on in classes" (T. Nolfi, personal communication, July 26, 1995).
6. Create internship experiences for graduate students which can be advertised to local graduate programs or through professional associations (e.g., the ACUHO-I internship, NODA internship).

ENTERING PROFESSIONAL PRACTICE

During the Spring of 1995, a flurry of stories on the STUDEV listserv about the job search process in student affairs brought both horror stories and models of excellence. The horror stories sounded like experiences with staff who have never taken a counseling course, never showed any amount of care to other human beings, and who enjoyed their power trips. The sensitive process of taking on the first job and the first three to five years as a new professional are critical. Several emerging issues deserve some attention.

Jobs and Candidates

National association and placement fair data (see Table 9-1) reflect a trend toward more candidates than positions available. From a ratio of two or more positions per candidate in the late seventies through most of the 1980s (R. Ward, personal communication, July 31, 1995), national placement center recruitment has seen a shift to about one job per candidate in the early 1990s, and a shift to about 1.4 more candidates than positions to the mid-1990s. While variations occur when national conventions are held west of the Mississippi or on the West coast, it is clear that more and more people are registering in these settings. There has been a fairly stable five-year pool of 621 openings at ACPA and 517 openings at NASPA. Data does not reflect how many candidates may have registered at both conventions or how many employers recruited at both. Some kinds of positions (e.g., academic advising, counseling) are rarely posted at these conventions and more traditional positions (e.g., residence life, student activities) predominate. We have no reliable national data base on entry employment in student affairs. This process of job openings, turnover, job mobility, and the like deserves greater study in this field.

Table 9-1
Profile of Positions and Candidates at National Convention Placement

Year		ACPA[1]	Oshkosh (WI)[2] Placement Exchange	NASPA[3]
Year		Location		Location
1989		Washington, DC		Denver
	candidates	NA	NA	322
	positions			462
1990		St. Louis		New Orleans
	candidates	NA		367
	positions			536
1991		Atlanta		Washington, DC
	candidates	931	NA	561
	positions	466 (652)[4]	NA	386
1992		San Francisco		Cincinnati
	candidates	613	907[5]	870
	positions	328 (459)	340[6]	410
1993		Kansas City		Boston
	candidates	757	738	957
	positions	412 (577)	324	453
1994		Indianapolis		Dallas
	candidates	1128	732	569
	positions	457 (640)	317	453
1995		Boston		San Diego
	candidates	1263	679	535
	positions	556 (778)	377	385

[1] Mike D'Attilio, personal communication, July 31, 1995
[2] Oshkosh Placement Exchange Summaries, 1993, 1994, 1995
[3] NASPA (1995). Career services registration history. Unpublished report. Washington, DC: Author.
[4] *Projected openings:* ACPA post convention studies demonstrate that the number of actual openings range from 1.3 to 1.5 of total positions listed. Numbers in parentheses are an extrapolation using the ACPA placement practice of using a 1.4 average for comparison. For example, one posted hall director position may reflect five actual hall director openings (Mike D'Attilio, personal communication, August 1, 1995).
[5] 1992 data are those registered; 1993-1995 data are those who actually attended.
[6] Actual number of positions available.

Contract and At-Will Employment

Many campuses have adopted flexible staffing models using contract employees to save on benefits or because they can hire in this category without adding "lines" and dealing with the hassle from state systems to gain approval for regular appointments. Unfortunately, this practice may mean that new professionals and others will have to take positions without benefits like heath insurance or tuition credits. Further, contract employees are often not considered regular staff and may not be included in staff meetings or policy decisions (just as part time faculty often do not have offices or participate in faculty meetings). Professional associations might explore the extent of this trend and determine if any association benefits like group health plans could be reasonably initiated, as is done by other professional associations, for those who practice independently, such as psychologists and lawyers.

Gaps in Competencies

A graduate program cannot possibly cover all the content, build all the skills, and create all the experiences needed for professional practice. Graduate programs in many fields make no effort to apply classroom learning to practice. Some do require a limited clinical experience (e.g., law) or an extensive clinical period (e.g., medicine, psychology) to build professional competencies. Today's "professional schools . . . mirror the priorities and work environment [for] their graduates" because of their "commitment to developing the whole student" (Boyatiz, et al., 1994, p. 132). Instead of expecting graduate programs to be all things to all people, we must proudly "move to where the learning occurs, create systems for just-in-time learning" (Baskett, Marsick, & Cervero, 1992, p. 112). After listing nearly three pages of competencies and skills one would need to be fully informed to enter professional work in the complex field of residence life, one professor concluded on an internet list recently "seriously, if students take graduate courses that adequately cover all these topics" and do everything else they have to do, like eat and sleep, "it would take them about 47 years to complete their masters program!" (C. Palmer, personal communication, May 12, 1995). While many student affairs programs do use the CAS standards for program design (see Chapter 7), many programs do not even design their curriculum around explicit competencies and leave it up to the student to translate what they are exposed to in classes to applications in practice. Practitioners can help fill this gap. In a collaboration between the graduate program and the Division of Student Affairs Professional Development committee, the University of South Carolina established a graduate assistant competency program in 1992 to link with formal academic experiences. The program is open to all divisional GAs, meets once a month in a two year cycle, has a formal completion certificate, is designed and sequenced after the CAS standards, and contains such useful elements as supervisor manuals for those working with the GAs in office settings (J. Doran, personal communication, July 27, 1995).

Setting aside differences of opinion on what can or should be covered in graduate education (see chapter 7), there is no doubt that the first few years of entry into professional work are times of intense continued learning and socialization. While practitioners are eager to hire a new graduate student who can hit-the-ground-running, it is more imperative than ever before to provide intentional continued learning experiences (see Chapter 8 on continuing professional education) and developmental, teaching supervision to ensure an effective transition. One of the hardest skills to teach in the classroom is supervision; by definition it is best learned when combined with the experience of working with others in a work setting. Too often new professionals are supervising other new professionals with little experience or knowledge to do this well. New professionals' workshops should regularly include sessions on enhancing supervision and leadership skills. Experienced supervisors should design intentional elements of their own supervision of new supervisors to allow time to reflect on and process their own supervision issues.

STATE, REGIONAL, AND NATIONAL LEVEL LINKAGES

Most campuses have no graduate preparation program in student affairs or higher education. Practitioners in those settings must be very creative to link with preparation faculty and, likewise, faculty must make extraordinary efforts to stay in touch with the issues in practice from those settings (for example, community colleges, regional state universities, liberal arts colleges, and many special institutions like historically Black colleges, women's colleges, and military academies). The primary opportunity point for such links comes through state, regional, and national professional associations.

Bring Students to Diverse Campuses

Even a remote campus without a nearby graduate preparation program can conduct professional development programs, bring in consultants, and provide opportunities for interns. Unique programs (e.g., community service, Native American culture centers) can be either linked to appropriate graduate programs or campuses can network with national associations to offer intern placements. Some graduate programs (e.g., Western Illinois University) require their students to engage in an off-campus internship; faculty help students make linkages with interested offices around the country.

The process of off-campus internship placements is primarily the responsibility of the graduate program and students become as limited as their pocketbooks and the knowledge and networks of their faculty. The ACPA/NASPA Task Force (1989) recommended that one of the national associations become a clearinghouse for summer internships so that a more systematic range of offerings would be available to students. Interested sites could begin to determine what elements of the offer (e.g., housing, stipend) would make their site more desirable. One of the most formal internship networks is through the American Psychological Association placing doctoral counseling psychology students in various clinical settings. Two of the most established informal national networks are the residence life internships offered through the Association of College and University Housing Officers-International (ACUHO-I) and the orientation internships established by the National Orientation Directors Association (NODA). They seek interns prior to their graduate preparation as well as those engaged in preparation. The ACUHO-I and NODA experiences could serve as models-in-practice of systems to do such linkages.

Technology and Learning

Technology is underused in formal linkages but holds good promise. One doctoral student singing the praises of various lists on the internet said "From the standpoint of e-mail and the internet . . . what can I say? You can bet I email Roger Winston and Ted Miller at Georgia and Barbara Mann at FSU if I have questions related to the field. From my vantage point . . . technology allows access to their ideas and reservoirs of knowledge when the occasion arises" (A. Bailey, personal communication, July 26, 1995). Alumni find the internet a useful way to share feedback and get support from their graduate faculty.

Indeed, some campuses are now bringing national faculty and practitioners into their classrooms via internet. For example, Carney Strange at Bowling Green State University established "electronic visiting professors" for one of his classes, inviting a pair of professionals to sign on to their class e-mail list and interact around topics over a period of several weeks! To date, other than teleconferences and some interactive conference presentations, student affairs programs have made little use of distance learning technology but this vehicle holds much promise for establishing linkages with sites across the country.

Linkages through Associations

Perhaps one of the strongest linkages is that faculty of student affairs programs and campus-based practitioners identify with the same set of professional associations. Faculty attend, present programs, and hold leadership roles in generalist national associations like NASPA and ACPA. ACPA has elected several full-time faculty to serve as president of the association in recent years (e.g., Bob Brown, Terry Williams, Harold Cheatham). These two associations provide many good examples of how faculty and practitioner dialogue is encouraged, including the ACPA and NASPA policy to appoint a faculty member and a practitioner as their two representatives to the Council for the Advancement of Standards (CAS), NASPA's waiver of the convention registration fee for one faculty member from each program, the NASPA convention breakfast for all faculty (adjuncts, affiliates, and full-timers), and the strength of the ACPA Commission XII (Graduate Preparation Programs) structure which regularly brings those interested in issues of preparation into the discussion. The Commission XII Syllabi Clearinghouse is a collaborative activity between faculty and those practitioners who teach to list their syllabi to help all who need to design new courses have ready access to materials of benefit.

Faculty will be increasingly pulled to the Association for the Study of Higher Education (ASHE) and the American Educational Research Association (AERA), associations that provide more focus on research about students and the higher educational experience. Should that trend develop and if there is a decrease in faculty attendance at NASPA or ACPA, these associations should study this phenomena with appropriate interventions to continue high level faculty involvement (e.g., registration fee waivers, grant support for research). Practitioners and faculty alike increasingly find associations like the American Association of Higher Education (AAHE) to be of interest with their emphasis on undergraduate education and student learning.

New professionals are the life blood of many professional associations. NASPA and ACPA have welcomed new professionals as student members and encouraged their involvement through committees that focus on their needs as members and specific needs at annual conventions. The graduate program receptions are well attended "family reunions" where current and former faculty interact with alumni and friends of those programs.

Specialty associations have a more challenging task to keep linkages meaningful. Faculty do not regularly attend specialty meetings unless their research or scholarship area is related to that specialty (e.g., counseling, leadership, financial aid policy). Various regional and national specialty associations (e.g., ACUHO-I and various ACUHO regions) sponsor linkage programs such as faculty-in-residence programs. Through their connection to CAS, specialty associations have identified areas of competence needed to practice in their areas. The National Association of Campus Activities (NACA) has developed perhaps the most comprehensive specialized competencies including a related curriculum for graduate study (Allen, Julian, Stern, & Walborn, 1987). Few specialty associations send their literature or recruitment materials directly to graduate programs, preferring instead to contact prospective members through field sites.

Both faculty and practitioners attending regional and national meetings is part of the solution; yet no meaningful dialogue may occur. The ACPA/NASPA Task Force (1989) recommended that "the profession needs to insure that multiple organizational structures are established and nurtured to provide continuous systematic dialogue between practitioners and preparation program faculties" (p. 25). More intentional and creative mechanisms like think tanks and joint issue-based task forces may be needed to promote essential dialogue. The ACPA/NASPA Task Force itself was a model of the type of faculty-practitioner dialogue needed on complex topics. This blue-ribbon commission (Johnson & Marcus, 1986) made specific recommendations about the interface of preparation and practice, yet accomplished little. Their fine report exists in archival records and resulted in little action, falling victim to the organizational malady of not being effectively translated into motions for governance action. The task force met all the criteria of effective blue ribbon commissions except one—"the members of the commission must be willing to advocate on behalf of their report once it is issued" (Johnson & Marcus, 1986, p. 72). As a task force, the members went out of business upon filing the report and the associations had no mechanisms to turn the report into action. As a member of that task force, I hope there is a lesson learned here that dialogue can be enlightening but unless it is designed to influence practice and policy, it becomes useless.

Few, if any, vice presidential councils of state systems or private consortia include any full-time graduate faculty to create an explicit link or dialogue, but many of those vice presidents are affiliated with their graduate programs and hopefully bring a broad view to their role with the program. (For a presentation on other multicampus and consortia programs see McDade, Andersen, White, & Santos, 1994). Although many state and regional associations have faculty-in-residence programs or faculty on advisory boards (e.g., Pennsylvania College Personnel Association, several NASPA regions, ACUHO-I), most regional associations assume that both faculty and practitioners will attend the conference as participants and that those links will informally happen. Many practitioners may attend such sessions because they are work related, but few full-time faculty are able financially to attend regional as well as national meetings. Few formal think tanks exist, but those that do hold good promise for faculty and practitioners to explore items of importance. For example, twenty vice presidents and several full-time faculty met about four times a year in a NASPA Region II think tank on such topics as creating moral campus communities (N. Evans, personal communication, July 26, 1995).

LESSONS FROM PRACTICE OF OTHER PROFESSIONS

It was affirming to explore how other professional fields link preparation and practice and conclude that the student affairs profession is very good with linkage. Most professional fields lament that their graduate faculty are not connected to practice and that practitioners make no effort to inform teaching. Those fields with a clinical component find some linkage through internship-type experiences offered through such university-sponsored practices as medical clinics and legal aid clinics. Fortunately, many professional fields are looking to infuse their preparation programs with concerns of practice.

> Medical schools are concerned about infusing a sense of compassion, caring for patients as human beings and not merely as disease-bearing problems to be solved . . . Law schools are worried about producing trial attorneys who can present their client's case . . . they are also turning attention to client management, diversity and globalization. Dental and nursing schools are attempting to prepare people for more activist roles in society, assuming more responsibility for the wellness or health of the whole person and family. (Boyatzis, et al., 1995, p. 4)

There are several promising aspects of linkages and new developments that might be useful to explore.

The Professional School Model

The Professional School Model is being initiated by many Colleges of Education to bring professors, student teachers, and administrators-in-training into meaningful involvement with teachers and administrators in practice. In addition to providing teacher in-service education, this model seeks to be grounded in real issues of the workplace and invites scholars and practitioners to interact about those problems (Abdal-Haqq, 1992; Nystrand, 1991). State systems, consortia, and state ACPA chapters might consider such a model to bring real issues in practice into a think tank and professional consultation setting. On some scale, this model could provide good outreach to state campuses, involve students in practical settings, and become useful local think tanks.

Extension Work

Agricultural and home economics extension work has long brought faculty and volunteers together through such programs as 4-H and cooperative extension work. Field faculty are often graduates of the local major program who then supervise internships and summer jobs of students in training. Each county has one or more advisory groups and there are intentional strong links between practice and field faculty although the link back to academic faculty may be uneven. These systems have benefited from strong external funding. Technology is making a major impact with interactive networks through which practitioners can access helpful information managed by an information coordinator (Meryl Miller, personal communication, July 14, 1995). Graduate student affairs programs might consider a network of field faculty from among their own graduates to intentionally develop campus-based outreach. Further, expertise based electronic consultation systems might be investigated by professional associations.

Practicing the Law

The legal field is fairly critical of their lack of emphasis in linking academic programs to practice. Indeed, the message is you "learn to practice law when you get out there" and learn a way of thinking in law school with less emphasis on how to apply or use that material. Some programs do not require a clinical experience. Many law faculty maintain a private practice, serve as arbitrators, or expert witnesses and maintain a practice-orientation with those involvements. Continuing legal education (CLE) is delivered separately from law school preparation and is not mandatory in some states. Most states do require CLE for licensure and for reputable professional practice. In addition to the Association of Continuing Legal Education Administrators, there is a professional education division of the American Bar Association (Michelle Lane, personal communication, July 10, 1995). Student affairs work is a long way from even deciding how continuing professional education is to be promoted (see Chapter 8) but if desirable, there are lessons in the medical and legal models.

CONCLUSION

Linkages between practitioners and faculty and between practice and preparation are essential for the health and continued vitality of this complex field. The dynamic reciprocity between faculty and practitioners at the local level and through national associations is a unique and encouraging element of this field. Where those campus-based linkages are underdeveloped, unhealthy, or unsupportive, they should be addressed anew. Of particular importance is to continue the realization that practitioners and faculty alike share a responsibility to educate generations of new professionals and that education transcends the years of formal graduate study.

REFERENCES

Abdal-Haqq, I. (Ed.). (1992). *Professional development schools: A director of projects in the United States.* Washington, DC: American Association of Colleges for Teacher Education Publications.

Allen, K. E., Julian, G., Stern, T., & Walborn, G. (1987). *Future perfect: A guide for professional development and competence.* Columbia, SC: National Association of Campus Activities Educational Foundation.

American College Personnel Association. (1993). Statement of ethical principles and standards. *Journal of College Student Development, 34,* 89-92.

American Council on Education. (1937). The student personnel point of view. Reprinted in G. Saddlemire & A. Rentz (Eds.). (1986). *Student affairs: A profession's heritage.* (pp. 74–88). Media Publication, 40. Alexandria, VA.: American College Personnel Association.

Baskett, H. K. M., Marsick, V. J., & Cervero, R. N. (1992). Putting theory to practice and practice to theory. In H. K. M. Baskett & V. J. Marsick (Eds), *Professionals' ways of knowing: New findings on how to improve professional education.* (New Directions for Adult and Continuing Education, no. 55, pp. 109-118). San Francisco: Jossey-Bass.

Bloland, P. A., Stamatakos, L. C., & Rogers, R. R. (1994). *Reform in student affairs.* Greensboro, NC: ERIC Counseling & Student Services Clearinghouse.

Boyatzis, R. E., Cowen, S. S., Kolb, D. A., & Associates (1994). *Innovation in professional education: Steps on a journey from teaching to learning.* San Francisco: Jossey-Bass.

Clement, L. M., & Rickard, S. T. (1992). *Effective leadership in student services.* San Francisco: Jossey-Bass.

Crosson, P. M., & Nelson, G. M. (1984). *A profile of higher education doctoral programs.* Paper presented at the annual meeting of the Association for the Study of Higher Education. (ED 245 604).

Johnson, J. R., & Marcus, L. R. (1986). *Blue ribbon commissions and higher education: Changing academe from the outside.* (ASHE-ERIC Higher Education Reports No. 2). Washington, DC: Association for the Study of Higher Education.

Keim, M. C. (1991). Preparation program faculty: A research description. *NASPA Journal, 28,* 231-242.

Keim, M. C., & Graham, J. W. (Eds.). (1994). *Directory of graduate preparation programs in college student personnel 1994.* Washington, DC: American College Personnel Association—Commission XII.

Komives, S. R. (1993). Advancing professionally through graduate education. In M. J. Barr & Associates, *The handbook of student affairs administration* (pp. 390-411). San Francisco: Jossey-Bass.

McDade, S. A., Andersen, K. E., White, F. L., & Santos, M. (1994). Programs sponsored by multicampus systems, consortia, networks, and associations. In S. A. McDade & P. H. Lewis (Eds.), *Developing administrative excellence: Creating a culture of leadership.* (New Directions for Higher Education, no. 87, pp. 41-54). San Francisco: Jossey-Bass.

Murphy, J. (1991). Bridging the gap between professors and practitioners. *NASSP-Bulletin, 75,* 22-30.

Nystrand, R. O. (1991). *Professional development schools: Toward a new relationship for schools and universities.* Washington, DC: ERIC Clearinghouse on Teaching and Teacher Education.

Task Force on Professional Preparation and Practice. (1989). *The recruitment, preparation, and nurturing of the student affairs professional.* A Report of the American College Personnel Association and the National Association of Student Personnel Administrators. Washington, DC: NASPA.

Teitel, L. (1994). *The advisory committee advantage: Creating an effective strategy for programmatic improvement* (ASHE-ERIC Higher Education Report, no. 1). Washington, DC: Association for the Study of Higher Education.

Part Four

Reactions: What, So What, Now What

The first three sections of this book have examined student affairs practice, the preparation of student affairs professionals, and linkages between practice and preparation. What does all this information mean, why is it important, and what do we do with it? In this section, three student affairs professionals react to the writings of our chapter authors and offer their thoughts about the implications of this material for the student affairs field. We chose as our reactors individuals who are at different points in their careers. Russ Jablonsky is an entry-level professional working in residence life and a relatively recent graduate of a leading masters program in student affairs. Jane Fried is a student affairs educator who has an extensive background in student affairs practice. She could be characterized as a mid-career professional. Lee Upcraft has had a long and distinguished career as a practitioner-scholar. He recently retired from his position as Associate Vice President for Student Affairs but continues to teach and conduct research on a part-time basis.

In his chapter, Jablonsky identifies two themes in the earlier writings. First, dramatic change is facing higher education and student affairs. Jablonsky urges the field to address this change proactively. Second, student affairs has been its own enemy in not resolving issues that have plagued the field since its inception. He notes that preparation programs have not adequately incorporated the standards the field has developed and that practitioners do not recognize the importance of preparation in hiring professionals. Both of these problems undermine professional identity. Jablonsky also addresses personal issues faced by beginning practitioners as they attempt to make decisions regarding their futures and map out a path for success in the field. He encourages more experienced professionals to take their roles as mentors seriously.

In Chapter 11, Fried expresses her concern about the either/or thinking she sees in some of the earlier chapters in this book. She encourages student affairs professionals to think with more complexity about the issues they face in order to come up with imaginative solutions. She also encourages student affairs professionals to look beyond their own area to the purposes and nature of the university as a whole. Fried sees ambiguity as a core component of the world in which we live and argues that its existence demands that we consider values and desired outcomes in student affairs practice relativistically and situationally. She also suggests a more flexible approach to preparation based on changing knowledge and skill requirements.

In Chapter 12, Upcraft expresses his opinions about the future of student affairs, which he believes will be more academically focused, more service oriented, and more reflective of the diversity of students entering higher education. He suggests that the survival of the field will depend on the degree to which it successfully incorporates these changing emphases. Upcraft advocates for changes in preparation that reflect these changes in the profession and better prepare professionals for the realities of practice. He also argues for closer links between student affairs faculty and practitioners and offers suggestions for accomplishing this goal.

In the Epilogue, Bob Young puts all the offered opinions and arguments into perspective with an "Alice-in-Wonderland, through-the-looking-glass" analysis. He humorously demonstrates that passions can run high as student affairs practitioners and educators argue their points of view. His basic premise is that student affairs professionals must each determine their own philosophy for carrying out their work, but that the basic goal of helping students is similar for everyone in the student affairs profession regardless of how they go about it.

Chapter Ten

The State of the Art: A New Professional's Perspective

Russ Jablonsky

The first nine chapters of this book describe student affairs at a crossroads. Institutions of higher education do not appreciate us; the general public does not understand what we do; our profession is still coping with its identity crisis; our students are diversifying in their cultural ethnicity, age, and readiness for college; and our graduate preparation programs fall short in preparing new professionals for today's organizational turbulence. Where is the off-ramp? It reminds me of the closing scene in every episode of the Jetsons cartoon show. George is calmly walking his dog Astro on the treadmill when the cat jumps onto the treadmill and entices Astro to start chasing it. Pretty soon George is on the treadmill by himself going around and around at full speed while yelling, "Jane, stop this crazy thing . . . Jane!" According to the authors of this book, the higher education treadmill is speeding up in ways that will significantly impact the student affairs profession.

As I read the chapters through my lens as a newer student affairs practitioner, two themes emerged for me. First, change in higher education, including student affairs, will occur in dramatic ways. We can either actively oppose change and have it thrust upon us anyway, passively await change, or assertively embrace change and help shape the evolution of higher education. Second, we as a student affairs profession are our own worst enemy. Our inability to resolve issues related to our profession since its inception weakens us as we face a future of significant change. I will respond to some of the pertinent issues raised by the chapter authors as they relate to these themes and conclude with some personal thoughts about our profession.

IMPENDING CHANGE IN HIGHER EDUCATION

Several authors in this book have appropriately cited the changing world of higher education as a major factor for student affairs practitioners. Woodard clearly states the case in Chapter 1 that higher education is changing because it has to change. The tough questions of "What shall we become?" and "How should we get there?" are yet to be finalized. In answering these questions, we are forced to address our core values of higher education and frame the greater context in which to view changes within student affairs practice. As higher education evolves, we will have opportunities to (a) establish more fluid organizational structures that allow higher education to take advantage of, versus succumb to, the speed of change, (b) examine the current university culture while shaping a more collaborative campus community for the future, and (c) choose our personal response to the change process. I will address these three issues in this section.

The recent trend sweeping across college campuses to downsize administrative structures has not lessened the outcry from politicians, governing boards, students, and taxpayers for increased fiscal accountability, more relevant career training, shorter time to degree, and less post-graduation debt. In the evolution of higher education, these restructuring exercises may only be the loosening of pebbles toward an impending avalanche of change. The future will require higher education to create organizational structures to be more responsive to and comfortable with the changedrivers of the future. In other words, as the rate of change increases, success and survival will correlate with an institution's ability to modify its curriculum, programs, services, and personnel. Currently, higher education is viewed publicly as slow to change. Recent criticism has interpreted this to mean higher education does not want to change or progress under its own direction and must be forced to do so.

Woodard describes current changedrivers in Chapter 1 that require extensive examination and definition of who we are and what our purpose is. I believe that the challenge facing higher education is to achieve a level of comfort with change that allows us to respond to future challenges in a more timely manner. Higher education seems to be reacting to changedrivers as opposed to being readily prepared for impending changes. One explanation for this perception may be the current state of our campus communities. Boyer (1990) describes universities as being organized into "bureaucratic fiefdoms" where efforts to meet the overall interests of students have to compete with efforts to maintain the status of a particular department, college, or division. The creation of dynamic universities more capable of changing to meet challenges requires a healthy campus community. The invisible walls of territoriality on a college campus must give way to collaboration and open dialogue in order for universities of the future to effectively face the challenges that lie ahead

Closely related to forming more dynamic organizational structures is the underlying professional relationships which form the campus culture. Love, Kuh, MacKay, and Hardy (1993) use a cultural perspective to describe the different values and perceptions faculty and student affairs practitioners have of each other. If the quality and quantity of institutional dialogue is a key factor in becoming more adaptive to change, then student affairs practitioners and faculty need to forge a deeper understanding of and appreciation for the roles each other play on a college campus. Similarly, student affairs practitioners must be generally knowledgeable about and collaborative with all student affairs functions. No person, department, or division can afford to operate in a vacuum. New professional partnerships must be shaped throughout the campus community while maintaining such relationships where they currently exist.

Moore and Neuberger note in Chapter 4 a "question everything" mentality that is taking hold among the various publics served by a university. How we respond to such questions says a lot about who we are as professionals. Depending on your daily perception, higher education is either going through an exciting metamorphosis, imminent chaos, or both simultaneously. From an exciting metamorphosis perspective, student affairs practitioners have a tremendous opportunity and responsibility to shape the future of higher education. From an imminent chaos perspective, impending change makes people feel ostracized and powerless. I have witnessed the emergence of two very different professional responses to the evolutionary changes facing higher education. One response focuses on communication, collaboration, empowerment, and consensus in creating the future of higher education through the chaos of the present. The other response focuses on using the chaos of impending change to limit information, gain political power, and manipulate decision making processes. Student affairs professionals knowledgeable about group dynamics and skilled at facilitating dialogue between various stakeholders can be a valuable asset to their colleges and universities in this era of change.

WE HAVE SEEN THE ENEMY AND IT IS US

The second theme that emerged for me is that our profession's unresolved problems are long-standing and perpetuated by ourselves through our professional organizations, graduate preparation programs, and daily practice. In particular, three inter-related issues continue to plague our profession. As a profession we are still wrestling with an identity crisis that emerged from our inception as we were created to assume responsibilities originally bestowed upon faculty. Graduate preparation programs which were created to service our profession as it grew into existence contribute to our search for identity with the variety of curriculum offered from program to program. As a result, practitioners do not operate from a common knowledge base. Consequently, student affairs practitioners learn to devalue the knowledge base of the profession. Without a common knowledge base, our profession will continue to struggle for its identity.

The student affairs profession is still trying to identify who we are and what role we serve within higher education. Fenske (1989) summarizes the struggle by stating ". . . that almost throughout the field's historical existence it has never had a single functional focus, has never been stable in its role over significant periods of time, and has never had a consensual integrative philosophy" (p. 27). Our profession's inability to establish a credible and coherent identity throughout our history within higher education makes us especially vulnerable as we face an uncertain future. Our inability to self-identify as a profession subjects us to being defined by others as higher education evolves. Functional areas will be judged by whatever criteria is established for the new higher education system. For example, if the main criteria is learning, then current student affairs functional areas will be judged by how they contribute to student learning. Functional areas that fall outside the established criteria will be identified as true services that could be outsourced, eliminated, or continued depending on the fiscal realities of the time.

So, who are we and what is our purpose? According to Rentz and Knock (n.d.), student affairs practitioners are designers of educational activities outside the classroom that enrich students. The 1937 *Student*

Personnel Point of View (American Council on Education, 1937) refers to the emerging student affairs practitioner as "a new type of educational officer to take over the more intimate responsibilities which faculty members had originally included among their duties" (p. 50). McEwen and Talbot report in Chapter 7 that the foundation of the CAS standards is to prepare student affairs practitioners as professionals in higher education who promote student learning and development. If students are to learn from us and we are designers of educational activities to foster that learning, then we are educators. Even though that may or may not be a profound statement, it raises some interesting issues. As educators, we should be able to

(a) define our curriculum and its learning objectives,
(b) understand the learning environment in which we work,
(c) demonstrate adequate teaching skills,
(d) understand the learning process,
(e) understand the students we teach, and
(f) assess the outcomes of their learning.

In Chapter 7, McEwen and Talbot describe the essential components of the master's degree curriculum in student affairs. Comparing these components to the preparation needs of student affairs educators shows that aspects of curriculum design, development of learning objectives, and teaching skills are noticeably absent. Assessment has been emphasized in recent years, but the implementation process is slow because we do not think in terms of learning objectives and measuring those outcomes. Other aspects, such as learning theory and environments, may or may not be adequately covered depending on the attention given to these components in the curriculum.

It is widely known that masters programs emphasize one of three tracks; administration, counseling, or student development. I have found that one must look beyond the title of the masters program and examine the core requirements of its curriculum in order to determine its emphasis. In viewing the *Directory of Graduate Preparation Programs in College Student Personnel* (1994), some programs devote a full third of their masters degree to counseling courses. Surely, these programs would be hard pressed to claim that they produce "educators" for our profession. What is professed as essential components for graduate preparation and what is actually taught do not appear to be consistent from program to program. Again, the profession itself can self-determine its path in relation to this issue.

McEwen and Talbot remind us in Chapter 7 of the importance of the CAS standards as a set of guidelines with which to evaluate graduate preparation programs. Even though I believe in the value of having some established set of standards guiding preparation programs, I question the overall effect it has on the profession. Practitioners also have a vital role to play. It is my contention that quality control measures implemented for graduate preparation programs are only as effective as the hiring practices implemented by practitioners. In other words, current practitioners must utilize hiring practices that value the educational background of those they recruit for job openings in order for that knowledge to be meaningful in practice.

A quick overview of job announcements implies that a masters degree in college student personnel or a related field is simply a yes or no issue without regard for the quality of that degree. It's as if the profession wants masters degrees, yet is indifferent to the knowledge represented by such a degree. Meanwhile, several stipulations are typically required regarding a candidate's previous job-related experiences. If our hiring practices are skewed toward differentiating candidates based solely upon their experiences, we lower the expected educational credentials of our candidates and in turn, devalue our profession. Because our profession does not reward people for their knowledge, there is little incentive to remain current with the literature. Given two candidates with masters degrees, a candidate with twice as much related experience is too often viewed to be a more qualified candidate for a promotion than one with twice as much knowledge. Fenske (1989) reports that historically our field has been viewed by others as a "haven for the incompetent" and "anti-intellectual" (p. 43). We perpetuate that perspective with our current hiring practices. Again, we can solve the problems we have created for ourselves.

PERSONAL ISSUES

The personal realm described by Hirt and Creamer in Chapter 3 resonates with me as a new professional. In talking with peers at my campus as well as student affairs professionals I know at other schools, I contend that these issues are important to the entire profession. Of particular importance is the issue of upward and lateral mobility. Hirt and Creamer point out that young practitioners tend to be highly involved in the professional association most relevant to their functional area. As a new professional enters the profession, one is immediately aware of the bottleneck to even move up to a mid-level position. With the chances of moving into a generalist senior-level position very unlikely, new professionals turn to the professional association of their functional area in hopes of distinguishing themselves and landing a solid mid-level position within their functional area. This creates a "catch-22" situation for new professionals. They are forced to choose between developing their generalist knowledge base for an uncertain position in their career or gaining professional prominence within their functional area. Those that try to do both expose themselves to increased chances for professional burnout.

The high attrition rate among practitioners is another key concern for our profession. With a masters degree considered to be the minimum level of education needed to work in the profession, the effort required to achieve such a degree does not appear to match the return on that investment. In addition to the individual effort made by graduate students in obtaining their masters degree, much support and training is given by graduate assistantship, practicum, and summer internship sites. In this sense, our profession expends a tremendous amount of time, effort, and money in the recruitment, training, and education of relatively short-term employees.

The high availability of entry-level positions within the residence life functional area plays a role in the attrition of new professionals. The live-in requirement associated with virtually all of these positions creates a fishbowl existence unlike that associated with any other profession. Live-out positions in residence life are highly sought after as practitioners attempt to move up professionally and gain more freedom in their living options. One contributing factor in particular is the residence hall director apartment which is typically a one-bedroom place with little chance for expansion. For hall directors with dependents beyond a spouse or domestic partner, these required accommodations weigh heavily when deciding how long to stay in a live-in position. With residence life positions dominating the entry-level ranks, the profession could potentially improve its attrition problem significantly by addressing the transient nature of live-in professionals.

In Chapter 6, Evans and Williams report that students in graduate preparation programs expect their faculty to be mentors. I concur that faculty mentoring was an element I sought when selecting a graduate program. But, the mentoring role also has implications prior to and beyond graduate preparation. Mentoring is part of the generative nature of our profession. My involvement as an undergraduate increased my access to and interaction with student affairs practitioners on campus. My hall director, in particular, was instrumental in encouraging me to consider a career in student affairs. Like most college students, I had no idea that our profession existed until it was explained to me and I was able to see it in action. Beyond graduate school, mentoring continues to serve an important role for new practitioners as they enter the profession and begin the process of applying their graduate education. Practitioners can mentor new professionals by identifying career development options, knowledge deficiencies, and professional opportunities. Similar to what Komives described in Chapter 9 as a "process of continuing conversation," a continuous cycle of learning can be supported and enhanced through a viable mentoring relationship. Seasoned professionals have a responsibility to reach out to less-experienced professionals to form meaningful mentoring relationships. All practitioners have a responsibility to reach out to undergraduates in order to recruit future practitioners.

SUMMARY

The future for student affairs practice is cloudy at best. In a world of organizational chaos that defines the current state of higher education, some are trying to chase the clouds away, some are seeking shelter from the storm, and others are searching for rainbows. The optimist in me says there will be a rainbow in the end, but the realist in me says don't count on a pot of gold. I am convinced that our willingness to change the organizational structure that created us will be the key to our success. I believe we should welcome the chaos, nurture it, and allow it to unleash new creative organizations. In these new organizations, student affairs practitioners will have to be more aware of the academy. We will need to integrate our work with more diverse stakeholders as we build multiple campus constituencies. Collaboration and communication within and among departments will have to far surpass what exists today. To get there, we need to critically examine all of our closely held beliefs in order to remain organizationally flexible, professionally sharp, and developmentally meaningful in our work with students.

REFERENCES

American College Personnel Association. (1994). *Directory of graduate preparation programs in college student personnel.* Washington, DC: Commission on Professional Preparation (Commission XII) of the American College Personnel Association.

American Council on Education. (1937). The student personnel point of view. Reprinted in G. Saddlemire & A. Rentz (Eds.). (1986), *Student affairs: A profession's heritage.* (pp. 74-88). Media Publication, 40. Alexandria, VA: American College Personnel Association.

Boyer, E. (1990). *Campus life in search of community.* Princeton, NJ: The Carnegie Foundation for the Advancement of Teaching.

Fenske, R. H. (1989). Evolution of the student services profession. In U. Delworth & G. R. Hanson (Eds.), *Student services a handbook for the profession* (pp. 25-56). San Francisco: Jossey-Bass.

Love, P. G., Kuh, G. D., MacKay, K. A., & Hardy, C. M.(1993). Side by side: Faculty and student affairs cultures. In G. D. Kuh (Ed.), *Cultural perspectives in student affairs work* (pp. 37-58). Lanham, MD: American College Personnel Association.

National Association of Student Personnel Administrators, Inc. (1989). *Points of view.* Washington, DC: National Association of Student Personnel Administrators.

Rentz, A. L., & Knock, G. H. (n.d.). *Student affairs careers: Enhancing the college experience.* Washington, DC: Commission on Professional Preparation (Commission XII) of the American College Personnel Association.

Chapter Eleven

State of the Art, Current and Anticipated, in Student Affairs *or* Is Imagination Really More Important than Knowledge as Albert Einstein Once Remarked? Reaction from a Proactionary

Jane Fried

I really do believe, with Albert Einstein, that imagination is more important than knowledge. More importantly, I believe that either/or thinking almost always gets you into trouble and dualistic descriptions of situations are almost always misleading. Reality is always very complicated and doesn't fit into sound bites, provide easy answers to frustrating questions or allow completely accurate predictions of unfolding events. Both knowledge and imagination are essential in this era. My perspective is shaped by many years of work in residence hall systems, training both paraprofessional and professional staff and supervising all elements of a department of residence life. If any experience can teach a person about unpredictability it is certainly the responsibility for "managing" a residence hall system. In fact, "managing" and "residence hall system" are almost mutually contradictory. One can guide, steer, monitor or oversee a system; but at any given moment, one cannot control events or outcomes. There are too many people, too many variables, too many details, too many feelings, too many ideas, hopes, wishes and fears to support even an illusion of control. Residence hall administration is very good training for predicting the future and trying to steer the ship, knowing that the power of events frequently overwhelms the best laid plans.

After more than twenty years of "res life," the opportunity to direct a masters degree preparation program was a delightful change for me. Henry Kissinger once remarked that he couldn't think and work at the same time. Teaching provided me an opportunity to reflect on my experience, to imagine the future, and to look at trends and predictions about the future of student affairs and higher education. This chapter represents my reflections about the unpredictability we are now facing in higher education as it internationalizes and becomes rapidly responsive to changes in global economics, politics and transnational communication. I have attempted to understand the points made by all the chapter authors from the perspective of my best guesses about what's going to happen to our profession. Resident, full-time students between the ages of 18 and 24 are already the minority. Cross-cultural communication and effective group skills have become an essential part of a college education. Faculty/student affairs collaboration is also becoming essential for the professional survival of many individuals and institutions, grounded in part by the need for students to develop the communication and group skills in order to work effectively. I believe that we must imagine our way into the future. To the degree that we can stimulate thinking within the academy by bringing people from many different groups together to solve problems and address issues, I believe that we can create the new structures which the emerging era requires. The one point in which I believe without hesitation is that we can't go back- because back isn't there anymore.

PROFESSIONAL PURPOSE AND CONTEXT

Several themes emerge clearly as these authors consider the future of student affairs—economics, technology, diversity, global context and organizational structure. All the authors recognize the on-going influence which all these issues have, singly or interactively, on higher education. In addition, Woodard raised two important additional issues: the multiple, often conflicting, expectations which various publics have for higher education and the accountability of these institutions for achieving multiple outcomes which may also be in conflict. Moore and Neuberger also address these issues, particularly with regard to the roles which professional associations can serve in helping particular institutions access resources to develop assessment measures on their campuses. Two metathemes emerged for me: (a) the effect of the author's framing of the issues on the limits of the author's ability to imagine new ways to address these issues, and (b) the absence of much explicit discussion about the purposes/nature of the university and the goals and processes of student learning in an electronically linked knowledge network. My reading of all the chapters was shaped by two questions which address the issues suggested in the metathemes: (a) what knowledge will we need, and (b) what skills will we need as student affairs professionals in order to remain effective during the next era in higher education?

It seems that these two questions should frame our professional thinking so that we push ourselves into a futuristic mode for evaluating knowledge creation and skill development. As with all bureaucratized professionals, we are ever in danger of committing a fundamental error, "the delusion of learning from experience" (Senge, 1990, p. 23). If the past is not prologue, as Woodard implies, then learning from the past and using approaches, methods, and philosophies which have served us in previous eras may hamper us in the future. Our efforts to remain effective in smaller, more responsive organizational structures which manage learning centers in cyberspace must be guided by extremely creative thinking and the willingness to transcend the limits of past practice. Of everything that we might learn or learn how to do, what knowledge and skills will most help us as professionals to advance the goals of student learning and institutional well-being? Phelps Tobin demonstrates this type of thinking when she acknowledges that using recruiting techniques which worked in the past with dominant populations probably will not work in efforts to recruit members of non-dominant populations to our profession. She has moved beyond the paradigm which has historically shaped student affairs thinking, from inclusion of non-dominant groups at the price of their unique world views to real diversity of perspective and purpose.

These questions raise the whole issue of the purpose of our profession in the larger context of higher education. In an era of global interaction in all spheres of public life, including economics, technology, science and culture, universities are most effectively understood as situated processes in complex, dynamic contexts. The profession of student affairs is embedded in the cultural/educational milieu of the United States and is historically grounded in the English college tradition. It presumes the existence of a physical rather than virtual campus and a student body which is culturally and chronologically homogeneous. Moore and Neuberger raise some key questions with regard to our emerging workplace. Who should professional associations serve? Do we need to train more generalists? What would a generalist do in a campus which serves a large number of its students via electronic means? Will specialists be more vulnerable in smaller, more narrowly focused institutions? Will institutions choose which particular student services to provide and hire only specialists to provide the services? How will institutions balance the financial benefits of outsourcing with less measurable benefits of service provided by institutional employees?

In multinational, multicultural higher education, every embedded assumption of our profession should be reexamined, particularly those shaped by Christianity, individualism, objectivism and the linearity of cause-effect relationships (Fried, 1995). Higher education has begun to move seamlessly toward continuing education. Carpenter makes this case powerfully in his suggestions for integrating preparation program faculty into the continuing education process for members of our profession. Integration of scholars from other relevant disciplines including anthropology, sociology, philosophy, management, health and educational technology, can easily be imagined. This type of integration evokes past, present and future themes in student affairs as a continuous loop beginning with Esther Lloyd Jones' call for professors from many disciplines to study student and institutional needs and then collaborate in the processes of meeting the needs and advancing the institution (Lloyd-Jones & Smith, 1954).

LEARNING AS A NON-LOCAL PROCESS: ANTICIPATED AND UNANTICIPATED LEARNING

The classroom as the major learning location is diminishing in importance while distance learning, courses offered on the internet, and continuing education for all of the professions is exploding in accessibility and availability. Bair, Klepper, and Phelps Tobin have described the potential effect of these changes by reminding us that the profession of student affairs will remain effective only by shaping its mission as integral to the entire learning environment. The role of the faculty has begun to shift although this change may be slowed significantly by tenure constraints. Involvement in service learning, diversity training and other forms of experiential and interdisciplinary education have begun to melt the boundaries between living and learning (Fried, 1995). The Student Learning Imperative (ACPA, 1993) calls for the integration of learning, personal development and student development including academic progress because, "the quality of one's job performance, family life and community activities are highly dependent on cognitive *and* affective skills" (p. 118). Yet this document calls for student affairs professionals to *support* the academic mission of the institution, rather than involve ourselves as central participants. The Student Learning Imperative suggests collaboration between academic faculty and student affairs professionals, but fails to grasp the need to transcend the dichotomy between academic and experiential education. This historically limited perspective constrains student affairs to continuing marginality at exactly the time when institutions are open to expanding the mainstream of teaching and learning toward another continuous feedback loop of practice-to-theory-to-practice, often called the action-reflection cycle (Kolb, 1984) or praxis (Friere, 1990). New roles are emerging in the academy such as interpreter/linguist, translator, and transformational architect (Sundberg & Fried, 1997) which transcend narrow professional roles and function as roles for enhancing professional practice by stimulating discussion of issues which affect the entire institution.

The purposes of student development education and student affairs administration must be redefined because the organizational structures of our institutions are changing rapidly. The goals, needs, resources, time constraints and demographics of our student bodies are changing even more rapidly. Those who are attempting to engage in theory-based practice often rely largely on theories which embody assumptions that may be irrelevant to many of our students. These assumptions include ideas about normative age, place of birth, full- or part-time status, sexual orientation, religion, ethnicity, family role and world view. More significantly, these theories are generally grounded in objectivist epistemology which has been severely challenged as the dominant research method for addressing research questions in our diverse and rapidly changing institutions (Lincoln & Guba, 1985; Patton, 1991; Whitt, 1991). Bair, Klepper, and Phelps Tobin do an excellent job of describing the effects of these demographics on institutional mission, curriculum and learning environment. Their presentation of the learning opportunities created at The College of New Jersey and in service organizations in the Trenton, NJ area demonstrates the potential for cross-fertilization and enriched learning within limited budgets. Imagination and diversity of interests, needs and cultures are the major resources of all the programs they describe.

Woodard and Carpenter seem to appreciate the need for viewing change as a continuing, often uncomfortable process shaped by the themes identified above. They are setting up models for evolution and evaluation of change as well as ways to think about guiding the process. They frame the issues as a dynamic and interactive process, pointing out the key ideas which ought to be considered and investigated in depth without prescribing generic outcomes. Carpenter does a particularly effective job of picturing the dynamic tension between professional diversity and inclusivity and the establishment of professional standards. By suggesting that standard setting generally tends to privilege certain groups and classes and juxtaposing that circumstance to the commitment of all professions to altruistic motivation of serving clients, he shapes a continuing dialogue whose outcomes may change as circumstances change while its basic value commitment endures.

AMBIGUITY, CRITICAL THINKING AND CLARITY

The ambiguity of a process approach is sure to frustrate many members of this profession who make their living solving problems and focusing on concrete outcomes. However, ambiguity is a very accurate descriptor of the world in which we continue to live our evolving lives. Rather than confuse issues, the presence of ambiguity helps individual problem solvers clarify issues because it does not take any value or outcome as given. Ambiguity demands that we consider values and desired outcomes in the light of problems to be solved and that we recognize that most problems have multiple solutions. Woodard alludes to this situation when he discusses "change drivers" in higher education. Decline in economic resources is coupled with the difficulty of reducing costs in a labor intensive environment. Unfortunately, Woodard adopts the concepts of unit price increases, labor costs and productivity from the business world and does not challenge the utility of these notions in thinking about the economic tension in an educational environment. In education, product is process; service, learning, and knowledge production are the goals, and productivity rarely has a clear definition. Bair, Klepper, and Phelps Tobin present an alternative model which might transform the limit setting of which

Woodard is so conscious. They describe a continuously unfolding learning process which occurs in several kinds of learning communities on and off campus and enhances resources available to all participants. In Woodard's discussion of student demographics, he references *Power-Shift* (Toffler, 1990) and *Generations* (Strauss & Howe, 1991). Both books describe the American population as if it were more or less homogeneous, without making explicit references to the different experiences and perspectives of African Americans, other non-dominant populations, recent immigrants and internationals, all of whom study in our universities and who do not typically conform to the descriptions. Many of the problems Woodard cites cannot be adequately resolved using old paradigm thinking or its unquestioned assumptions. They can be productively explored, however, if the people exploring them can critique their own thought processes, make their assumptions visible and risk the loss of the privilege which current structures and belief systems permit them (Giroux, 1992; Sanchez & Fried, in press).

deBono (1994) suggests a simple exercise called the PMI to help people think outside the borders of their preconceived ideas. Use of the PMI suggests that all situations be explored by writing down their **P**lus aspects, their **M**inus aspects and their **I**nteresting aspects. People write individually and discuss what they have written. As people begin to realize that one element of a situation can appear on all three lists as prepared by three different people, the conversation begins to push the boundaries of the accepted. Interesting is a category beyond evaluation which can change the basis on which values judgments are made and make values visible. Increased tolerance of ambiguity, respect for the values and perspectives of others and ability to articulate the values of one's own group will be increasingly important in our diversely populated and valued institutions of the future. At the present time it appears that student affairs professionals have not spent enough time articulating the basic assumptions of the profession, challenging each other via **PMI** or any other critical thinking system or seeking out conversations with people outside our own profession in order to take advantage of the current state of ambiguity in higher education. I am not sure I share Carpenter's optimism about inertia as a non-problem in the current environment. Ambiguity and random activity can lead to innovation. They can also lead to entrenched repetition of beliefs as if they were dogma, and, in the best tradition of Maslow, reversion to meeting the basic security needs of all participants wherein academic cannibalism can easily result (Crookston, 1975).

RECRUITMENT, RETENTION AND PREPARATION

Ambiguity and dynamism as organizing constructs provoke some questions about the approaches to graduate preparation programs as well as recruitment and retention of students. By emphasizing skills and knowledge necessary for professional effectiveness, one becomes less concerned with length of program, quantitative admission and evaluation criteria and more concerned with learning experiences and outcomes. Should we continue to frame our ideas about professional preparation in terms of completion of a particular degree or should we integrate structures for continuing professional development, peer learning activities and student/faculty dialogue about student needs as part of an on-going learning process for the profession?

Carpenter and McEwen and Talbot explore these issues from contrasting perspectives. Carpenter acknowledges the fluidity of working contexts, client needs and so forth while calling for professional consensus about values and purpose. Carpenter's approach to the design of the CPE process reminds me of suggestions made by Schön in *Educating the Reflective Practitioner* (1987). Schön remarks that problems which are easily understood and solved by available technologies are satisfying to work on, but typically not very important. The most difficult and significant work occurs in unpredictable field settings where "naming and framing" (p. 4) problems becomes the most important task. Problems are not clearly defined. Generating solutions depends on the professional's ability to identify key elements and organize the response in order to move the situation forward. The key decisions are value decisions. Technology and resource allocation follows. In contrast, McEwen and Talbot present what is currently the best practice in the preparation of student affairs professionals, but they do this without reference to the context in which future student affairs professionals will work. Phelps Tobin, in her discussion of recruitment and retention, takes context clearly into account, both as it affects the current situation and as it might be improved to enhance recruitment in the future. By building on the strengths student affairs professionals typically have in relationship development, she can see our way to future transformations in an encouraging and hopeful manner, taking constraints into account but not being paralyzed by them.

It seems that knowledge and skill requirements should shape learning formats in preparation programs and that structure should become more flexible in response to changing delivery systems and student and institutional needs. Consequently preparation program faculty should have a significant role in this evolution as Carpenter suggests because of two resources they have—time to think and skills to conduct research. Despite the depressing picture which Evans and Williams present in terms of the multiple and often conflicting demands on faculty members' time, faculty productivity seems quite impressive. The typical scholarly output in a five-year period was one book, one edited book, several articles and several presentations at local and national conferences. In addition, Carpenter and Komives cite numerous types of consultation and service which many faculty provide to their institutions, particularly in the practitioner area of our discipline, the Division of Student Affairs. Administrators, in complementary fashion, tend to have first-hand knowledge of problems and access to more resources with which to conduct research and often are willing to speak to students in class about real-life problems and issues in professional practice. We should probably be blurring the role distinctions and increasing opportunities for dialogue so that the "problem to theory to research to practice" loop gets a lot of use. Komives' chapter on linkages provides an excellent map and numerous examples for this type of collaboration and mutual support.

DUALISTIC PERSPECTIVES AND INSOLUBLE PROBLEMS

The Creamer and Hirt chapter raises the issues of author perspective and framework. I believe that the reader can learn as much by examining how they think as what they think. The authors use a binary, or dualistic approach in which they acknowledge tension, but do not inquire about resolution or transformation. Because of the complexity of the current era, tension is inherent in everything we do or think about, but it is not a steady state. Rather than using "either/or thinking" which is traditional in science and American culture, the profession needs to develop "both/and/what next? thinking" to emerge from the paralysis and despair that seems to pervade this chapter. An either/or approach blocks movement toward a synthesis or a transcendence or a new paradigm. This chapter illustrates, through its binary approach, the limits of the old paradigm, zero/sum approaches. Particularly obvious to me is the identification of ethics as an area for personal concern, but not for institutional concern (Banning, 1997; Talley, 1997). Ethics for individuals without ethics in context leads only to the next job, the fruitless search for ethical perfection and a blame the victim mentality. The discussion of quality assurance displays another dimension of the traditional mind-set which will tend to block progress. What is quality in our evolving world? Is it more important to come to a mutual understanding of the term's meaning or to assume that we all mean the same thing and then try to identify ways to measure its presence or absence? What if quality has different definitions under different circumstances? Is quality a dynamic phenomenon or a static attribute, measured scientifically, appearing in similar form under widely varied circumstances? I believe that we should be raising these issues, rather than assuming agreement. Quality is profoundly affected by diversity, organizational structure, technology and economics.

Readers of this book would do well to engage actively with all the material presented and ask themselves how they might shape the next steps in their own professional development, what new areas they need to learn about and how they can use the information presented to shape their contributions to evolving post-secondary education. In the words of e.e. cummings "tomorrow is our permanent address—and there they'll scarcely find us (if they do, we'll move away still further: into now)" (1968, p. 412).

REFERENCES

American College Personnel Association. (1993). *The student learning imperative: Implications for student affairs.* Washington, DC: Author.

Banning, J. (1997). Assessing the campus' ethical climate: A multideminsional approach. In J. Fried (Ed.), *Ethics for today's campus: New perspectives on education, student development, and institutional management.* (New Directions for Student Services, no. 77, pp. 95-105). San Francisco: Jossey-Bass.

Crookston, B. (1975). Milieu management. *NASPA Journal, 13*(1), 45-55.

cummings, e. e. (1968). "all ignorance toboggans into know." In *Poems.* New York: Harcourt, Brace & World.

deBono, E. (1994). *deBono's thinking course.* New York: Facts on File.

Fried, J., & Associates (1995). *Shifting paradigms in student affairs: Culture, context, teaching and learning.* Washington, DC: American College Personnel Association.

Friere, p. (1990). *Pedagogy of the oppressed* (M. B. Ramos, Trans.). New York: Continuum.

Giroux, H. (1992). *Border crossings.* New York: Routledge.

Kolb, D. (1984). *Experiential learning.* New York: Praeger.

Lincoln, Y., & Guba, E. (1985). *Naturalistic inquiry.* Newbury Park, CA: Sage.

Lloyd-Jones, E., & Smith, K. (1954). *Student personnel work as deeper teaching.* New York: Harper and Brothers.

Patton, M. (1991). Qualitative research on college students: Philosophical and methodological comparisons with the quantitative approach. *Journal of College Student Development, 32,* 389-398.

Sanchez, W., & Fried, J. (in press). Giving voice to students' narratives: Cultural criticism and education in the helping/service professions. *College Teaching.*

Schön, C. (1987). *Educating the reflective practitioner.* San Francisco: Jossey-Bass.

Senge, P. (1990). *The fifth discipline.* New York: Doubleday.

Strauss, W., & Howe, N. (1991). *Generations: The history of America's future, 1584-2069.* New York: William Morrow.

Sundberg, D. C., & Fried, J. (1997). Ethical dialogues on campus. In J. Fried (Ed.), *Ethics for today's campus: New perspectives on education, student development, and institutional management.* (New Directions for Student Services, no. 77, pp. 67-79). San Francisco: Jossey-Bass.

Talley, F. J. (1997). Ethics in management. In J. Fried (Ed.), *Ethics for today's campus: New perspectives on education, student development, and institutional management.* (New Directions for Student Services, no. 77, pp. 45-66). San Francisco: Jossey-Bass.

Toffler, A. (1990). *PowerShift: Knowledge, wealth and violence at the edge of the 21st century.* New York: Bantam Books.

Whitt, E. (1991). Artful science: A primer on qualitative research methods. *The Journal of College Student Development, 32,* 406-415.

Chapter Twelve

Do Graduate Preparation Programs Really Prepare Practitioners?

M. Lee Upcraft

My reflections on how we train and prepare student affairs professionals are based on my experience both as a student affairs practitioner and affiliate graduate faculty member, as well as what I believe to be the future of student affairs in the next century. In this chapter, I will first present my own personal context for these reflections, then discuss what I believe to be the future of student affairs, and conclude with my recommendations for improving graduate preparation programs, based, in part, on a critique of the excellent writings of the authors of this monograph.

MY PERSONAL CONTEXT

I spent 31 years "in the trenches" administering and leading at almost every level of student affairs, in virtually every functional area, including residence halls, psychological services, career services, health services, health education, orientation, veterans affairs, women's services, adult student services, disability services, Greek life, student activities, student unions, off-campus student services, and many others. I have recruited, selected, trained, supervised, and evaluated literally hundreds of student affairs professionals, many of whom were products of student affairs graduate preparation programs.

Concurrently, I served as an affiliate faculty in two graduate preparation programs, teaching a wide range of courses, and advising scores of graduate students. I have supervised internships, directed theses at both the masters and doctoral level, and written more letters of recommendation than I care to remember. Along the way, I managed to write and publish, based on both my experience as a practitioner and my research.

So I have seen, first hand, the dilemmas of both the practitioner and the faculty who prepare practitioners. Unfortunately, I also saw tensions between these two groups. For example, some of my practitioner colleagues believe that preparation programs are run by people with little or no practical experience, or recent practical experience, who are disconnected from the realities of practice, and unable to translate their wonderful theories into practice. Many practitioners believe that many graduate programs focus too much on counseling and not enough on more general interpersonal skills and administrative skills. The result: they believe they spend too much time "reorienting" graduates of student affairs preparation programs to the realities of practice.

On the other hand, some of my faculty colleagues see my administrative colleagues as people, who are, at best, too busy to keep up-to-date on current theory, literature, and research, and at worst, distrustful of anything theoretical or impractical. They lament the lack of scholarly rigor of many practitioners, who often act in ignorance of, or knowingly contrary to relevant literature and research. Many faculty believe that student affairs programs are too bureaucratic and institutionally oriented to serve the best interests of students and their development. The result: they believe they devote a lot of time to developing attitudes and skills that are quickly eroded by administrative environments where student development gives way to bureaucratic priorities and political agendas.

Nowhere is this schism more evident than in our two major professional organizations: practitioners are more typically drawn to NASPA, while faculty are more likely to affiliate with ACPA. While some practitioners and faculty are active in both organizations, when one looks at the conference programs, NASPA tends to be practitioner and administratively focused, while ACPA tends to be more theory, research, and counseling based. This schism is also evident in those institutions where the preparation program and the student affairs division operate independently from one another. The schism sometimes becomes a chasm, particularly if the practitioners are trained in fields other than student affairs.

So I offer my reflections in the context of having been on both sides of the preparation equation, although I must admit to a bias in the direction of the practitioners.

THE FUTURE OF STUDENT AFFAIRS

Before I can offer my reflections on preparation programs for the 21st century, I must first map what I see as the future of student affairs. Based on the trends of the past ten years, I have concluded that student affairs operations will be quite different from the ways in which we have done business since the demise of in loco parentis in the sixties, and the emergence of student development as the *raison d'etre* of our existence: it will be more academically focused, more basic service oriented, and reflect the broadening diversity of our students.

Unfortunately, the student affairs profession is somewhat divided on the reason for its existence (Upcraft, Schuh, & Associates, 1996). One view is probably represented best by the NASPA publication, *A Perspective on Student Affairs* (1987) in which the first assumption identified is that the academic mission of an institution is preeminent.

> Colleges and universities organize their primary activities around the academic experience: the curriculum, the library, the classroom, and the laboratory. The work of student affairs should not compete with and cannot substitute for . . . that academic enterprise. As a partner in the educational enterprise, student affairs enhances and supports the academic mission. (pp. 9-10)

A second perspective is best described as promoting student development. That is, there are certain developmental goals (such as psychosocial development, attitudes and values formation, moral development, and career choice and development) which are related to, but somewhat apart from academic goals such as verbal, quantitative, and subject matter competence, and cognitive and intellectual growth. In this view, student affairs assumes the primary responsibility for the achievement of developmental goals, while faculty assume the primary responsibility for the achievement of academic goals. Thus, everything we do in this scenario must somehow contribute to students' development (Upcraft, Schuh, & Associates, 1996).

To complicate matters even further, according to Upcraft, Schuh, & Associates (1996), a third perspective holds that while academic and developmental outcomes are important, other equally important institutional and societal expectations must be addressed. Providing basic services, such as housing, financial aid, admissions, and registrar, is vital to an institution, somewhat independent of any educational or developmental outcome. For example, students need money to pay for college, and institutions assume some responsibility for helping them do this, not necessarily because of students' educational or developmental interests, but because if students can't afford college, they won't attend.

Of course, in reality, we do all three: our services and programs contribute both to academic and developmental goals of students, as well as providing basic services to students and other clientele. It is also a reality that in an era of declining resources, the academic and basic services rationales are much more likely to be supported by faculty budget committees and upper-level administrative officers (Upcraft, Schuh, & Associates, 1996).

There is substantial evidence to support this conclusion. Over the past ten years, as resources have become more scarce, there are strong indications that "student services have borne the brunt of budget cuts . . . For college administrators, it was a Hobson's choice: to shield academic programs from severe cuts, all other budget categories had to suffer a disproportionate share of reductions" (Cage, 1992, p. A25). Examples include substantial cuts in student activities and support for student government, reduction in career and psychological counseling staff and outright elimination of programs and services, such as legal counseling. In addition, some student services have survived only by initiating fees for services such as placement, health services, student activities, and counseling (Cage, 1992). Another trend is to eliminate selected services and programs, on the assumption that student needs can be met by off campus and community services (Upcraft, Schuh, & Associates, 1996).

Of course, the increasing diversity of our students will be a powerful factor in the future of student affairs. Diversity is typically defined as the increasing representation of students based on race, ethnicity, gender, age, sexual orientation, country of origin, disability, veterans status, and other descriptors. However, as Upcraft (1995) points out, above and beyond these shifts, other significant changes are occurring. Our campuses today include students who are more politically and religiously conservative, less politically active, more likely to come from dysfunctional or abusive families, more likely to have been raised in single parent or blended families, more likely to suffer from serious psychological pathology, more likely to have histories of health problems such as drug and alcohol abuse, more likely to be paying a greater share of the cost of their education, and less likely to have sufficient academic preparation to succeed in college.

They also include students who study part time (now nearly 40% of the total enrollment in higher education), and live off campus. These students often have family and work responsibilities which limit their collegiate experience to going to classes. They often miss the enriched out-of-class environment experienced by their full time, residential colleagues. In fact, according to Upcraft (1995), only one in seven students in higher education is (a) 18 to 22 years old, (b) studying full time, and (c) living on campus. The problem is that often we develop student services and programs as if most of our students have these combinations of characteristics, when, in fact, they do not.

I believe that for the foreseeable future, the survival and effectiveness of student affairs lies in the extent to which (a) we provide basic services, (b) our mission, services, and programs promote students' academic development, and (c) we respond to the broadening diversity of our students, as defined above. In fact, a recent ACPA (1993) statement tries to move our profession more in this direction. *The Student Learning Imperative: Implications for Student Affairs* proposes to refocus the rationale of our profession to the concept of student learning. While not abandoning student development as a viable rationale, this document clearly moves our rationale more in the direction of our responsibility for students' learning and academic development, including complex cognitive skills and knowledge acquisition. It also calls for us to be committed to meeting the needs of our increasingly diverse students.

So I believe the profession for which we are preparing graduate students will undergo profound changes in the next ten years. Put simply, those services and programs which are considered "basic" to the institution, or contribute directly to the academic mission of the institution, or contribute directly to meeting the needs of our increasing diverse students will receive priority. Other services will be downsized, eliminated, "outsourced" to the community, or continued on a "fee for service" basis.

The implications for our profession are enormous. It means, among many other things, more involvement of faculty with our services and programs, more partnerships with academic units, greater efforts to assess our impact, using academic outcomes such as knowledge acquisition, cognitive development, academic achievement and retention to assess our effectiveness, and more use of the classroom by student affairs in pursuit of our mission in the areas such as orientation, health education, multiculturalism, and leadership development. Put another way, as Bair, Klepper, and Phelps Tobin argue, there must be a stronger integration of the curricular and the co-curricular.

It also means that those involved in "basic" services, or administering academically focused services and programs, must have administrative skills such as problem solving, mediation, decision making, planning, organizing, budgeting, assessment, and public relations. It will also mean the ability to recruit, hire, select, train, supervise, and evaluate staff. It means knowing and understanding the political dimensions of organizations, and how to work within the interpersonal realities of an institution. It also means being on the cutting edge of the applications of technology to our services and programs as well as exploring the implications of technology for individual student development, and for the various human environments in which we are involved.

And finally, it means that we must be prepared to meet the needs of our increasingly diverse students. It means focusing our services and programs on traditionally underrepresented groups, both individually and collectively. It means helping both minority and majority groups relate to one another in positive and collaborative ways. It also means going beyond a narrow definition of diversity to include meeting the needs of our students who differ on other dimensions discussed above.

IMPLICATIONS FOR GRADUATE PREPARATION

Given this vision of the future of student affairs, within the context of the writings in this monograph, I see the following implications for graduate preparation programs:

1. The theoretical foundations must be restructured to reflect more broadly the realities of our profession.

I believe both McEwen/Talbot and Evans/Williams are right when they argue that the components of an effective preparation curriculum should include the theoretical foundations of higher education, as well as the student affairs profession. The problem comes in translating this principle into practice. Too often, the historical and philosophical foundations of higher education are omitted, and the theoretical foundations of the student affairs field are too narrow. For example, many masters programs focus exclusively on developmental/psychological/counseling theoretical foundations as a basis for practice, giving little or no attention to the context of higher education, organizational theory, environmental theory, and learning/pedagogical theory.

2. The curriculum must be revised to reflect the present and future realities of our profession.

If I am right about the future of our profession, then the curriculum must be made more relevant to practice. If we are educating people to be administrators and teachers, as well as advisers and counselors, then our courses should reflect a greater emphasis on organization and administration, and less emphasis on counseling and development. Further, there must be more emphasis on practice and less emphasis on theory, and perhaps more importantly, more emphasis on the translation of theory to practice. As both Woodard and Hirt/Creamer point out, there must also be some consideration given to technology. And finally, as McEwen/Talbot and Phelps Tobin have pointed out, there must be some emphasis on how to deal effectively with the increasing diversity of students, particularly relations among diverse students.

I recently reviewed a promotional brochure from what most would consider an outstanding masters preparation program offered at a first rate regional state university. The brochure says the program will prepare graduates to succeed in a variety of student affairs units, including admissions, housing, residence life, financial aid, orientation, placement, student activities, etc. The content is summarized to include (a) theories of student development, organizational development, and historical context, (b) dimensions of professional practice such as ethical, multicultural, and political issues, and (c) administrative issues such as leadership, budgeting and planning, and assessment.

So far, so good. Based on this information, I would conclude that this program would meet all of my expectations for preparing graduates for the 21st century. But a look at the courses purported to meet their stated objectives belies what they say they are doing. Of the required credit hours, one third are in individual counseling and psychology. (The reader will note that "counseling" does not appear as one of the units listed above for which the student will be prepared). One can assume the designers of this program assume one or more of the following: (a) most of their graduates will be in counseling positions (which is unlikely), (b) if one successfully masters individual and group counseling skills, one is prepared to do any masters level job in student affairs (which is debatable), and (c) most of their graduates will not teach in the classroom (which is unlikely, over the span of their careers).

On the plus side, practica and internships make up about 20 percent of the program, and other courses include technology in student affairs, social and cultural diversity, research methods, and student development. But there is only one course on administration, no courses on environmental theory and practice, no courses on learning/pedagogy, and the practica and internship sites are entirely within student affairs. Based upon the courses taken by students, I can only conclude that this program will be very unlikely to deliver on its claim to adequately prepare students for the jobs they list in their brochure.

3. The curriculum must be revised to prepare graduates to meet the needs of our increasingly diverse student population.

I agree with McEwen/Talbot that preparation curricula must be responsive to changing student demographics, and in general, I would give our preparation programs very high marks for accomplishing this task. However, too often these efforts are focused too much on individual student development, and not enough on the collective impact of this diversity, and on the issues of how various campus groups relate to one another. Racial tensions abound on campuses across the country, and women continue to experience "chilly" climates, both inside and outside the classroom, yet very little is included in graduate preparation programs to address group and community issues. As McEwen/Talbot point out, development of a caring community is an overarching curricular issue which pervades all other issues.

Further, as demonstrated earlier in this chapter, our definition of diversity is too narrow. Our preparation programs must be expanded beyond race/ethnicity and gender diversity to include meeting the needs of part time students, those living off campus, and older students. They must also address the needs of increasingly troubled students, students with different sexual orientations, international students, disabled students, those with insufficient academic preparation, those from non-traditional families, those from troubled families, and politically and religiously conservative students.

4. Full time faculty must be transformed to reflect closer connections with practice.

While I agree with Evans/Williams that one of the qualifications for preparation faculty should be professional experience, I would argue in more specific terms: it is essential that faculty have had significant experience in student affairs, not only at entry and mid-levels, but preferably at high levels as well. Too often, preparation faculty do not have sufficient breadth and depth of professional experience needed to train practitioners.

Further, because this experience becomes less relevant as time goes by, faculty must have some continuing role in practice on a part-time basis. For example, faculty teaching counseling courses should carry a few clients in personal counseling or career centers. Faculty with professional expertise on issues such as race relations, drug and alcohol abuse, gender equity, conflict management, or assessment might be used as consultants to the student affairs leadership for policy development, decision making, and problem solving.

One of the more disturbing findings of a survey of graduate students reported by Evans/Williams is that they felt they learned more from practitioners in the field than from faculty. In part, this is a reflection of students who are in too much of a hurry to learn practice before they learn theory and research. It is also an indictment of faculty who are unable or unwilling to help students make connections between theory and practice.

On a more personal note, while I always suspected that the longer faculty are estranged from practice, the less effective they are, I am now experiencing that disconnection. I retired about two years ago, and as every day goes by, I feel more out-of-touch with practice. My graduate seminar on students, which was liberally infused with practical issues when I was an administrator, is less and less becoming a course based in the context of current practice, and that does not serve my students well.

5. Practitioners must become more connected to preparation programs.

Faculty aren't the only ones in need of a role transformation. Komives argues that one way for graduate programs to link to practice is for practitioners to be involved in graduate programs. I couldn't agree more. However, while she argues that there are often mixed reactions on whether academic appointments for administrators are positive, I believe that on the whole, they are not only positive, but needed. Practitioners must become more involved in preparation programs, and I don't mean just teaching and advising students. It won't work unless practitioners become more committed to scholarly endeavors, keep up to date on the literature in the field, and collaborate with faculty on research. Nothing is a bigger waste of time than uninformed practitioners who believe all they have to do is show up for class after class and "share their experiences" as a practitioner.

Further, practitioners should see their work setting as a learning environment for graduate students, creating and supervising practica and internships. But this means more than just giving students a few hours a week in some office. It means framing these experiences in the light of theory, literature, and research in the field. This assumes, of course, that practitioners are up-to-date scholars, which is often not the case.

Phelps Tobin has pointed out that graduate students often choose the student affairs profession because one or more student affairs staff served as role models. The involvement of practitioners in graduate programs can provide a continuing opportunity for students to stay involved with professional role models, and integrate the shared values of the profession.

Going back to the brochure mentioned above, only one full-time faculty member was listed, so I must assume that other faculty are drawn from other disciplines. I happen to know of two respected and fairly well known practitioners at this institution who, apparently, have little or no connection to this program, and that is a tragic missed opportunity for strengthening this program.

6. Students must be recruited to preparation programs on the basis of present and future realities of our profession.

Too often, students are interested in pursuing student affairs as a profession, or recruited to student affairs graduate programs for the wrong reasons. For example, resident assistants may find a great deal of satisfaction in their job, and most likely worked with student affairs professionals whom they respected and admired. Flattered by the student's admiration, and impressed by his or her abilities, the mentor suggests going into student affairs as a career, and encourages immediate enrollment in a graduate program.

While I agree with Phelps Tobin that professional role models can be an important factor in choosing a career in student affairs, this scenario, while typical, is sometimes lethal. For one thing, there are no professional jobs in student affairs that come anywhere close to an RA's job, and to decide upon a student affairs career based upon the satisfaction gained from an RA job is, in my opinion, a mistake. Half of the persons entering our profession leave after five or six years, and I believe one of the reasons is that this profession is not like the RA job or student leadership role they experienced as undergraduates.

While I prefer that graduate students have some full time experience before enrolling in a graduate program, I also know this is not very realistic (the impossible dilemma: in order to get experience, a graduate degree is required; in order to get a graduate degree, experience is required). However, both practitioners and faculty can do a better job of providing more realistic pictures of our profession, and helping the student make a more reasoned career decision.

We should also be mindful of the job market. It is wrong to mindlessly recruit students to fill admissions quotas if we know, with some degree of certainty, that there are too many graduates and not enough jobs. Too often, the number of students admitted to graduate programs is based upon the enrollment needs of the program, rather than a realistic assessment of the job market.

7. Practica and internships must involve not only traditional student services, but academically related services and programs, and teaching in the classroom.

I have discussed earlier the importance of practica and internships to a graduate preparation program. I now argue that we should not restrict these experiences to student affairs settings. If I am right about the necessity to connect student affairs and academic affairs, and the viability of using courses to implement our goals, then internship and practica should include not only student services, but also academic support services and opportunities for supervised teaching in the classroom. This means all of us, both faculty and practitioners must know a lot more about teaching and learning, student learning styles, teaching methods, and other pedagogical issues.

8. The gender balance of students in preparation programs and in student affairs must be addressed.

An issue not discussed in this monograph, but frequently whispered about by faculty and practitioners, is the gender imbalance in preparation programs and in the profession: Up to 75 percent of graduates in preparation programs are women. Twenty years ago, this ratio was approximately reversed. At the risk of being labeled a sexist, I would argue that a student affairs profession dominated by women is as detrimental to our profession and our students in somewhat the same ways as when our profession was dominated by men. We need a balance of men and women, and currently that is not the case. We must actively recruit men and women to our profession, but it appears we must make a special effort to attract men. This issue has been little discussed, and to my knowledge, little studied to determine why men are increasingly disinterested in our profession. But we must talk more about and do more about this imbalance.

9. The gender imbalance among faculty in preparation programs must be addressed.

While women students are dominating graduate preparation programs, and becoming a majority of student affairs professionals, as pointed out in this monograph, a majority of faculty in graduate preparation programs are men. We must do more to remove barriers which prevent women from assuming greater responsibility for graduate preparation programs, such as valuing research which is based upon non-traditional assumptions and methods, extending time limitations for promotion and tenure, eliminating sexist and discriminatory administrative practices, and providing more mentoring opportunities for women.

10. Continuing professional education of both faculty and practitioners is essential.

Carpenter argues that since many people enter the student affairs profession with no student affairs training or background, professional development is even more essential than in other professions. Moore and Neuberger's chapter outlines the importance of professional associations in this endeavor. I agree with both points of view, because without professional education, both our profession and our professionals will become less relevant to higher education and the students we serve.

CONCLUSION

Preparation programs must, above all, be connected to and reflect the realities of current and future practice, if they are to *really* prepare practitioners for the millennium and beyond. So my answer to the question posed by this chapter, "Do graduate preparation programs really prepare practitioners?" is "Not yet." To achieve this goal, I believe that both the curriculum and faculty of preparation programs must change substantially, and practitioners must get more involved if we are to produce professionals who will be successful in our field. We owe them, our students, and ourselves, nothing less.

REFERENCES

American College Personnel Association. (1993). *The student learning imperative: Implications for student affairs.* Washington, DC: Author.

Cage, M. C. (1992, November 18). To shield academic programs from cuts many colleges pare student services. *The Chronicle of Higher Education*, pp. A25-A26.

National Association of Student Personnel Administrators. (1987). *A perspective on student affairs.* Washington, DC: Author.

Upcraft, M. L. (1995). Teaching and today's college students. In R. J. Menges, M. Weimer, & Associates, *Teaching on solid ground: Using scholarship to improve practice* (pp. 21-41). San Francisco: Jossey-Bass.

Upcraft, M. L., Schuh, J. H., & Associates (1996). *Assessment for student affairs.* San Francisco: Jossey-Bass.

Epilogue

A Heretical Bit of Whimsy

Robert B. Young

"Who are you?" said the Caterpillar.

This was not an encouraging opening for a conversation. Alice replied, rather shyly, "I—I hardly know, sir, just at present—at least I know who I *was* when I got up this morning, but I think I must have been changed several times since then."

"What do you mean by that?" said the Caterpillar sternly, "Explain yourself."

"I can't explain *myself*, I'm afraid sir," said Alice, "because I'm not myself, you see."

Lewis Carroll
Alice's Adventures in Wonderland

What is Alice doing in some commentary about student affairs preparation and practice? Both nothing and everything as Lewis Carroll might say. *Alice's Adventures in Wonderland* had nothing to do with higher education but everything to do with an individual who was trying to understand her surroundings. Just as Carroll used Alice, the "only person with self-control," to "make sense and order" out of his England (Auden, 1962, p. 5), we shall see how Alice deals with some of the mangle in our profession.

We can extend her conversation with the Caterpillar [who sounds very much like a weary career counselor]:

> "Well, if you cannot explain who you are, then tell me what you do," said the Caterpillar.
>
> This seemed a much simpler question, so Alice said, "I do all sorts of things. I'm an R.A. and president of student government and a member of the track team and . . . oh yes, a business major, and a sorority member and I listen to *everybody* and. . . ."
>
> The Caterpillar had heard enough. "Enough," he said. "Do you mean to tell me that you are interested in student leadership and all such stuff?"
>
> "Oh no sir," Alice responded, "I would not go that far. All I know is that these days I seem to be just about anything that people want me to be."
>
> "If you cannot explain yourself, you cannot find yourself," said the Caterpillar. "Go on your way."
>
> "But which way, sir?" said Alice.
>
> "Every which way, since that seems to be where you are heading . . . But, oh bother, just follow one of the signs. Perhaps you will find someone out there to help you," the Caterpillar replied.

Poor Alice, caught at the crossroads between every which way and unable to explain herself to the only one who knows the directions. She sighs, turns around, and reads the signs before her. Turn right and she could go to Tish, the realm of student affairs practitioners. Turn left and she heads toward Fess, the strange world of professors . . . or she could go straight ahead to the student union.

Alice chooses the union. She might see some friends there and maybe help them with THEIR problems. That seems so much easier than deciding what to do for herself when she graduates from college.

Alice orders decaf at the coffee bar and takes it over to the table where Rob and Dorothy are sitting. Rob is drinking Maxwell House, black of course, and Dorothy is spooning extra sugar into her mocha latte. Alice is surprised to see Rob there. He was the president of student government when Alice was a sophomore. He finished graduate school last year and he's working somewhere in Tish. Dorothy was her big sister in the sorority; she's trying to get a masters degree over in Fess, in "student affairs," what a weird name. Alice sits down and sips her coffee while Rob talks to Dorothy. He seems pretty intense, but then Rob is ALWAYS intense.

Rob began, "Like here's how it is, Dorothy; it's all about practice. Just do it! It's on my Nikes and in my heart. I don't care what degree you've got or how much time you spend talking to students. If you don't give them something solid and make the rest of the administration happy while you're doing it, then you aren't a good professional."

He continued, "Like my mentor, Friday, says, 'If you are sitting alone behind a closed door, you aren't doing anything.' So morning, noon, and night, I'm in meetings, on the phone, or working with people in the office. That way I'm really proactive. What's that? Oh yeah, occasionally I see people in other offices. I'm on a couple of committees. But I've got my role in my area and that's where I see my career heading: not as some sorta generalist." Rob was on a roll.

"And Friday says, 'If you don't live by the numbers, then you die by the numbers.' So, I crank out assessment data all the time for Friday and he and the VP show it to the president: they're happy, the institution's happy, students are helped, and I keep my job. Yeah, it's tiring; sometimes I'm exhausted, but I'm still EXCITED about the work.

I remember when I first met my man Friday. I was a sophomore. He showed me what I needed to do as a student leader and look where I am today! Working with him!

The only problems I ever had with him were when I was in the program. Everyone convinced me that he was just doing administrative crap. All the professors and students wanted to talk about was student development. Now I see that he was right and they were wrong. Providing real services is what the field is about. Students might like to know what their vectors are, but they would rather have you give them money and food and someplace to sleep and something to do.

For a while, I was like you and thought that spending hours with every student was what we should do. Just talk and listen and talk and listen. But all that counseling crap doesn't keep the place going. And that's the secret: we keep the institution humming. Our services keep students in school.

You KNOW what sorta counselor I am anyway. I just dreaded those labs! I wish I'd had more experience in administration when I was in the program. I wish I hadn't done anything else. Just take practica and my assistantship, not theory after theory after theory. Nobody in the real world uses theory anyway.

Now if they'd teach more about administration in the program, there might be a chance, but they'd still teach it wrong: telling you about it instead of letting you do it. Have you had the class on budget yet? What a farce. Everybody's scared to death of it and it's taught like it's out there or something. I do budget stuff every day; in fact, I learn more in any single day on the job than I did in those two years in the program.

I'll tell you what they should be teaching: TECHNOLOGY. It's a new age out there. Computers can do EVERYTHING! Why I've got a 133 burner with a 2 gig and 16 Megs of RAM in my office. And I taught myself how to use it! Well, actually, some of the secretaries and other people helped me at first. It was great. Everybody learning from everybody else: not some dumb professor pretending to know everything about it. Hands-On. Learning something important by doing it. That's the way it is with technology and that's the way it should be with the whole program. Second class technocrats? Oh yeah, that stuff. Yeah, you should hear some people in the office bitch about that. They all whine that people think they're technicians or custodians or housemothers or something: turn the heat on, keep the dogs off campus, and make sure that Jennifer doesn't get pregnant. But they're the ones who don't do what I do—put up the numbers that SHOW what we're doing. They aren't proactive like I am. They aren't good administrators and pretending to be like faculty won't get them any more accepted than they are now. Who cares what professors think anyway! We represent the *institution*; they're off in their own separate worlds. Hey, sometimes I don't even care what some of the students think. They aren't the only ones who've ever been here and they won't be the last ones either. The university was here before them and it will last a long while after they're gone.

Who cares about the professors in the program either? All your grades don't count when it's job time: what you need are good recommendations from your field supervisors. You pay attention to THEM because your career's on the line! And be honest, you never listen to the professors anyway except when they bring guests to class, people who are *doing* the job. Now Friday had the right program a zillion years ago. He was taught by a retired Dean. Friday says that this old guy knew all the ropes. Nobody in the program knows the ropes; they're too busy writing articles about theory crap . . ."

◈ ◈ ◈

She had had enough, thank you. "Old paradigms," muttered Dorothy. "Old paradigms. Get real, Rob. Everything you do just follows the same old quantitative, administrative, Eurocentric male model of the field."

"But I'm African American," protested Rob.

"It doesn't matter," said Dorothy. "You're caught up in the old way of doing things. And worse yet, you're justifying it!" Dorothy gulped some latte and continued. "Now my mentor, Glenda, wasn't teaching in the program when you were in it, and you could learn a lot from her. She's amazing!

Glenda knows that it's WRONG to quantify everything. You have to study students qualitatively. Why you're an African American . . . ["I know," Rob muttered.] . . . and you KNOW how multicultural needs are abused by the power structure. We need new models that embrace diversity, ones that tell us how different groups see the world. We can't just give everybody the same old student services. 'Services,' the word makes me shudder: everything is so specialized and so separated and so, so *administrative*.

I remember the first time I went into the financial aid office. It was really strange and the only one who wanted to help me was the secretary. She pointed out somebody to talk to, and all I could think of was, 'Sure, another old white guy to tell my problems to. He'll make me fill out some forms, give me some mom and pop advice, and I'll never hear from him again.' And I was RIGHT. And that's what I believed student affairs was about until I met Glenda. Rob, I'm not in the field because I was helped by administrators like Friday, but because I *wasn't*.

And you want those good old boys teaching in the program. Pretty chauvinist. Maybe they could just teach good old boys too, just like in the old days. And, yeah, I guess that would please a lot of the blockheads in the program. They know how to be cheerleaders, but they've never had an IDEA in their lives. No idea, Rob, just like you.

And it's just as bad over in Fess. The good old boys in charge over there don't understand *anything* about new paradigms. They expect Glenda to publish and publish and all of it is driven by numbers. She told me that she thought that she was coming to the U to be a *teacher*. Now she's found out that she has to be a *professor* instead. That means research, at least around here.

Now Glenda did a great qualitative study for her dissertation but nobody understands that it's GOOD even though it's just about six students. It's *thorough*. The same thing happened to Carol Gilligan! Nobody at Harvard understood her techniques and where would women's theory be without her? Just tell me how many tenured full professors are women anywhere? They're hiring women but we don't get the goodies. That's why we have to band together, students and faculty, to make sure that new ways and new people get their proper share of the power!

And that begins and ends with *education*, not *administration*. Honestly, Rob, I'd think that you of all people would understand the need for transformative leaders who can counteract the dominant paradigm. Everything else is crap, including those transactional managers that you call mentors. Friday, a mentor? Honestly!

And that's why I'm not buying into the power thing. I'll just work with my students and do my thing and not even pretend to fight the system. I'll be an educator and a counselor and proud of it. And while you're getting all those management techniques down pat, I'll be sabotaging all your efforts by changing the hearts and souls and minds of my students."

"Yeah, all six of them," Rob sniped.

"So?" Dorothy countered. "I'll be finding out how and why they operate. And I'll care about *all* their needs, not just the ones they bring to your tiny office in some far off corner of some humongous building. I can't imagine any real professional ignoring *any* of the learning needs of her students, inside the classroom or out. And so I'm taking every course on communication and qualitative research and diversity that I can find. I want a real ACADEMIC program, not just fun and games."

"But what about respect and keeping your job?" argued Rob.

Dorothy replied, "They'll come around eventually. The system has to. The Fridays of this world are getting old. Hey, they were born old. Soon they'll retire and people like us will replace them. Women, people of color, internationals: the new majority is going to triumph and YOU should be fighting *with us*, not against us!"

⊞ ⊞ ⊞

Alice got up from the table and walked outside. "What was that all about?" she wondered. The sun was bright as she walked down the steps. Looking for some shade, Alice saw Beatrice, the advisor to student government, sitting at a table. Alice walked over to her, sat down, and told her about the conversation that Rob and Dorothy were having. Beatrice laughed.

"I've heard it all before, many, MANY times over the years. Rob and Dorothy used different words, maybe, but they were just talking about some age old problems . . . and opportunities . . . in the field. You should have seen how Ed Williamson carried on about services! He thought they were the be-all and end-all! And Esther Lloyd-Jones? How she would rail against specialization!

It's easy for Rob to like the field just as it is. He found a mentor early on who is still helping him; Friday's advice works for Rob. Dorothy is here because she wasn't helped by anyone when she was in school. That person that she met in financial aid was a mentor to her, too: he just taught her what NOT to do. Dorothy wants to change an uncaring system but she's not sure how. It's easier for her to think about it than to 'just do it.' But both Dorothy and Rob are deeply interested in helping other people. They both have great communication skills, too, but different ones, and they can help students in different ways.

Basically, student affairs . . . ["There's that term again," Alice noted.] . . . has always had its administrators and educators, its extraverts and intraverts, its individualists and community advocates, and its specialists and generalists. Each group has been in power for a while and each has been out of power, as the times have changed. Different ways of helping people are important at different times. But none of these groups has ever gone away, thank goodness, because they're all necessary.

What's funny is that they all think that they have come up with new answers instead of new terms to deal with age old questions. Rob talked about assessment, right? Well, in the 1970s he would have been talking about accountability. And Dorothy talked about multiculturalism, right? People were talking about student cultures in the 1960s just before student activism began. Why in 1968, Phil Tripp was warning about the dangers of being caught in 'old paradigms!' Then some people in the field got a lot more activist than Dorothy is now: 'power to the people.' Doesn't that sum up most of what she was talking about?" Beatrice asked.

Alice replied, "Yes, I suppose . . . but . . ."

Beatrice continued, "But the problems don't go away. As long as there are 'college students,' people who are forming or re-forming their lives will be working within a structure built on other people's lives. The tension between the past and the future, the society and the individual, will always be there. The institution organizes what is known in order to teach it. Students are ahistorical; they're bound together by the process of becoming. The important thing is that they need each other, the institution and the individuals. The university needs its students in order to survive and students need the knowledge and the time that they can find there. And *good* student affairs folks stand right in the middle of them, sometimes defending the institution and sometimes the individual: so it's hard for them to be fully accepted by either!"

This was all getting to be a bit too much for Alice, so she tried to change the subject. "But what *are* they studying and how should they study it? Rob and Dorothy I mean."

Beatrice answered, "Student affairs: that's what it's called now, but it also includes words like student development and student services and even student personnel. Student development is about growing and student services are how we help students grow. Both of these fit under a bigger notion: student *service*, with no plural "s" attached. Rob and

Dorothy would agree about that; they just think it's important to serve students in different ways.

Sometimes we serve students by counseling them, and sometimes through programming, and sometimes it means being an administrator at the institution. It's all of those things and each is inseparable from the other. To manage well, I have to be able to listen to students. And students won't come to me if I can't get them the stuff they need to know, to do, or to have."

"But how do you learn about all those things?" asked Alice.

Beatrice responded, "You don't learn them all in graduate school, that's for sure. And you don't NOT learn them there, either. It's not an all-or-nothing proposition, Alice. You learn different skills in different ways in school and on the job. The times and the locations change, but you change, too. It's never whole and it's never ended. I learn new things all the time and that's a big reason why I'm still here. My work is *always* about learning!

Nowadays, though, most masters programs are the same, even though people like Rob and Dorothy, graduate students or professionals, want to help undergrads in different ways. It didn't used to be that way. A few years ago, Rob could take an administrative program and Dorothy could take an educational or counseling one. But that's not a major problem to me. If you have to make a choice, then I think that you should *start* with the educational purposes of the field. Ultimately, you'll need it all. Dorothy's right; you need to listen to people who are different from you. And Rob's right, too; budgets aren't the Great Satan. You need to learn about both in time. But at least, graduate programs are a lot better than they were in the old days when any retired administrator could teach whatever he wanted. (Yes, Alice, the emphasis is on *he*.) So, I can accept today's standardized education, even if it's too vanilla for my taste. But if I had my way, I'd teach students a little differently than they do in the program here."

"What do you mean?" Alice queried.

Beatrice explained, "I wouldn't change the content as much as when it's offered. First, most new students come to school like you would, as recent graduates who choose our field because they liked doing 'college' more than their classroom studies. So, instead of starting them off with regular courses, I'd get them into practica right away. They would have virtually nothing but practica for their first term, except for an occasional seminar where they'd share logs about their work and identify what they need to know about their jobs. This would do three things: it would make students ready for classes, it would give them self-confidence, and it would help them learn whether they can make a career commitment to the field. About half of our people leave the field a few years after their masters programs; I'd like them to find out early if it's the right place for them to be. And I'd make sure that every student had a couple of mentors, people to talk with about what they're doing: a professional and a second year student would be good."

"Well, I know that would make Rob happy," Alice suggested.

Beatrice continued, "But it wouldn't stop there. The next term, they would have virtually nothing but academic classes: Tough ones, too. They would build knowledge on top of their experience. Their experience would have shown them what they need and it would provide case studies that they could apply to the lessons in the classroom. The students would want to learn everything they could, because they would know that the classes were relevant to their futures."

"And after that?" Alice asked.

"Then it's back into the field, to apply their knowledge-in-action," Beatrice replied. "That third term, students would examine professional decision-making and the theories-in-practice that they were using and creating. And after that term, they could synthesize their learning into a professional portfolio and an action research project."

"Was your program like that?" Alice asked.

Beatrice admitted, "Uh, I don't have a degree in this field, Alice, but I wish I had. And as I said, I'm always learning about it. But I was older when I got into the field and it was a long time ago. My ideas fit people like Dorothy and Rob better than they fit people like me and Dan Alighieri, who's standing over there. Dan can't go to school full-time. He's older. Has a family and he needs to change jobs. Nobody in the field has paid enough attention to teaching Dan and others like him, and I'm not even sure that Dan will even get a job later, except maybe in a community college where they understand about older students. But I'm going to stick with him to see how it all works out. Oh, and I need to see him now, so would you please excuse me, Alice?"

◈ ◈ ◈

Alice got up and went back down the path toward the crossroads. Beatrice and Dan were talking by the doorway. She saw Friday and Rob walking back toward Tish. And that must be Glenda over there. She and Dorothy were laughing about something. But poor Alice has nobody, at least not yet. Somebody might come along, but even if nobody does, all gentle readers of the story know that Alice needs nobody but herself to make her way forward in life. As the caterpillar said, "If you cannot explain yourself, you cannot find yourself." Sometimes that's good advice for a profession as well as people, and Alice knows more about herself than she thinks. . . but look up ahead. A lop-eared critter is leaning on one of the road signs, munching a carrot. "I've been waiting for you," he says. "Tell me what you've been doing?"

Alice admits, "I'm afraid I'm rather confused. You see I've been listening to Rob and Dorothy and Beatrice talk about work and school and . . . I thought it would help me find myself, but even though they're supposed to be doing the same thing, it seems to me that there are two sides to everything that they're doing. There's the administrative side and the educative side, the doing side and the thinking side, the quantitative side and the qualitative side, and the institution side and the student side and . . ."

"Do you want to help people?" the creature asks.

"Yes," Alice acknowledges.

"Good," states the rabbit. "Rob and Dorothy do, too. It means that none of you has to worry about working in business. That's about dollars and cents, not about helping others. It's easy to tell if you're a success in business, but it's hard knowing if you ever really help somebody. That's what's confusing about that. But now I've got another question for you, whom do you want to help?"

Alice replies, "People like me, who don't always know exactly what they're doing or what they need sometimes. But people who are okay basically, not whacky."

The rabbit continues, "Okay, right now that means people like college students. And some of them fit the system and some of them don't, but they're mostly okay. And that means that you probably don't want to be a psychotherapist; a sometimes counselor is a good enough role for you. But I have to warn you that you won't FEEL like a student for very long. Pretty soon you'll notice that they aren't quite like you anymore. Now, *where* do you want to help them?"

Alice acknowledges, "This place is pretty cool. On a college campus, I mean."

The rabbit explains, "Well, someday you'll know that there are lots and lots of different college campuses with lots and lots of different purposes, but right now that's enough. We're done for the day."

"But aren't there other things I need to know? Other questions I should be asking?" Alice protests.

"Of course, Alice," the rabbit calmly states, " and they'll come in time, especially when you'll be *living* them instead of just asking them. Today it's just talk, but someday you'll need to assemble the same answers for yourself that Rob and Dorothy are putting together for themselves today. And you might be *just* as convinced as they are that you're right. But those questions are only hows and whats and whiches, and those types of questions aren't as important as these others: at least at first. You've already told me that you want to help and that's the first best answer of all. Now let's go get a cup of coffee; I could use a double espresso. You want to help. That's a good enough start for any person."

And maybe, for any profession.

REFERENCE

Auden, W. H. (1962, July 1). Today's 'wonder-world' needs Alice. *New York Times Magazine*, p. 5.

About the Contributors

Carolyn R. Bair is a doctoral student at Loyola University Chicago. She completed the B.A. in Psychology in 1970 and M.A. in Counseling Psychology in 1974 at Northern Michigan University, Marquette. She has 19 years of professional experience in student affairs, 14 of which were as a senior student affairs officer. She has made presentations at NASPA and ACPA conferences and she is also involved in AERA and ASHE. She is working on a dissertation in the area of doctoral student persistence; other research interests include leadership in higher education, gender differences, and innovative practices in student affairs.

D. Stanley Carpenter is professor of educational administration at Texas A & M University and executive director of the Association for the Study of Higher Education. He holds a Ph.D. in Counseling and Personnel Services (Higher Education Administration concentration) from the University of Georgia (1979), M.S. in Student Personnel and Guidance from East Texas State University (1975), and a B.S. in Mathematics from Tarleton State University (1972). Dr. Carpenter has held professional positions in student affairs at Oglethorpe University and University of Arkansas-Monticello, and in university development at Texas A & M University. He has received numerous professional awards including the Distinguished Service Award from ASHE (1996), Distinguished Teaching Award, TAMU College of Education (1996), and the ACPA Annuit Coeptis Senior Professional Award (1995). He is active in ACPA, NASPA, SACSA, TACUSPA, ASHE, and AERA. He has published over 50 articles, chapters, and reviews and continues to be interested in student affairs professional development issues and college student volunteerism.

Don G. Creamer is professor of educational leadership and policy studies at Virginia Polytechnic Institute and State University (Virginia Tech). He holds the Ed.D. degree from Indiana University and the M.Ed. and B.A. degrees from East Texas State University. During his 37 years in the student affairs profession he served as administrator of various functional areas, including dean of students, for 17 years, and as professor, including coordinator of masters and doctoral preparation programs in college student affairs and higher education, for 20 years. He is past president of ACPA, a recipient of the Annuit Coeptis Senior Professional Award, a diplomat of senior scholars, and currently serves as one of ACPA's representatives to CAS where he has taken a leadership role in promoting quality assurance in the profession. He is also a trustee for the ACPA Educational Leadership Foundation. His most recent work, co-authored with Roger Winston, is titled, *Improving Staffing Practices in Student Affairs*. He is the author of three other books in student affairs and more than 70 articles in journals and other scholarly media.

Jane Fried is associate professor in the Department of Health and Human Service Professions at Central Connecticut State University. She earned her doctorate in Counseling Psychology and Human Development from the Union of Experimenting Colleges and Universities in 1977, her M.A. in Student Personnel Work from Syracuse University in 1968 and her B.A. in American and World Literature from Harper College, SUNY-Binghamton in 1996. Dr. Fried received the Annuit Coeptis Senior Professional Award from ACPA and has served as chair of several ACPA committees. Her most recent publication is *Ethics for Today's Campus: New Perspectives on Education, Student Development and Institutional Management* (1997). Other books include *Shifting Paradigms: Teaching, Learning, Culture and Context* (1995), *Different Voices: Gender and Perspective in Student Affairs Administration* (1994), and *Education for Student Development* (1981). Her current interests include developmental education across the lifespan, creation of a multicultural perspective for ethical counseling practice, and integrating the educational functions of student development into the mainstream of higher education.

Joan B. Hirt is an associate professor in the Department of Educational Leadership and Policy Studies at Virginia Polytechnic Institute and State University (Virginia Tech). She holds a Ph.D. degree from the University of Arizona, an M.Ed. from the University of Maryland at College Park, and a B.A. degree from Bucknell University. During her 17 years as a student affairs administrator, she worked in residence life and in the dean of students area where she was associated with the management of numerous administrative units. She is a past president of the Western Association of College and University Housing Officers, chaired the Major Speakers Committee for the 1997 ACPA Convention, and is a current member of ACPA's Commission XII Directorate Board. A recipient of the 1997 ACPA Annuit Coeptis Award for Emerging Professionals, her research interests focus on the professional evolution of student affairs administration and the changing nature of professional practice in higher education. Her recent publications include articles in professional journals and chapters in forthcoming books on the professions in higher education.

Russ Jablonsky is currently a residence hall director at the University of Wisconsin-Stout. He received his M.S. degree in College Student Personnel from Western Illinois University in 1992 and his B.S. in Physical Education from Moorhead State University in 1990. He was a 1995 recipient of the ACPA Annuit Coeptis Emerging Professional Award. Mr. Jablonsky also received the 1995 Outstanding New Professional Award given by the Committee for New Professionals and Graduate Students of ACPA. His professional interests include identity development, self-organizing systems, transitional issues for college students, and leadership for social change.

William M. Klepper currently holds the position of vice president for student life at The College of New Jersey where he has been a student affairs administrator for over 25 years. He received his Ph.D. in Education (Higher Education) in 1975, M.Ed. (College Student Personnel) in 1967, and B.S. (Biology and Chemistry) in 1966 from St. Louis University. He was the founding editor of *The Journal of College and University Student Housing*, and has written for ACPA, ACUHO-I, ACU-I, and NASPA publications. He is the co-editor with Martha Stodt (1987) of *Increasing Retention: Academic and Student Affairs Administrators in Partnership*. He has served in leadership positions within a number of student affairs associations, including as president of the Mid-Atlantic Association of College and University Housing Officers.

The primary emphasis in his work, teaching, and writing has been on achieving community. During the 1996-97 academic year, he was on leave from The College of New Jersey to serve as academic director of executive education in the Graduate School of Business at Columbia University where he has been an adjunct professor since 1986. He will continue in this role after his retirement from The College of New Jersey in August, 1997.

Susan R. Komives is associate professor of counseling and personnel services at the University of Maryland at College Park where she also serves as faculty affiliate for the division of student affairs. She received her B.S. in Mathematics (1968) and her M.S. in Higher Education Administration (1969) from Florida State University. Her Ed.D. in Educational Administration is from the University of Tennessee (1973). A former vice president for student life at Stephens College and the University of Tampa, she was president of ACPA in 1982-83. She is an ACPA Senior Scholar and recipient of the Esther Lloyd Jones Professional Service Award. Dr. Komives is co-editor of the 1996 *Student Services: A Handbook for the Profession* (Third Edition) with Doug Woodard. She is a member of the board of editors of *About Campus* and research editor for *Concepts & Connections* from the National Clearinghouse of Leadership Programs.

Marylu K. McEwen is associate professor in the College Student Personnel program, Department of Counseling and Personnel Services, University of Maryland at College Park. In 1968 she received a B.S. in Mathematics and in 1973 a Ph.D. in Counseling and Personnel Services from Purdue University. She also completed an M.S. Ed. in College Student Personnel Administration from Indiana University in 1970. Dr. McEwen is active in ACPA, NAWE, and NASPA. She received the Annuit Coeptis Senior Professional Award from ACPA, the Contribution to the Profession Award from the Standing Committee on Multicultural Affairs of ACPA, and the Elizabeth A. Greenleaf Award from Indiana University. She also has served as a NAWE senior scholar. Prior to being at the University of Maryland at College Park, Dr. McEwen was affiliated with Auburn University and Purdue University. Her primary professional areas of interest include theories of college student development and multiculturalism in student affairs and student affairs graduate programs. She also serves as associate editor of the *Journal of College Student Development*.

Leila V. Moore is vice president for student affairs at the University of New Hampshire. She received her Ed.D. in 1975 from the State University of New York at Albany in Counseling and Personnel Services, her M.A. in 1963 from Syracuse University in Student Personnel Administration, and her B.S. in 1961 from Carnegie Institute of Technology in English Literature. She is a former president of ACPA and has held numerous leadership positions in the association. In 1988 she was named an ACPA Annuit Coeptis Senior Professional. Dr. Moore has held a variety of professional positions in student affairs at the Pennsylvania State University as well as serving as a faculty member in college student personnel programs at Penn State, Bowling Green State University, College of St. Rose, and SUNY-Albany. She is editor of *Evolving Theoretical Perspectives on Students* (1990) and the author of numerous monographs, book chapters, and journal articles on student development theory, professional development, and diversity in higher education.

Carmen Guevara Neuberger is executive director of the American College Personnel Association. She holds a Certificate in Institutional Management from Harvard University (1987), a J.D. from Washington College of Law, American University (1983), an Ed.D. (Higher Education Administration, 1977) and M.Ed. (Student Personnel Administration, 1973) from American University, and a B.S. in Institutional Management and Chemistry (1955) from the University of Maryland. She has received numerous professional awards, including the Ethnic Woman of Achievement Award from NAWE in 1997. Dr. Neuberger has held many leadership positions in NAWE and NASPA, including president of NAWE (1983-84). Other professional positions she has held include president of the Tuition Exchange, Inc. and dean of educational services and student affairs at Dickinson College. She has a number of journal articles and book chapters to her credit on a variety of topics including Greek Life, international students, and campus conflict.

Donna M. Talbot is assistant professor and coordinator of the student affairs in higher education graduate programs in the Department of Counselor Education and Counseling Psychology at Western Michigan University. She received her B.A. in Sociology from Amherst College (1981), her M.Ed. in Special Education from Lesley College (1985), her Ed.S. in Counselor Education with an emphasis in Student Personnel Services from University of Florida (1987), and her Ph.D. in College Student Personnel Administration from the University of Maryland-College Park (1992). Dr. Talbot is chair-elect of ACPA Commission XII: Professional Preparation and has held numerous leadership positions in ACPA and NASPA. She is a recipient of the ACPA Annuit Coeptis Emerging Professional Award (1993), The Nevitt Sanford Research Award (1992), and the NASPA Dissertation of the Year Award (1993). Prior to becoming a faculty member, Dr. Talbot worked in student affairs as a college counselor, researcher in residence life, judicial affairs staff member, and multicultural affairs director. Her research focuses on diversity and multiculturalism, especially as related to training issues for counselors and student affairs practitioners.

M. Lee Upcraft is assistant vice president emeritus for student affairs, affiliate professor emeritus of higher education, and a research associate in the Center for the Study of Higher Education at Penn State University. Dr. Upcraft received his B.A. in History (1960) and his M.A. in Guidance and Counseling (1961) from SUNY-Albany. His Ph.D. in Student Personnel Administration is from Michigan State University (1967). Dr. Upcraft is a senior scholar of ACPA, the 1966 recipient of the Outstanding Contribution to Research or Literature Award from NASPA, and the 1994 recipient of the Outstanding Contributions to the Orientation Profession Award from NODA. Dr. Upcraft is the principal author of three books: *Residence Hall Assistants in College* (1986), *Learning to be a Resident Assistant* (1986), and *Assessment in Student Affairs: A Guide for Practitioners* (1996) with John Schuh. He has authored or edited six additional books. Dr. Upcraft continues to have scholarly interests in student retention, race relations, program assessment, teaching and learning, and the transition to college.

Terry E. Williams is associate professor in the Department of Educational Leadership and Policy Studies at Loyola University Chicago. He received his B.S. in Business Administration from Illinois State University in 1970, his M.S. in College Student Personnel Administration from Indiana University in 1974, and his Ph.D. in Higher Education from Florida State University in 1979. In 1980, Dr. Williams received the NASPA Dissertation of the Year Award. In 1992-93 he served as president of ACPA and in 1994 he received the Elizabeth A. Greenleaf Distinguished Alumnus Award from the Indiana University graduate program in College Student Personnel Administration. Dr.

Williams has served as graduate program director, academic department chairperson, and in 1996-97 as interim dean of the Loyola University School of Education.

Dudley B. Woodard, Jr. is professor and director of the Center for the Study of Higher Education at the University of Arizona. A 1962 alumnus of MacMurray College, he majored in Psychology. He received his M.A. in Human Relations (1965) and Ph.D. in Counseling and Guidance (1969) from Ohio University. He is the co-editor of *Student Services: A Handbook for the Profession* (Third Edition), editor of two monographs, and author of several book chapters and journal articles. He was the vice president of student affairs at Arizona University and the State University of New York at Binghamton, a past president of NASPA, a member of the NASPA Monograph Board and national chair of the Minority Undergraduate Fellows Program. He also serves on the NASPA Journal Board. He currently is directing a national research project on retention in land grant and research I universities and is involved in several international projects.

Robert B. Young is professor of higher education and coordinator of educational leadership at Ohio University. He received his Ph.D. in Higher Education from the University of Illinois in 1975, his M.S. in Counseling from California State University at Los Angeles, and his A.B. degree in History from the University of Rochester. Dr. Young previously held faculty positions at Kent State University, the University of Vermont, and the University of Connecticut. He also served as a counselor and student affairs professional at several institutions of higher education. Dr. Young has held a variety of leadership positions in ACPA and NASPA, including chair of ACPA Commission XII: Professional Preparation. For his efforts on behalf of the profession, Dr. Young has received an Outstanding Contribution to Teaching Award from the Midwest Region of NASPA, the Phillip Tripp Distinguished Service Award from the Ohio College Personnel Association, and the ACPA Annuit Coeptis Senior Professional Award. He is the author of *No Neutral Ground: Standing by the Values We Prize in Higher Education*, the editor of four books related to student affairs administration, and the author of numerous other book chapters and over 40 articles. His interests include values, mid-level management, and professional education.

About the Editors

Nancy J. Evans is associate professor, Department of Professional Studies in Education, at Iowa State University. She received an M.F.A. in Theatre (1991) from Western Illinois University, a Ph.D. in Counseling Psychology (1978) from the University of Missouri-Columbia, an M.S.Ed. in Higher Education (College Student Personnel) (1972) from Southern Illinois University, and a B.A. in Social Science from SUNY-Potsdam (1970). She previously held faculty positions in College Student Personnel programs at Penn State University, Western Illinois University, and Indiana University. She also held positions in counseling, residence life, and student activities at a number of institutions of higher education. Dr. Evans is a recipient of the ACPA Annuit Coeptis Senior Professional Award. She is a past chair of ACPA Commission XII: Professional Preparation and currently serves as the commission's representative to the Core Council on Professional Development. Dr. Evans' previous books include *Beyond Tolerance: Gays, Lesbians and Bisexuals on Campus* (1991) with Vernon Wall and *Facilitating the Development of Women* (1987). Her scholarly interests focus on the impact of the college environment on student development, particularly with regard to members of oppressed populations.

Christine E. Phelps Tobin is a visiting assistant professor at Loyola University Chicago in the Educational Leadership and Policy Studies Department teaching in the College Student Personnel and Higher Education programs. Dr. Tobin received a Ph.D. in Counselor Education/Student Development in Postsecondary Education in 1990 from the University of Iowa, an M.S. in College Student Personnel (1984) and a B.S. in Business Administration (1982) from the University of Wisconsin-LaCrosse. She has held faculty positions at the Center for the Study of Higher Education at the University of Arizona, Eastern Michigan University, and the Pennsylvania State University. She also served as a financial aid advisor at Bradley University. Currently chair of ACPA Commission XII: Professional Preparation, Dr. Tobin chaired the Commission's National Week for Careers in Student Affairs Committee for several years. She has authored numerous articles on student development, faculty-student involvement, and graduate students of color. Current professional interests and research revolve around the issue of quality assurance in the preparation of student affairs professionals.